D0075563

Faculty Vitality and Institutional Productivity

Critical Perspectives for Higher Education

Faculty Vitality and Institutional Productivity

Critical Perspectives for Higher Education

Shirley M. Clark and Darrell R. Lewis, Editors

Teachers College, Columbia University
New York and London

Published by Teachers College Press, 1234 Amsterdam Avenue, New York, N.Y. 10027

Copyright © 1985 by Teachers College, Columbia University

Library of Congress Cataloging in Publication Data

Main entry under title:

Faculty vitality and institutional productivity.

   Includes bibliographies and index.
   1.   College teachers — Vocational guidance — United
States — Addresses, essays, lectures.   2.   College
teachers — United States — Psychology — Addresses,
essays, lectures.   3.   College teachers — United States —
Supply and demand — Addresses, essays, lectures.
I.   Clark, Shirley Merritt, 1936–   .   II.   Lewis,
Darrell R.
LB1778.F29   1985   378'.12'02373   84-17058

ISBN 0-8077-2763-6

Manufactured in the United States of America

90 89 88 87 86   2 3 4 5 6

Contents

Preface

The development of *Faculty Vitality and Institutional Productivity: Critical Perspectives for Higher Education* arose from our concern about the lack of understanding that many faculty members and administrators seem to have about how faculty careers develop and about how faculty career development relates to professional vitality and institutional productivity. Equally important was our concern for how faculty vitality would be maintained in light of the demographic and economic trends now emerging and those projected for higher education in the next two decades. The major consequences of these trends indicate greatly diminished faculty mobility with few new hires along with an increasingly underpaid and aging faculty. It is very clear that knowledge about the implications of these trends on faculty career vitality and institutional productivity is of critical importance for rational decision making in higher education today.

In partial response to these concerns, we developed a colloquium series in higher education at the University of Minnesota in the winter and spring of 1982 in order to address systematically the topics and issues surrounding faculty career vitality. We reviewed the literature, developed the topical outline, consulted with our colleagues both in related disciplines and in the field of higher education, contacted the speakers and authors, conducted the colloquium series with faculty and graduate students in higher education, and subsequently edited this publication as the collective product of this effort.

In the development of the colloquium series, special assistance and support was provided by the University of Minnesota — through the Center for Educational Policy Studies, the Teacher Center, the Graduate Program in Higher Education, and the College of Education. The faculty and graduate students in an adjunct seminar (Educ 8-229: Issues in Higher Education) were especially helpful in assisting the contributing authors in developing their topics and papers. Throughout this project, the advice and assistance from a number of key people at the University of Minnesota were essential to whatever success it enjoyed. Such a list must include Mary Corcoran, Theodore Kellogg, Carol Boyer, and Donna Rosenthal, our efficient secretary.

In *Faculty Vitality and Institutional Productivity: Critical Perspectives for Higher Education,* we have brought together a group of scholars who individually have made significant contributions to the field of higher education and their respective disciplines. Each author was chosen because he or she was the best person available to address specific issues and problems in one or more parts of the book. Some of the authors are nationally known in their fields or specialties, and each drew heavily from his or her own work.

Part I in *Faculty Vitality and Institutional Productivity: Critical Perspectives for Higher Education* serves as an introduction to the theoretical and conceptual issues inherent in the concern for faculty career vitality. Attention is given both to reviewing the literature and to defining better the issues and problems of institutional and faculty vitality.

Part II focuses on a number of the empirical questions surrounding the issues of faculty vitality. The data on a relatively immobile and aging faculty in American higher education and the influences affecting this group are reviewed in the context of faculty career development theory and practice. Special attention is given to the effects of the following factors on productivity and other measures of vitality: institutional characteristics, career events, discipline-related characteristics, and aging.

Part III addresses the major institutional policy options that are available as possible responses for maintaining faculty vitality in light of the empirical evidence presented in the preceding parts of the book. Attention is given to the problems and opportunities inherent in faculty development programs, external professional consulting, mid-career change alternatives, collective bargaining, and early retirement programs.

Part IV reviews and summarizes the demographic and external pressures that currently influence faculty vitality in higher education. Suggestions are given for the use of policies and strategies that follow from the preceding chapters of the book.

Although the major institutional focus throughout most of this book is on universities, much of what is discussed applies to other higher education institutions as well. In considering the problems of faculty vitality across higher education, we recognize that a mixed situation exists in terms of institutional mission and academic aspirations, reward systems, motivations, and productivity of individual faculty in the 3000 institutions of higher education in this country. However, since there are many similarities, especially in terms of demographic concerns, we are confident that many of the policy inferences drawn from the chapters in this book can be generalized to much of higher education today.

Shirley M. Clark
Darrell R. Lewis

Part I

INTRODUCTION

Part I serves as an introduction to the theoretical and conceptual issues inherent in the concern for faculty career vitality. Attention is given both to reviewing the literature and to defining better the issues and problems of institutional and faculty vitality. Drawing from existing work in the organizational behavior sciences, the authors develop guidelines for vitality perspectives in order to operationalize the concept and its related issues for purposes of assessment and policy formulation.

Chapter 1

Faculty and Institutional Vitality in Higher Education

Shirley M. Clark, Carol M. Boyer, and *Mary Corcoran*

Interest in issues of performance and productivity in academe has taken many forms. At the individual level, examples include faculty work load reporting, student evaluation of instruction, and faculty scholarly output. At the institutional level, accountability and performance budgeting are familiar indicators. Present and anticipated conditions in American higher education have added to the vocabulary of the higher education community another, more encompassing term, *vitality,* that is widely used but infrequently defined. Vitality refers to those essential, yet intangible, positive qualities of individuals and institutions that enable purposeful production. Just as performance and vitality are associated, so individual and institutional vitality are intertwined and mutually reinforcing (Kirschling, 1978).

In this chapter, we will examine the idea of faculty and institutional vitality and suggest its utility, to higher education, along with some of its problems and limitations. We will begin by noting the conditions that have given rise to concern for vitality. Then we will consider it as a theoretical concept and review several contemporary definitions of faculty and institutional vitality. Next we will turn to a discussion of various approaches to the study of vitality. Then, drawing from the organizational behavior literature, a foundational perspective for understanding vitality will be presented; problems in assessing it also will be discussed. And finally, we will conclude by suggesting several criteria that should be considered as attempts are made to refine further the idea of faculty and institutional vitality.

CONCERN FOR VITALITY:
A RESPONSE TO CHANGING DEMOGRAPHIC
CONDITIONS

The conditions that have brought concern for vitality sharply to the fore are largely demographic and arise in a broader economic context of concern about slowed growth in the nation's productivity. Student enrollment projections suggest a leveling or declining phenomenon, with faculty position replacement demands estimated at a modest proportion of all new doctorates in the 1980s (Carnegie Council on Policy Studies in Higher Education, 1980; Commission on Human Resources, 1979; National Science Foundation Advisory Council, 1978; and others). Enrollments within institutions have shifted from one program area to another—for example, away from the social sciences and humanities and into the professions—while tenured faculty members have remained in their specialties (Carnegie Foundation for the Advancement of Teaching, 1977). The annual turnover rate in tenure-track positions slowed from around 8 percent per year in the 1960s to less than 2 percent per year in the 1970s, with no hope for reversal in the 1980s (Hellweg & Churchman, 1981). Changing birthrates, expanded access patterns, and innovative high-school curricula allegedly have contributed to the phenomenon of the underprepared student on many campuses—a phenomenon that challenges the kind of teaching for which faculty have been prepared (Baldwin, 1982; Edgerton, 1980; Watkins, 1982a).

How will these and other selected shifts affect the vitality of faculty members and their institutions? We could elect to take what surely is a minority stance and argue the advantages of the stability that accompanies such shifts; for example, opportunities to review programs unhurriedly and to consolidate gains, to benefit from the experience of established and loyal faculty who do not expect to play the academic market or to move to other institutions, and to reduce class sizes and focus more deliberately on student development. It even is conceivable that the very lack of mobility might encourage faculty to make an effort at incremental, if not revolutionary, change in curriculum quality (Grant & Riesman, 1978).

On the other hand, the majority stance in response to these sobering shifts is to perceive them as highly problematic. For example, economic stringency doubtless will lead to fiscal and programmatic cutbacks, and shared governance may deteriorate as institutions centralize their decision-making process to meet financial exigencies (Kirschling, 1978; Bruss & Kutina, 1981; Oi, 1979). The "tenuring-in" of the faculties and the advancing average age of those faculties will lead to a "lost generation of scholars" as new PhDs come on stream but are not able to locate positions in which to begin their academic careers (Radner & Kuh, 1978). Those faculty members who do have security of employment may feel immobilized in the profession, unable to revitalize and advance their careers by the prevalent pattern of the past, namely, by moving to another position in another institution (Baldwin, 1982; Edgerton, 1980). Under such conditions, it will be most difficult for women and minority doctorates, who now have the force of regulation and moral imperative on their sides, to gain firm footing on the tenure ladder and opportunities to enrich and diversify the student experience (Newman, 1979). Considering the effects of inflation on faculty salaries over the past decade and the reality of current institutional roles such as dealing with the underprepared student, faculty members may feel that they are giving more and getting less (Edgerton, 1980). Moreover, the aging of the faculty cohort will result in questions being raised about the relationship between productivity and role performance (Reskin, 1979b) and about the appropriateness of a tenure system that virtually assures continuous employment until mandatory retirement age (Hellweg & Churchman, 1981). In sum, these are among the assumptions of those researchers and commentators of the higher education scene who foresee widespread problems affecting faculty and institutional vitality.

THE STUDY OF VITALITY

Vitality as a Theoretical Concept

As far as we have been able to determine in our review of literature, there is no theory of faculty and institutional vitality, at least not in the strict scientific sense of the term. Sometimes, however, the word *theory* is used to refer to other, usually abstract types of formulations such as vague conceptualizations or descriptions of events and things, prescriptions about socially desirable behaviors or arrangements, and untested hypotheses (Reynolds, 1971). Certainly all three of these formulations can be found in the literature on faculty vitality. Frequently, however, no attempt is made to define vitality (or related terms such as renewal or revitalization or productivity). Even when the term appears in the title, it usually is not referenced again in the body of the work; rather, events are described and/or solutions to the "problem" such as faculty development programs are set forth. It could be that contemporary writers assume that an adequate degree of agreement about meaning (intersubjectivity) exists with respect to the concept. This assumption may be open to question.

Vitality is probably more of an imprecise than a precise concept. Usually it is thought that precise concepts are more valuable and that the social/behavioral sciences as well as education already seem burdened with ill-defined notions. However, as Bacharach and Lawler (1980) point out in their exposition on power — an important but imprecise concept to be sure —

the theory-construction literature of the last fifteen years reveals that ill-defined terms sometimes are critical to the theory-construction enterprise. This literature distinguishes two general types of concepts: *primitive* and *derived*. The value of primitive terms is primarily heuristic, functioning to sensitize us to phenomena without providing precise ideas or hypotheses. Among their strengths, primitive concepts often: "(1) reveal the complexity and multidimensionality of phenomena that might otherwise be treated in an oversimplified or unidimensional manner, (2) serve as integrative devices for analyzing seemingly disparate ideas, and (3) lead to more specific well-defined ideas" (Bacharach & Lawler, 1980, p. 14). The more specific, less abstract terms are derived terms (Hage, 1972; Reynolds, 1971). Whereas derived terms facilitate concrete operationalization of the ideas included in primitive terms, primitive terms can be conveyed by examples and are best used in a loose sensitizing fashion.

According to these guidelines, then, vitality is a primitive concept that is currently considered useful for describing a complex phenomenon in higher education. As we shall see, however, it is difficult to say precisely what vitality *is*. Nonetheless, what we can do is ask two questions: First, to what phenomena does the concept of vitality sensitize us? And, second, what more concrete phenomena or ideas can we attempt to specify or measure that are derived from the concept of vitality?

Definitions of Faculty and Institutional Vitality

Let us look at several contemporary definitions of faculty and institutional vitality. (See Table 1.1 for a schematic guide.)

Several writers who have wrestled with the meaning of vitality as it applies to late twentieth-century higher education credit John W. Gardner with stimulating their thinking generally (Peterson & Loye, 1967; Maher, 1982; Centra, and Clark & Corcoran in their contributions to this book). In two of his popular works, Gardner presents the reader with several kinds of theoretical statements or hypotheses about the capacities of individuals, institutions, and societies for adaptation and change. For example, from his earlier book, *Self-Renewal* (1963), the following ideas emerge:

> Continuous renewal depends upon conditions that encourage fulfillment of the individual (p. 2).
>
> When organizations and societies are young, they are flexible, fluid, not yet paralyzed by rigid specialization and willing to try anything once. As organization or society ages, vitality diminishes, flexibility gives way to rigidity, creativity fades and there is a loss of capacity to meet challenges from unexpected directions (p. 3).
>
> Too often in the past we have designed systems to meet all kinds of exacting re-

TABLE 1.1. Definitions of Vitality

Author(s)	Terms	Central Idea
Gardner, 1963, 1978	"Renewal," "vitality," "regeneration," etc.	The capacities of individuals, institutions, and societies for adaptation and change
Peterson & Loye, 1967	Institutional vitality	Definition should be multidimensional, dynamic, include individual vitality, and allow for institutional differences
Ebben & Maher, 1979	Institutional vitality	Interaction of mission, goals, programs, and institutional climate that enables individuals both to contribute to the mission, etc., and to realize the benefits that come from "a creative, productive, and energizing work life"
Maher, 1982	Institutional vitality	Same as above, but with added focus on individuals within an institutional context
Smith, 1978	Faculty vitality	Interaction of faculty and institutional vitality
Planning Council, University of Minnesota, 1980	Faculty vitality	"Sustained productivity" in teaching, research, and service activities, with focus on the faculty as a collective

Note: Faculty vitality seems to be context-specific (i.e., it varies with the institution). Therefore, definitions of vitality must reflect both the type of institution and its mission.

quirements except the requirement that they contribute to the fulfillment and growth of the participants. . . . It is essential that in the years ahead we undertake intensive analysis of the impact of the organization on the individual (pp. 63–64).

And from a later book, *Morale* (1978), Gardner provides some synonyms for vitality, and some further statements of meaning:

regeneration (p. 13).

re-creation (p. 27).

physical drive and durability (p. 59).

physical vigor (p. 60).

dedication to beliefs that require action (p. 60).

enthusiasm . . . zest . . . sense of curiosity . . . care about things . . . reach out . . . enjoy . . . risk failure (p. 62).

A society concerned for its own continued vitality will be interested in the growth and fulfillment of individual human beings — the release of human potentialities (p. 73).

In a vital society, the forces making for disintegration and death are balanced — or more than balanced — by new life, growth, and health (p. 144).

whatever the odds . . . men and women of vitality have always been prepared to bet their futures, even their lives, on ventures of unknown outcome (p. 152).

In his introduction to *Conversations Toward a Definition of Institutional Vitality,* Richard Peterson acknowledges the creative stimulation provided by John Gardner's concepts to the undertaking that would culminate a few years later in an inventory for measuring institutional functioning (Peterson & Loye, 1967). (We will return to this inventory toward the end of this chapter, when we consider problems in assessing vitality.) Peterson and his colleagues, in their extended recorded conversations, struggled with defining both institutional vitality and an idealized institution of higher learning. Discussants suggested that the definition should be multidimensional, should include the notion of the institutionalization of individual vitality, should not be elitist but open to the diversity of institutional types in the United States, and should allow for the notion of dynamic (ebbing and flowing) vitality. The exercise of abstracting comments from those discussions yielded statements about institutional vitality, including: "educational effectiveness in terms of some change in the behavior of the students, and institutional adaptability in terms of progressively changing rather than going through periods of reaction and reform," and "an energetic institution with some sort of self-selected, distinguishing [institutional] purpose" (Peterson & Loye, 1967, pp. 24–25ff).

This early work by scholars at the Educational Testing Service predated the range of systematic attempts in the 1970s to undertake curricular reviews and reforms, to initiate and institutionalize faculty development, to improve and evaluate instruction, and to experiment with organizational and administrative development activities. However, conditions and issues in academe continued to change throughout the 1970s, and while the effect seems to have intensified concern for faculty and institutional vitality, it has also added to the complexity of the matter. Although some of these conditions were mentioned earlier, we should also consider institutional-environmental shifts such as the economic straits of the nation and the states, the increase in regulations and statutes that affect many areas of academe including personnel policies (and along with this a more litigious climate generally) and, of course, the movement to embrace collective bargaining.

Persuaded that maintenance of institutional vitality and survival are linked in small private colleges that expect to survive in the 1980s, James Ebben and Tom Maher (1979, p. 2) viewed institutional vitality as involving:

> A clearly designed and accepted mission for the unit in question.
>
> Direction, attainable goals, and programs which enable fulfillment of the mission.
>
> A climate which empowers individuals to be participants in the fulfillment of the mission and to have the sense of being involved in a creative, productive and energizing work life.

Later, Maher (1982) elaborated this definition by focusing on the faculty in the life of the institution: by providing for their security and respect, by providing a continual process of challenge and stimulation, and by recognizing those who contribute significantly to the institution. Maher's most recent statement of institutional vitality summarizes these earlier efforts:

> In essence, then, the quest for vitality might be said to focus on the capacity of the college or university to create and sustain the organizational strategies that support the continuing investment of energy by faculty and staff both in their own career and in the realization of the institution's mission. (1982, p. 7)

This intertwining or interacting of institutional and faculty vitality is an important theme. Donald K. Smith sets "durable truisms" before us: "A university is its faculty," and "The excellence of a university is the excellence of its faculty" (1978, p. 1). These truisms suggest to him that inquiry into faculty vitality needs to address academic personnel policies, including how faculty members are selected, socialized, promoted, and rewarded. These policies and procedures evolve from the philosophy and mission of an institution and from the form of governance appropriate to such a mission. This strikes us as a very interesting and significant observation, implying as it does that ideal types of faculty vitality will differ according to institutional type and mission. Thus, for example, at a large, land-grant, research-oriented institution such as the University of Minnesota where the mission is tripartite (i.e., teaching, research, and service), a draft position paper on planning strategies contains the following definition of faculty vitality:

> A faculty is vital if it exhibits sustained productivity in its teaching, its research, and its service activities. Productivity is characterized not by quantity of output but by quality of these outputs as judged by faculty peers. A faculty is vital if it is continually creating important, new knowledge and expanding our understanding of the world in which we live. A faculty is vital if the instructional programs of the University are continually being monitored and developed. A faculty is vital if there is a balance between innovative and traditional approaches to teaching and research. The University faculty is vital if it is responding to the needs of the state, the nation, and the world for new knowledge. On occasions, this vitality is recognized through awards and prizes for scholarship. Perhaps most important, a faculty is vital if its members find their work stimulating, enjoyable, and satisfying. (Planning Council, University of Minnesota, 11 February 1980, p. 4)

Since it is well known that a division of either labor or functions exists between teaching and research institutions in higher education, and even within these kinds of institutions, value-laden definitions of faculty vitality will differ in their emphases for, say, two-year community colleges, liberal arts colleges, and universities with greater or lesser research orientation. As Fulton and Trow (1974) have suggested, the expectation of continuing research activity is included in ideal types of academic roles in some universities and colleges, but not in others; in yet other institutions, teaching is emphasized and research is not a normal expectation.[1] Prevailing ideal types of faculty roles may be assumed to affect patterns of recruitment and socialization of faculty members. Reflected and reaffirmed in the reward structures, these ideal types may be linked with personal preferences, social origins, and other variables about which relatively little is known.

In sum, notions of faculty vitality seem to have a situational, contextual dimension that makes defining the concept difficult at best without taking into account institutional type and mission. Doing so leads us to consider institutions both as employer and workplace, and as organizations in which faculty members pursue careers as scholars, teachers, and researchers.

APPROACHES TO THE STUDY OF VITALITY

Many avenues of approach might be taken to illuminate the primitive concept of faculty and institutional vitality if our goal is to understand it better.

As will be seen in a later section on organizational behavior, such approaches may include theory, research, or practice, or some combination of all three modes. Another approach would be paradigmatic relative to groups of academic disciplines. For examples, humanists and historians might select institutional histories or biographies of vital institutions and vital individuals, whereas social and behavioral scientists would be more likely to undertake organizational analysis, career studies, or performance and productivity measurement. Practitioners such as faculty developers, on the other hand, might focus on strategic approaches to the improvement of instruction, or more broadly, to faculty career development and personal growth. We will take up some of these approaches, briefly, in turn.

Reputational Method (Focus on Institutions)

When Richard Peterson, his Educational Testing Service colleagues, and other scholars were brainstorming the development of an instrument to measure institutional vitality and struggling to define the term, they considered a plan for validating an instrument that would ask some broadly informed people to identify a number of colleges that they thought possessed vitality and a number that lacked that quality (Peterson & Loye, 1967). The experimental inventory would then be administered to both groups, and items that proved to discriminate between groups subsequently would be selected. During their extended conversation, one discussant suggested that one of the many problems with such an approach was the lack of consensus upon a definition of vitality. Or, as he put it, "Perhaps one might say that it's a little less precise than a rifle but not quite as diffuse as a blunderbuss" (Peterson & Loye, 1967, p. 54).

The idea of selecting vital institutions by a reputational method is an interesting approach, but one that is fraught with numerous obstacles. We could, for example, follow Grant's and Riesman's (1978) ethnographical approach and study colleges and universities whose protean qualities were manifest in experimentation and broad-scale reforms in the 1960s and 1970s. Yet, although many of the reforms echoed the passionate commitments of those times, by the middle 1970s the winds of social/political change in the external environment and the stresses and strains inside the institutions resulted in phasing out some of the reforms and making others more conservative. Nonetheless, study of institutional histories of both continuing and moribund colleges (e.g., Black Mountain, Ladycliffe, and Merrill-Palmer) of our own time and of a century past might stimulate further ideas about organizational vitality and social change.

Biographies and Autobiographies (Focus on Individuals)

A second approach to a better understanding of the concept of vitality — and one that provides the latent pleasure of inspiration — is the study of biographies and autobiographies of great teachers and scholars. There are many biographies from which to choose, but the writing tends to differ substantially in both format and content, and in the degree of analytic rigor. Moreover, like institutional histories, sometimes there is even a celebratory quality to the writing. For example, *Masters: Portraits of Great Teachers* (Epstein, 1981) collects "critical appreciations" written by eighteen well-known students of famous teachers and scholar/artists, all of whom were highly productive in both roles though not equally so. It is interesting to note that this single collection of essays illuminates the little understood relationship over time between teacher and student from the perspective of the student.

The study of autobiographical sketches rendered by older persons whose productive careers span several decades also may be useful for examining subjective perceptions of what influenced career development, generational differences, attitudes, discoveries, and more. Although the frequency of such autobiographies is not known, both a recent and an historical example come to mind: the former is Earl J. McGrath's "Fifty Years in Higher Education" (1980) in which he traces personal influences on his development; the latter, Justus von Liebig's reflections about the founding of organic chemistry and the establishment of teaching-research laboratories (Brown, 1893).

Consequences of Changing Conditions (Focus on Individuals Within Institutions)

One of the most seminal of concepts arising in response to the "new circumstances" in higher education is that of *opportunity structure,* a concept presented by Rosabeth Moss Kanter in her book about organization life (1977) and applied more specifically to academe in her later essay (1979). In contrast to approaches taken by humanists and historians, Kanter's approach is decidedly sociological and organizational. Although the concept of opportunity structure has not been extensively measured in higher education, and thus has some of the same primitive characteristics as does the concept of vitality, it is a useful sensitizing idea. As Kanter explains, when times are prosperous and expansion is automatic, career prospects tend to take care of themselves; but when times are bad, opportunities for personal and professional development decrease, job satisfaction drops, motivation declines, and people may feel that they face lack of both challenge and prospect for advancement. Since opportunity is structured in paths, tracks, and ladders in academic institutions, it is difficult to cross over from one track to another. Moreover, paths to promotion and administrative positions sometimes are unspecified, and ladders of rank and salary increase are short and relatively flat, respectively. Much of Kanter's concern with opportunity structure is with the responses of faculty members to the reality or the perception of being "stuck" versus having opportunities to "move." Reduced mobility is associated with numerous negative responses, including lowered aspirations and self-esteem, disengagement from work, and destructive forms of coping behavior. In short, although these and other formulations such as Kanter's conceptualizations about power and reward structures appear valid, they are in need of further study and hypothesis testing.

Marvin Peterson (1980) draws from observer and consultant experiences in imperiled institutions to develop another perspective that attends to the importance of maintaining the morale and institutional loyalty of continuing faculty during a period of real resource decline and retrenchment. In a series of charts, he links changing institutional, governance, and faculty conditions with observed consequences for faculties and programs. Ways of bolstering faculty career vitality under these conditions of actual decline also are proposed.

Academic Career Development (Focus on Individuals)

Both Kanter's and Peterson's emphasis on the effects of decline in higher education on faculty careers leads us into the emerging literature on issues in academic career development.

Adult- and career-development stage theories.   Robert T. Blackburn, whose review of adult-development theories as applied to faculty productivity appears in this book, has synthesized the current literature, including his own several studies of academic careers, to produce nine assertions:[2]

1. The productivity of faculty over an entire career is predictable.
2. The institution determines to a high degree a faculty member's productivity.
3. Organizational factors influence faculty productivity.
4. How time is structured affects productivity.
5. Faculty interests and desires for different types of work change over the academic career.
6. Age is not a predictor of productivity over a career path.
7. Mentorship/sponsorship in the first year is critical for launching a productive career.
8. Faculty productivity over a career is affected by security and by challenge (competition).
9. Rewards affect faculty performance, and intrinsic rewards dominate extrinsic ones. (Blackburn, 1979, pp. 25–26)

These assertions include both sociological and psychological, organizational and personal "truths" and, of course, lend themselves to proposals for both inference and intervention.

Other perspectives on academic careers emerge out of attempts by researchers to apply the adult-development theories of Erik Erikson (1978), Daniel Levinson (1978), and a number of other career-development psychologists. These development stage theories have been applied to academic careers by Baldwin (1979b) in his research on faculty at various professorial ranks and years of experience, and by Rice (1980) in his study of former Danforth Fellows at midcareer that apparently is a watershed regarding reconciliation of the realities of their work situations with the idealism of their graduate-school days.

The one life–one career imperative. Based on concerns about the declining conditions in academe and the immobile, aging professoriate, W. Todd Furniss (1981a) of the American Council on Education has embraced Seymour Sarason's concept of the *one life–one career* imperative (1977) to explain what is wrong with the traditional single model of the faculty career. As Sarason puts it:

> The conventional conception of career has long had a restricted scope: one life, one career, period. The developmental task of the individual is to decide from a smorgasbord of possibilities the one vocational dish he will feed on over the course of his life. This has been so accepted a view, reflected in institutional practice and rhetoric that from the standpoint of the individual the choice of a career becomes a self-imposed, necessary, and fateful process. . . . If as we shall see later, the cultural imperative may not only be dysfunctional but is increasingly being questioned, the fact remains that for most people the imperative is ego syntonic, i.e., it should be obeyed. (1977, p. 123)

Both Sarason and Furniss conclude that academics and their professional counterparts, except those in business and industry, are prime examples of the operation of this imperative. Moreover, both argue that under present conditions the imperative has become increasingly dysfunctional for academics conditioned to spend their careers in the single model (i.e., probationary assistant professor to tenured professor to retirement). Thus, when denied the opportunity to begin their faculty careers after earning a PhD or when forced to leave their careers in the middle years, academics become upset, disillusioned, and sometimes consider themselves failures. To ameliorate this situation, Furniss advocates moving toward a new, more flexible career vision that will enhance and legitimize other career options for advanced graduate students and faculty members. In his book, *Reshaping Faculty Careers* (1981b), Furniss also proposes specific institutional policy changes that fundamentally would recast the relationships between faculty member as employee and institution as employer.

Others who are interested in approaches to maintaining faculty vitality also noted that faculty development strategies have undergone a significant shift in recent years, from emphasis on instructional development to emphasis on academic career development. Foundations and national associations of higher education have supported this shift, as reflected in their funding and research programs (Rice, 1981).

Professional role socialization.   If we are to succeed in loosening the one life–one career cultural imperative, and if we are going to attempt to maximize career vitality in institutions, it will be important to give attention to another area which appears promising, that of adult role socialization. While few studies of faculty role socialization have been done to date, studies of professional socialization in other occupations might provide some useful guidelines. One of the most relevant of such studies for academe is Dan Lortie's *Schoolteacher* (1975), an occupational ethnography that probes how career decisions are made, what the strengths and weaknesses of the preparation program are for long-term professional role performance, how peer relationships relate to professional success, how expectations of performance affect its quality, how rewards are structured, and more. Several dimensions or strategies of organizational socialization also have been identified, along with their consequences for both the individual and the organization (Van Maanen, 1978). Moreover, much more appears to be known about the impact of socialization on earlier rather than later career and under circumstances of resocialization (Wheeler, 1966).

ORGANIZATIONAL BEHAVIOR: A FOUNDATIONAL PERSPECTIVE FOR UNDERSTANDING VITALITY

The search for insight into the idea of faculty and institutional vitality is benefited by attention to the more generic, foundational literature on organizational structures and processes, including how they change. This section is intended merely to suggest the rich possibilities of pursuing the elusive concept of vitality through study of the vast literature on organizations that exists in sociology, psychology, economics, administrative sciences, anthropology, and other fields. We are not likely to find the term *vitality* in the vocabulary of the organizational scholar.[3] However, we do find attention to organizational change, effectiveness, and efficiency, and also to roles and individual behaviors that arise in the context of interaction.

Organizational Change

An understanding of faculty and institutional vitality at present and in the future will require an understanding of the organizational consequences in colleges and universities that result from modifications in the larger economic milieu. Organizations shape their own environments somewhat, but the critical agents of change "are probably exogenous, often international in scope and of a scale that compels both organizations and individuals to play a reactive role" (Presthus, 1978, p. 252). In our time, changing demographic and economic conditions are among the factors in a relatively turbulent environment that influence organizational change. Thus, among the primary issues of organizational change that might be pursued in the interest of understanding the concept of vitality are those related to differential survival and success. Why do organizations (or colleges and universities) with similar objectives, products, or services differ rather drastically in terms of survival and success? Emergence in the past decade of the resource-dependence perspective represents a recognition of the importance of external constraints on organizational change (Aldrich, 1979). However, rather than impinging directly on organizational structures and activities, environments are mediated by participants' choices (Child, 1972). The latter has come to be known as *strategic choice,* and it has opened new issues for the study of institutional viability by drawing attention to the political determinants (e.g., elites, leaders, and dominant coalitions) of organizational activities—given that environment, technology, and size are not totally responsible for organizational change or stability.

Boundaries and Boundary Maintenance

Macro approach.   Another potentially fruitful area of exploration in the quest for understanding the concept of vitality—and one that also relates to organizations and their environments—is the study of boundaries and boundary maintenance. Who controls entry and exit? Are there alternatives available from other organizations to supply the product or service? How sensitive is management to exit (loss of client) and to voice (expression of dissatisfaction), and to what extent are organizational responsiveness and viability related? Boundary-spanning activity, both information processing and external representation, links organizations to their environments. Information-processing functions include scanning the environment, gathering intelligence, and protecting an organization against information overload, whereas representation includes resource acquisition, maintaining or improving the political and social legitimacy of the organization, and enhancing its image (Aldrich, 1979). When environments are resource scarce and unstable, boundary roles increase insofar as institutional viability becomes somewhat dependent upon the spanner's ability to mediate critical contingencies for the organization. Although little research exists about how spanners go about their work or about how critical that work is to the capacity of an institution to realize its mission, the activity itself would appear to be positively related to the adaptive capacities of institutions.

Micro approach.   In addition to the macro-institutional approach just described, we suggest that attention to boundaries should also be cast within a systems context. The idea of using open-systems concepts to study individuals, groups, and organizations has been with us since the early 1960s; organizational psychologists, sociologists, and others have emphasized both boundaries in organizational life and within organizations as the different parts relate to each other (Argyris, 1960; Bennis, 1962; Katz & Kahn, 1968). Miller's (1965) conceptualization of systems and their exchange relationships with environments on which their survival depends has been summarized by Alderfer (1976) in this way: "through exchange with the external environment, an open system can forestall its death, guarantee its life, or even increase its vitality over time" (p. 1593). Persons, groups, and organizations may be conceptualized as open systems, insofar as (theoretically) parts of an individual's body may be replaced by other living or artificial organs, and as groups or organizations live indefinitely through the process of recruiting new people to replace senior members who leave the system. Therefore, whether a human system (individuals, groups, or organizations) flourishes depends upon boundary permeability and exchange at some appropriate level. Finding and regulating that level may be the key to survival and productivity. For example, in a study of productive work climates of scientists in three settings (i.e., university, government, and industry), Pelz and Andrews (1966) produced some findings about scientific effectiveness that seem related to conceptualizations about boundary permeability and relationship exchange. They found that the most effective scientists were characterized as having mutually reinforcing relationships; not only did these scientists have several sources of influence over their goals, they also spent more time with colleagues than did the less effective scientists. Moreover, the most effective scientists often initiated such contact with their colleagues. This, then, is but one example from an extensive literature that suggests that at any level of analysis — individual, group, or organization — support can be mustered for permeable boundaries and mutual relationships as favorably affecting survival, health, and innovative products or outcomes.

Internal Environment for Individual and Group Behaviors

Environment often is thought of as that which is external to the organization. However, the organization itself does provide an environmental setting for individual and group behaviors. As Payne and Pugh state, "Discovering how the organization is a psychologically meaningful environment for individual organization members has led to the concept of 'organizational climate'" (1976, p. 1126). Organizational climate research has examined context and structure by undertaking direct assessments and by obtaining people's perceptions. Dimensions of such climate include individual autonomy and responsibility; degree of structure imposed on the position;

reward orientation; and consideration, warmth, and managerial and peer support. At present, challenges and problems of methodology and interpretation are so great that little can be said with confidence about the effects of different climates. Payne and Pugh (1976) conclude their exhaustive review by suggesting that the approach needed to study climate should include cross-sectional surveys coupled with case studies and in-depth involvement of the members of the complex system to gather data that will reflect their experiences meaningfully and realistically. This is advice to be considered in the future by researchers who explore institutional climate and its possible implications for faculty vitality.

Control Systems

Another area of organizational structure that may affect vitality is that of control systems. All viable, complex organizations introduce control systems to accomplish coordination and information processing. Moreover, large organizations with specialization of functions typically contain a number of these control systems. Lawrence and Lorsch (1967) have shown that the way in which organizations manage their coordination problems significantly influences their effectiveness. In higher education, we are familiar with a variety of control systems, including rules, regulations, standard policies and procedures, budgets, management-information systems, student evaluation of instruction, and faculty activity (productivity) reports. Lawler (1976) has framed a set of questions about what is measured and how well, who sets the standard and acts as the discriminator, what rewards and punishments are used as motivators, who receives information, and whether motivation sources are extrinsic or intrinsic. How people react to a particular control system and whether control systems produce dysfunctional consequences (e.g., invalid information, resistance to change, rigidly bureaucratic behavior, goal distortion) should be of concern in academic institutions.

Reward Systems

Reward systems tend to be tied closely to control systems. In the positive sense, reward systems provide the motivational mechanism that makes the control system viable. Inasmuch as they have received extensive attention in higher education (Lewis & Becker, 1979), reward systems are assumed to be related to faculty performance and vitality, but not in simple or well-understood ways. The effects of reward systems seem to be mediated by professionalism, self-control, and personality variables. However, just which control systems and reward systems affect the vitality of which faculty favorably or unfavorably, in which kinds of institutions, and under which kinds of conditions is not well understood at present.

Job Satisfaction and Morale

Probably no area of individual behavior in organizations has been subjected to as much research as has job satisfaction and morale. Locke (1976) estimates that to date there are well over 3,000 published studies of job satisfaction and morale. The schools of approach have evolved from those initially that focused on physical conditions of work, to those that emphasized the social or human relations aspects, to those recognizably contemporary thrusts that focus on work itself and the growth in skill, efficacy, and responsibility that challenging work affords. We are intrigued by Locke's conclusion that only negligible relationships have been shown between satisfaction and level of performance or productivity (1976, pp. 1332–1333). The latter seem to be separable outcomes of the person-work interaction. Interesting questions arise about conditions under which high productivity would lead to job satisfaction as well as the reverse of that; what past experiences are influential, what the bases of satisfaction are, how an individual responds to his or her level and quality of performance, and whether an individual's ability and skills enable a high level of performance. More organizationally oriented considerations that affect productivity might include level and quality of performance with regard to expectation set, values manifest in the reward structure, and actual working conditions.

Other Approaches

Although it would be presumptive indeed to make any direct leaps from the foundational study of organizations to issues of individual and institutional vitality in higher education, it appears that there is much theory and research in the field of organizational behavior from which hypotheses could be framed for investigation in the academic setting. Although the focus here has been on research and theory, we might also look at practice or applications of theory and research to organizational change, especially where the intent is to enhance productivity and/or to improve worker morale and job satisfaction. Recently, with the ascendance of Japan as an international economic power in clear competition with the economic-growth ranking held by the United States, much interest in and out of academe has arisen over a genre of writing that both explains and advocates a Japanese management style that focuses on company philosophy, corporate culture, staff development, and consensus decision making. A prime example of this writing is *Theory Z: How American Business Can Meet the Japanese Challenge* by William Ouchi (1981) who asserts that organizations can and should: "change their internal social structures in a manner which simultaneously satisfies competitive needs for a new, more fully integrated form, and the needs of individual employees for the satisfaction of their individual self-interest" (p. 222). Perhaps certain well-developed "practices" such as Theory Z management style should be scrutinized for the light they might shed on the nature of worker and work organization vitality.

PROBLEMS IN ASSESSING VITALITY

Measuring and quantifying an imprecise, descriptive concept such as faculty vitality obviously are difficult if not impossible tasks. However, several different ways of looking at the measurement of vitality or related phenomena have been attempted by adventurous scholars. The most direct way was embodied in a project of the Educational Testing Service that was initiated through collaborative efforts of the Kettering Foundation and Columbia University. During the conversations toward a definition of institutional vitality that were held in the late 1960s, the term *vitality* came under repeated fire for possessing "emotional overtones" that render it unsuitable for objective research (Peterson & Loye, 1967, p. 5). It was decided, therefore, that the underlying concept was "institutional functioning" rather than institutional vitality and that the goal of the project was to create an instrument for describing the relative well-being of colleges and universities. The instrument, designed to elicit perceptions of respondents for self-study purposes, included eleven scales: intellectual-aesthetic extracurriculum, freedom, human diversity, concern for improvement of society, concern for undergraduate learning, democratic governance, meeting local needs, self-study and planning, concern for advancing knowledge, concern for innovation, and institutional esprit. Values attached to high and low scores on these scales, according to the test designers, must come only from consideration of the institution's traditions, priorities, and purposes. No a priori position on vitality was to be taken.

Studies of Organizational Effectiveness

Scholars of faculty and institutional vitality are not alone in their perception of problems in assessing vitality. Cameron (1978) reports that organizational researchers have been concerned with "effectiveness" of organizations for some fifty years, yet confusion persists regarding its definition. Since few common criteria exist for indicating effectiveness, studies are seldom comparable. Even when there is agreement on criteria (e.g., adaptability, flexibility, sense of identity, absence of strain, capacity for reality testing), there may be both differences in organizational goals, constituencies, and characteristics, and methodological disagreements about such things as level of specificity for criteria, level of analysis, and objective versus subjective sources of data. All of these problems or issues are present in higher education where almost no studies of organizational effectiveness have been conducted. Cameron (1978) claims that the Educational Testing Service's Institutional Functioning Inventory was not intended to assess criteria of effectiveness, and that studies of program quality or other individual variables do not focus on effectiveness per se.

Assessing Effectiveness in Higher Education

Why is it so difficult to select and assess criteria of effectiveness in higher education? Cameron (1978, pp. 609–610) suggests four reasons: First, it is difficult to specify concrete, measurable goals and outcomes because of their diffuse and complex nature. Second, evaluation of institutional effectiveness sometimes arouses skepticism and defensiveness in academe because of concerns about attempts to extend external control. Third, financial concerns of institutions have led to research on efficiency (e.g., costs per student and student faculty ratios) rather than on effectiveness that, in turn, has led to the confusion that efficiency and effectiveness mean the same thing. A good example of the latter is Scott's (1980) extensive list of sixty-five indicators of "institutional vitality" that combines efficiency and effectiveness ratios. And finally, even the applicability of the concept of organizational effectiveness to higher education has been questioned by writers who suggest that concepts such as "organized anarchy" (Cohen & March, 1974) or "complex garbage cans" (March & Olson, 1976) or "loosely coupled systems" (Weick, 1976) describe the special nature of these organizations although considerable variation might be expected among institutions.

If we turn from problems of measuring organizational effectiveness to those of measuring faculty effectiveness or performance or vitality—although the three terms may not be synonymous—the level of analysis shifts to that of individual behavior. Nonetheless, the first three of Cameron's explanations for the difficulty in assessing organizational effectiveness continue to confront the researcher; namely, the goals and outcomes to be measured may not be easily agreed upon, the evaluation of individual effectiveness may indeed arouse concerns about control over cherished autonomy, and the indicators may focus on efficiency rather than on effectiveness. Moreover, none of the faculty performance domains is without issue vis à vis the criteria, the constituencies, the data types (objective versus subjective), and the input-output problems of measurement. Whether we are attempting to assess instructional effectiveness, scholarly distinction, or service contributions, these kinds of issues will arise and will need to be dealt with. An example will be drawn from just one of the three areas of individual performance, that of scholarly work. Scholarly performance is significant because clearly it is related to the two major purposes of colleges and universities; that is, the generation and the dissemination of knowledge. Usually reputational measures are used to assess the scholarly quality of academic departments, although most ratings of individual scholarly performance are based on individual ratings. Since recognition as determined by various honors and awards is unduly influenced by the prestige of current academic affiliation (Crane, 1965), scientific achievement is usually determined by publication count. However, since quantity measures of productivity also have their own limitations, measures that include quality as well as quantity usually are preferred. Of the latter, citation measures seem to be least contaminated by factors such as prestige of the scholar's department or university or the sheer number of published papers. According to Smith and Fiedler (1971), while citation measures are not without problems, they seem to be the preferred quality measure of scholarly performance at present.

CONCLUDING REMARKS

In this chapter, we have described and assessed the idea of faculty and institutional vitality in higher education as it is currently treated. While our review of the literature on vitality suggests that the concept is *imprecise, primitive,* and in other ways problematic, we do conclude that vitality is a useful concept, sensitizing us as it does to complex, multidimensional phenomena in circumstances that do not lend themselves to easy simplification. In advancing knowledge, there is no substitute for a good idea, including one whose current formulation may be ambiguous and clumsy. Vitality *is* a good idea.

Those who have struggled to define the concept of vitality have proposed one or more criteria that should be kept in mind as work proceeds toward eventual shared agreement on its meaning, operationalization, and assessment. These criteria include:

1. Individual and organizational vitality are interrelated. *Individual* faculty vitality focuses on the person in the career, with the latter being viewed as a series of positions in organizations. *Organizational* vitality refers to interactive strategies and processes that enable faculty, staff, and students to fulfill mutually agreed upon expectations.
2. Vital institutions should not be considered synonymous with elite institutions vis-à-vis institutional type, resource status, student body, or mission. Although there doubtless is some overlap between vital and elite institutions, the concept of vitality neither necessarily nor exclusively characterizes prestigious institutions.

3. Ideal types of vital faculty and performance emphases will differ according to institutional type and mission. Whereas some will emphasize teaching, others may emphasize research or scholarly productivity. Moreover, the service dimension may also be emphasized differentially. In defining vitality, therefore, the situational and contextual aspects must be given consideration. (It is particularly important, for example, that faculty development programs be constructed with this in mind, and that they be individualized rather than standardized.)
4. Productivity and efficiency are inherent in the concept of vitality, but they are not the whole of it. Since vitality should include qualitative as well as quantitative aspects of productivity, measures of effectiveness as well as efficiency must be developed.
5. Consideration also should be given to a currently nonspecific, abstract dimension of vitality that is variously termed as "enthusiasm," "energy," or "esprit." The latter refer to the embodiment of a set of values in the spirit of the organization that, in turn, energizes people to work in continually productive, satisfying, and occasionally innovative ways.

Throughout this chapter, we have suggested that the external environment imposes serious constraints upon faculty members and their institutions. That situation is likely to continue into the foreseeable future. Moreover, higher education seems to be undergoing a gradual paradigmatic shift, termed variously from faculty hegemony to student consumerism (Riesman, 1980) and from education community to economic industry (Kirschling, 1978; Hodgkinson, 1981). This shift is accompanied by emphasis on exchanges of goods and services and on measures of efficiency (e.g., student credit hours), and by a general valuing of performance and vitality that is based more on economic criteria than on academic, human, or social criteria. What we need to develop is a definition of vitality that goes beyond that of simple productivity, that is compatible with the "business" we are in, and that includes measures of productivity, effectiveness, and quality. Emphasis on productivity alone imitates a standard that is fast becoming obsolete in the business and industrial sectors of our society as they join the quality-of-work-life movement (Hodgkinson, 1981). Measures of vitality in higher education also should reflect concern for added values of a qualitative nature, including longitudinal perspectives on careers in organizations, development of job-related skills at different career stages, opportunities for internal mobility (both vertically and horizontally), relationship building that facilitates the psychological sense of community and sponsorship, and participation in shaping the direction of the institution or some major segment of it.

In a final sense, then, it may be that value-added approaches to productivity will lead to vitality, the state of grace that higher education seeks.

NOTES

1. Ladd (1979) argues that the research role holds sway throughout American higher education in the minds of faculty members, regardless of institutional type, and adversely affects the weighting of reward structures.

2. For the fuller exposition of each assertion and supporting research and references, see Blackburn (1979).

3. For example, *vitality* is not listed in the subject index of the 1,740-page comprehensive *Handbook of Industrial and Organizational Psychology* (Dunnette, 1976). Neither is it referenced in two popular sociology textbooks by Hall (1977) and Aldrich (1979).

Part II

EMPIRICAL ISSUES IN FACULTY VITALITY

The five chapters in Part II address a number of the empirical questions surrounding the issues of faculty vitality. To what extent is the faculty changing and aging in American higher education? How do faculty careers develop? And, if the faculty is relatively immobile and aging, what are the implications for both individual and organizational productivity? In answering these questions, the authors review both the theoretical and empirical literature and offer evidence from their own work. Chapter 2 introduces Part II by focusing on the changing demography of faculty in higher education. Assessment is given through simulation and empirical models as to the likely forms of adjustments to forecasted changes in the 1980s and 1990s. Special attention is given to a faculty flow model concerned with assumptions about current age profiles, limited budgets, enrollment declines, changes in student–staff ratios, tenure practices, and retirement policies and practices. It is shown that the academic labor market is becoming highly immobile and "graying." In this rather bleak context, Chapter 3 examines how existing faculty careers can be enhanced for the sake of institutional productivity. Existing career development theories are reviewed and assessed against empirical evidence in the literature dealing with specific data on faculty research productivities, teaching, service, personality, and career stages. A new conceptual framework is introduced that focuses on career events rather than age stages as being more critical and useful for influencing institutional policy and practice. Chapters 4 and 5 address more directly the probable relationships between faculty age and scientific research productivity. As a result of recent and contemplated federal legislation dealing with compulsory retirement, special attention is given to the case of older faculty. Chapter 6 employs an institutional case study to examine empirically those individual and institutional characteristics that contribute most to faculty vitality. Focus is given to institutional characteristics and policy areas that lend themselves to influencing productivity and vitality.

Chapter 2

Changing Demography
of Faculty
in Higher Education

W. Lee Hansen

Both the recently slowing growth and the impending contraction of the
academic sector as the size of the college-age youth population declines have
produced widespread concern about how to maintain faculty vitality. The
changing pattern of growth means that fewer new faculty members will be
required; consequently, the average age of faculty members will rise, and we
will face the prospect of a serious imbalance in faculty age structure a
decade from now when enrollments are projected to begin rising again. This
chapter explores the changing demography of college and university teachers. It begins with a brief review of the major influences on faculty demography and the concerns produced by the likely pattern of change. Then a
more detailed analysis of these changes is presented, as revealed by simulations or projections of the faculty age structure over the next two decades.
After considering various ways by which the projected age patterns might
be altered, a brief set of conclusions is offered.

BACKGROUND

The changing demography of college and university faculties is of much
concern because of the mutually interacting relationship between teaching
and research. Established scholars seek not only to transmit existing knowledge to oncoming generations of students and to society as a whole but also
to discover new knowledge through close interaction with younger scholars,
both those just starting their research careers and those engaged in research
training. But as the demand for new faculty positions slows dramatically
there is concern that over the next decade faculties, students, and institutions will suffer because of the relative absence of "new blood." By "new
blood" we mean new PhDs who are freshly trained, full of enthusiasm, and

filled with new ideas and ways of looking at matters that will spill over and affect their older colleagues, and who invigorate instruction and assure a continuing flow of new and innovative research for the benefit of society. Moreover, to the extent that younger faculty members often perform somewhat different roles than more senior faculty members, as reflected in the nature and mix of their teaching and research, there will be inevitable changes in the "output" of the higher education sector as faculties age. Most observers see the prospective "graying" of the professoriate as a not altogether happy development but feel powerless to do much about it.

These concerns are exacerbated by two related developments in social policy. The first is the change from age 65 to 70 in the minimum allowed age of mandatory retirement which took effect on 1 July 1982, with the expiration of the special exemption given tenured faculty members by the 1978 amendments to the Age Discrimination in Employment Act of 1967. Whereas prior to this legislation many colleges retired their faculty members at age 65, this practice is no longer possible. The likely result is that appreciable numbers of faculty members will continue teaching until age 70. Doing so will further reduce opportunities for new PhDs to find academic posts and to exert their stimulating effects on the profession (Hansen & Holden, 1981). Higher education interest groups had mixed opinions when this legislation came up for consideration. Most institutionally oriented associations opposed the change, whereas faculty groups generally favored the change. Taking positions on this legislation was complicated because the joint position of the American Association of University Professors (AAUP) and the Association of American Colleges (AAC) had long stated the need for a fixed retirement age but allowed that the age could range between 65 and 70, depending on the needs of individual institutions and their faculty members.

The second development is still pending but appears increasingly likely to occur. That is passage of Representative Claude Pepper's bill that would completely eliminate the mandatory retirement age for all workers, including college faculty members. This "uncapping" of the retirement age would give all faculty members opportunities to continue teaching until the infirmities of old age caught up with them or they succumbed with the chalk still clutched in their fingers. President Reagan recently endorsed the idea of uncapping the retirement age, reasserting a fall 1980 campaign promise (a similar promise was also made by then President Carter). The word from Washington insiders is that little opposition exists within Congress to eliminating the mandatory retirement age. Moreover, there is little or no opposition elsewhere either. The business sector appears to believe that it can adapt to uncapping without undue difficulty. Whether this is true for the academic sector remains unclear. It appears that many higher education organizations and institutions are fearful of the adverse effects of uncapping. In fact, the American Association of University Professors went on record in June 1982 opposing uncapping. The adverse effects on tenure were explicated by AAUP's Committee A on Academic Freedom and Tenure in a special report ("Uncapping the Mandatory Retirement Age," *Academe,* September/October 1982b, pp. 14a–18a). Academic opposition to uncapping was registered in testimony by Professor John Dunlop of Harvard (and a former Secretary of Labor) presented before a Pepper subcommittee hearing in August 1982 (Dunlop, 1982).

To round out the picture, the prospects for higher education itself are not buoyant. Enrollments are projected to decline, thereby reducing the demand for new faculty and hastening the aging of the academic profession. Graduate enrollments are also likely to decline, even more so because job prospects for new PhDs will continue to be poor. Present faculty members are likely to retire later not only because they are healthier and live longer than people from most other occupational groups but also because recent inflation and declining real salaries have sharply reduced the real value of retirement benefits from retiring early.

The enrollment projections indicate declines from 5 to 40 percent in undergraduate enrollments from 1980 to 1990, with the recent projections showing from a 20 percent increase to a 47 percent decrease in undergraduate enrollments from 1980 to 2000. Much of the uncertainty about future enrollments depends on the behavior of adults (i.e., how many of them will return as older students) and on the assumed responsiveness of college-age students to the declining economic benefits from college attendance. To the extent that enrollments decline and student–faculty ratios remain relatively constant, this implies commensurate percentage reductions in faculty size.

This slackening of demand for undergraduate education will be even greater at the graduate level. Not only will the pool of potential students be reduced, but in addition the greatly reduced job prospects of future PhDs will undercut the incentive of many young people to pursue graduate training. Despite these prospects, projections of the number of PhDs awarded indicate substantial overproduction of PhDs until the year 2000 (Bowen, 1981). This reflects only a slight lessening of the dismal picture presented by Cartter in 1976 (Cartter, 1976).

The likelihood that existing job slots will be opened up by the exit of present faculty members has been reduced by several factors. The evidence shows that prospective male faculty annuitants at age 60, for example, can expect to live another 22 years, five years more than for the average male worker of the same age. Moreover, faculty members display remarkably good health, which permits them to continue working longer than most occupational groups. Finally, the surge of recent inflation combined with the substantial decline in real faculty salaries in the 1970s has produced among older faculty members greater concern about the adequacy of their prospective retirement benefits, particularly in view of their increased longevity (Hansen & Holden, 1981, Chapter 3).

Taken together, all of these developments make it more important than ever to examine faculty demography. By how much is the age structure likely to change over the next two decades? How might this structure be affected by changing the retirement age? How will the numbers of new positions for newly trained PhDs be affected? What will be the impact of such constraints as limited budgets, enrollment declines, and changes in student–staff ratios? And finally, what if anything can be done to deal with these problems?

OPTIMAL AGE STRUCTURE

Before we discuss any formulated faculty flow model, we need some organizing framework for thinking about faculty-age structure and faculty vitality. There are two important elements to this framework: the objectives of higher education institutions and the optimal age structure to help achieve these objectives.

College and universities can be thought of as organizations that attempt to maximize the present value of their outputs of teaching, research, and service, taking account of both quantity and quality of these multiple outputs. In hiring new faculty members, professors and administrators alike desire to attract individuals who show great promise for highly productive careers. A check on the effectiveness of the selection process occurs a half dozen years after hiring when, routinely, assistant professors are reviewed for tenure; at that time a decision must be made about both their adequacy of performance to date and their potential for continuing high levels of future performance. Once tenure is awarded, institutions have less control over the performance of their personnel. At many institutions, merit salary increases serve to stimulate faculty members to greater levels of effort and performance. Individual faculty members cannot, however, be discharged because of slightly below-average performance. If some of them should slip into incompetence they can be discharged, but the process of proving such charges is not easy.

The focus of institutions is on what its faculty members can do, and yet institutional personnel policies necessarily have important age dimensions. Individuals who attain tenure by their early to mid 30s have the opportunity to continue in their jobs until reaching the age of retirement. This means that institutions possess relatively little flexibility in altering the age mix of their faculties. In the absence of growth, the age mix of the faculty can be changed only as individuals retire or leave for other positions and are then replaced with younger people or are not replaced at all.

Given the age composition determining the effects of these long-standing personnel policies, we can think of institutions as being concerned about the age structure of their faculties and questing for what might be called an optimal age structure. This structure can be defined as that distribution of faculty members by age whose present value of total output, now and into the future, is at a maximum. If institutions are concerned about the mix of outputs, it is with that distribution of faculty members by age whose total output, present and prospective, is at a maximum, provided the desired minimum quantity and quality of each type of output is attained. In a sense, this is an empty statement; yet it helps us to conceptualize the issue because of its focus on the present level and continuing flow of output. As noted before, the key to change lies in being able to influence the flow of retirements and of exits to other jobs and to control access to tenure. Given this latitude, the balance between younger and older faculty members can be affected to a significant degree, but only slowly.

Implicit in this shift of focus to age is the belief that age represents a reasonably good proxy variable for academic productivity. In fact, academic productivity varies enormously among individuals as well as among fields (which will be treated by Reskin in Chapter 4). The demands of various fields also differ substantially and the age-performance or age-productivity link varies widely. Productivity levels also vary by type of institution, given that two-year colleges emphasize teaching while universities focus more heavily on research output.

Several barriers exist to the attainment of any particular age distribution that would maximize total institutional productivity over the long run. First, age discrimination legislation prevents the use of age as a factor in personnel decisions. Indeed, the pursuit of some optimal age structure might itself be deemed a manifestation of age discrimination. Second, salary policies militate against the attainment of any particular age structure. Not only is it almost impossible to reduce a person's nominal wages, as a device to help induce their leaving, but it is often difficult to offer the higher salaries needed to attract new faculty members or to retain those who are tempted by other opportunities. The idea of relative uniformity in salaries seems to be based on the notion that faculty members represent some community of interests and that substantial salary differentiations among them, whether because of market or other forces, are inappropriate.

Even if we could determine the configuration of an optimal age structure, the problems of maintaining it would be severe. The principal reason is fluctuations in the overall demand for higher education. The college-age population, while not fluctuating erratically from year to year, does vary systematically over time — as reflected by the post–World War II baby-boom cohorts reaching age eighteen beginning in the mid-1960s and the birth-dearth cohorts that will reach age 18 in the late 1980s. We have earlier examples of the latter in the 1930s depression-induced reductions in birth cohorts which reached age 18 in the early 1950s. Additional variation results from the combination of wars, which temporarily reduce enrollments, and their aftermath, which not only raises enrollments to offset the earlier decline but typically expands enrollments because of educational benefits offered to ex-servicemen. And finally, we have a more recent development whose future effects are still difficult to predict; namely, the expanding enrollments of older students, many of them women, who are preparing for new careers.

Even if some optimal age structure could be achieved and maintained, there is less reason to hope that the same could be done for broad subdivisions of faculties or individual departments within these subdivisions. Many of these units are small and this necessarily makes it more difficult. More important, changes in the pace of knowledge development, shifts in student preferences, and the like cause some units of an institution to expand and others to contract. Newly emerging disciplines will necessarily have younger faculties because only younger people are available to staff these positions. Fields in decline and not hiring new people will achieve contraction through attrition.

In light of these difficulties does it make sense to think about an optimal age structure? It does in that changes in the age distribution of existing faculty members, aside from any concerns about quality, affect not only faculty compensation costs, given that older faculty earn on average twice as much as new younger faculty members, but also the rate at which new young PhDs can be added to the faculty. To explore the effect of faculty demography on these two important factors, we must turn to our faculty flow model.

FACULTY FLOW MODEL

A faculty flow model is simply a device to trace out future changes in the age composition of faculty members. The faculty flow model used here (Figure 2.1) traces the movement of faculty members through their careers which have four distinct phases: nontenure status, tenure status before eligibility for early retirement, tenure status while eligible for early retirement (prior to normal retirement), and finally retirement itself. In most cases, these phases can be characterized by age with appropriate age divisions within each of the phases. The volume of movement through the age structure would indicate what percentage of a cohort of tenured faculty members, say, age 40–44 in year 0, would remain in the teaching profession in year 5 when the cohort is age 45–49.

A faculty flow model of this kind can be used in a variety of ways. One possibility is to employ recent or current values of entry, retention, and exit

FIGURE 2.1.   Faculty Flow Model

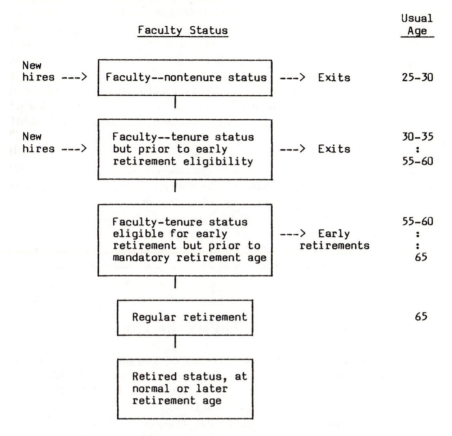

rates to work out the pattern of future changes in age composition. Another possibility is to incorporate policy changes and other expected or known changes to show how the pattern of already projected future changes in age distribution might be altered. Still another possibility is to allow patterns of future changes in age distribution to be influenced by behavioral responses to these changes. Attention will be concentrated on the first two of these three approaches.

To implement this model, we start with an age distribution of faculty members. To this we add transition rates from age group to age group that reflect patterns of physical aging, mandatory retirement, early retirement, voluntary exit to other jobs, involuntary exit through failure to gain tenure, and new entrants (both new PhDs as well as others who enter at somewhat later ages). Because the data are so scanty, these various transition rates are often rather crude approximations of reality. We next add the overall constraints, such that faculty size remains constant or that the faculty compensation budget remains constant. These constraints yield different results, largely because the average, older faculty member earns twice as much as a younger faculty member. These results can also be altered by allowing for differences or changes in the age-salary profile.

The resulting patterns of change depend on any number of additional considerations. The initial age distribution will vary depending on whether the faculty can be described as "young," "mature," or having a "balanced" age structure. The first is represented by relatively new institutions which have few older faculty members; and the latter is represented by long established nongrowing institutions whose faculties will be considerably older. The extent to which nontenured faculty members are renewed and subsequently tenured will differ. The age of mandatory retirement and early retirement provisions will affect the rate at which people retire. Similarly, exits to other occupations will vary in a variety of ways, depending on institutional location, compensation level, and orientation (liberal arts versus a greater emphasis on preprofessional training, e.g., engineering).

FACULTY DEMOGRAPHY IN THE 1970s

The demography of the faculty is not easy to ascertain. Various surveys from the 1970s show an array of results that are generally similar and move in anticipated ways over time. Some sense for what has been, is, and is likely to be comes from the work of Froomkin (1978). Starting with 1970 census data on the age distribution of faculty members, he estimates the 1977 distribution and then projects it forward to 1980 and 1985. From these distributions it is possible to calculate the median age and, in addition, the proportion of faculty members over age 60.

The results in Table 2.1 show the median age of faculty members rising from 34.5 years in 1970, to 35.7 years in 1977, and to 37.4 years in 1980: the median continues to rise during the 1980s, reaching 39.4 years by 1985 for the high projection and 40.3 years for the low projection. The percentage over age 60 rises from 6.5 percent in 1970, to 6.9 percent in 1975, and to 8.1 percent in 1980. The 60+ age group is expected to rise to between 11 and 12 percent of all faculty members by 1985.

These estimates leave out a number of factors. First, they fail to take account of the financial stringencies of higher education that developed in the middle to late 1970s. Second, they fail to consider prospective enrollment declines in the 1980s that will reduce the need for faculty members.

TABLE 2.1. Actual, Estimated, and Projected Distribution of
            Full-Time Faculty Members by Age and Estimated
            Median Age, 1970-85

Age	Actual, 1970	Estimated, 1977	Projected to 1980 High	Projected to 1985 High	Low
<30	19.5	13.2	8.7	6.7	6.8
30-34	14.7	17.0	12.7	8.9	5.1
35-39	17.4	17.6	19.7	15.5	16.0
40-44	14.5	17.3	18.4	21.4	21.2
45-49	12.5	10.5	13.5	15.4	16.2
50-54	8.5	10.2	9.3	12.2	13.3
55-59	6.5	7.3	9.5	9.2	9.7
60-64	5.0	5.3	6.2	8.5	9.3
65+	1.5	1.6	1.9	2.4	2.7
Totals	100.0	100.0	100.0	100.0	100.0
Estimated Median Age	34.5	35.7	37.4	39.4	40.3

Source: Calculated from Joseph Froomkin, "Full-Time Faculty in Higher Education--Numbers and Ages," Proceedings of the Social Statistics Section, American Statistical Association, 1978, pp. 657-662.

Third, they neglect changing patterns of retirement such as those likely to result from the 1978 amendments to the Age Discrimination in Employment Act. Fourth, they ignore possible reactions to the pressures of all three of these forces that may give rise to important new policy changes such as the development of early retirement or midcareer change programs. The impact of any or all of these changes will depend heavily on and, in turn, affect the age distribution of faculty members.

Of key importance for our discussion here is the impact of the mandatory retirement exemption. With the lapsing of this exemption in 1982, causing the minimum mandatory retirement age to change from 65 to 70, the aging of the faculty will be accelerated. The extent of the change will depend on what fraction of faculty members decide to continue teaching. For individual institutions, however, the near-term impact will vary, depending not only on the proportion who opt to continue but also on the relative age distribution, that is, what proportions of their faculty members are already age 60 and above. How substantial will this effect be? To answer this question, we must turn to a number of simulations.

BACKGROUND OF SIMULATIONS

The results of simulation studies depend critically on the nature of the faculty flow model used and the data they incorporate. A major difficulty with most of these studies is that they utilize what can be called "synthetic" rather than actual data, that is, "made up" numbers that seem plausible in the absence of actual numbers or averages of existing data that reflect representative situations. Typically, the data needed are difficult if not impossible to obtain. Now, however, we are in a position to offer more realistic simulations by drawing on new information from surveys of institutions and of faculty members undertaken for our recent evaluation of the impact of the special exemption for tenured faculty members from the provisions of the 1978 amendments to the Age Discrimination in Employment Act of 1967 (Hansen & Holden, 1981b). Our most important addition is for attrition rates, that is, the rates at which people of different age groups exit from their academic jobs. We have this information for both institutions and faculty members. However, several important differences in the attrition data for institutions and faculty members require explanation. (For more details, see Hansen & Holden, 1981b.)

The attrition rates based on the institutional survey were derived from information provided by institutions on the number of people who retired by age from 1978–79 to 1979–80. Given the availability of data on the age distribution of faculty members in 1979–80, we were able to calculate age-specific attrition rates appropriate for our simulations. One difficulty with this approach is that the data for a single year may not be representative of normal attrition patterns.

The attrition rates for faculty members differ somewhat in that they are prospective, being based on the expected age of retirement as reported by those faculty members who were surveyed. With this information it became possible to estimate for each cohort what proportion of its members expect to work for how many more years. The difficulty with using faculty responses is that expected ages of retirement may deviate substantially from actual ages of retirement. We have no way of knowing how accurate the expected retirement age will be. Nonetheless, we can infer the effects of a change in the mandatory retirement age (MRA) by comparing the patterns of expected retirements for faculty members at institutions with different mandatory retirement ages.

The faculty data offer additional advantages by showing how respondents might alter their expected ages of retirement in response to other factors, among them inflation and various early-retirement options. Even if the expected age of retirement is found to be in error after the fact, there may be reason to believe that reported changes in expected retirement age are indicative of how faculty members will respond. For this reason, we have run additional simulations that use the expected age of retirement to reflect faculty attrition rates, both with and without early retirement incentives.

These simulations are carried out under the two alternative constraints employed in Hansen's earlier simulations, namely, constant faculty size and a constant compensation budget (Hansen, 1979). In addition, enrollments are assumed to remain constant or to decline by 10 percent or alternatively by 30 percent during the 1982–87 period. Because of the possibility of additional pressures on institutions, the faculty–student ratio was also allowed to drop by 10 percent, again during the 1982–87 period. Of course, numerous combinations of these assumptions, keyed to different periods, could be incorporated that would modify some of the results but not change them substantially. The specific assumptions and data sources used are described elsewhere (Hansen & Holden, 1981b, Appendix F).

All simulations start with the age 65 mandatory retirement situation and, in the absence of any change, reflect the retention rates for faculty and institutions with an MRA of 65. To estimate the impact of the expiration of the exemption in 1982, we allow retention rates to change beginning in 1982 by employing several alternative retention patterns. One is that of faculty at institutions with an MRA of 70. Next, we build a "worst" case situation which assumes that large proportions of older faculty members continue teaching until age 70, after the exemption expires. Finally, we incorporate faculty expectations to construct another alternative set of retention rates based on the expectations of faculty members currently at institutions with an MRA of 65.

STEADY-STATE SIMULATION RESULTS

We first present the most general case, based on the overall age distribution and the assumption that higher education is in a "steady-state" environment, with constant faculty size or constant budget size as a constraint. The simulations begin in 1979 when the 1978 amendments took effect and the exemption permitted mandatory retirement to continue at age 65. Table 2.2 shows how budget size changes and the proportions of new hires vary when faculty size is held constant. Lines 1–2 portray the "base case," that is, the course of events based on the assumption that faculty members continued to retire at age 65; lines 3–4 indicate the effect of lifting the exemption in 1982 (so that the minimum mandatory retirement age rises to 70), on the assumption that faculty members who are affected take on the retirement patterns of faculty members at institutions where the MRA has for some time already been set at age 70; lines 5–6 present a "worst" case, with substantially larger proportions of faculty members choosing after 1982 to continue teaching until age 70; and lines 7–8 indicate what happens after 1982 based on the statements of affected faculty members about their expected retirement plans. (For more details, readers are again referred to Hansen & Holden, 1981b.)

Even in a base case situation (lines 1–2), budget size rises by 1982 to a level 4 percent higher than in 1979 and remains above the 1979 level through the end of the century. New hires decline from 1979 to 1982 and then remain about constant at the 1987 level. With the expiration of the exemption (lines 3–4), there is relatively little change in either budget size or proportion of new hires. This is not so with the worst case (lines 5–6). By 1987 annual costs rise to a level that is 2.5 to 3 percent higher than in lines 1 and 3. By 1987 new hires drop by more than 25 percent (to 12.8 percent from 17.5 percent in line 2) and then gradually rise, but never regain their old level. The impact of faculty expectations (lines 7–8) falls roughly between the previous two cases. By 1987 budget costs are 1.7 percent higher than in line 1, and they are 2.2 percent higher in 1992 remaining more than 1.5 percent higher through the end of the century. New hires in 1987 drop by about 18 percent (line 8 versus line 2) and then rise, but not quite to the levels that would occur if the exemption remained in force.

What happens under the constant budget assumption as shown in Table 2.3? With the continuation of the age 65 minimum mandatory retirement age shown in lines 1–3, faculty size drops modestly initially and then regains its 1979 level in the 1990s, and finally begins rising sharply after 1997. New hires drop in 1982 but then regain their 1979 level and hold at that level. The expiration of the exemption and the assumed change in retirement behavior to that characteristic of faculty members under an age 70 MRA has little effect (lines 3–4). However, with larger proportions of faculty members continuing to work after the exemption expires in 1982 (lines 5–6), faculty size by 1987 is almost 4 percent lower than with the exemption; this situation continues throughout the simulation period. More striking is the almost 50 percent drop by 1987 in new hires — 10.9 percent in line 6 versus 18.9 percent in line 1. Incorporating faculty expectations into these simulations reduces faculty size by just over 2 percent in 1987 and necessarily reduces new hires less sharply — by about one-third in 1987 (line 8) — but more sharply than if the MRA had not been changed (line 2).

The interpretations we give to these results depend in part on which set of retention rates seems most reasonable. The assumption that affected faculty members take on the patterns of those who are not affected is hard to accept, inasmuch as the affected faculty members have been conditioned to an age 65 MRA and in all likelihood to different retirement plan contribution rates. In the long run, this assumption might be appropriate but it is not so now. The worst case may be equally difficult to accept because the retention rate selected is quite arbitrary, assuming that three-quarters of

TABLE 2.2. Index of Changes in Budget Size and Percentage of New
            Hires (Based on Assumption of Constant Faculty Size
            for Different Retirement Patterns)

	1979	1982	1987	1992	1997	2002
Base Case--Retirement at Age 65						
1. Budget size	100.0	104.0	103.2	102.5	101.8	100.6
2. New hires	16.5	8.9	17.5	17.2	16.5	17.8
Retirement Based on Age 70 MRA Pattern						
3. Budget size	100.0	104.0	103.3	102.7	102.0	100.8
4. New hires	16.5	8.9	17.2	17.0	16.6	17.5
Retirement Based on Worst Case-- Age 70 MRA						
5. Budget size	100.0	104.0	105.8	105.6	104.7	103.1
6. New hires	16.5	8.9	12.8	15.3	15.8	16.8
Retirement Based on Faculty Expectations						
7. Budget size	100.0	104.0	104.9	104.7	103.8	102.3
8. New hires	16.5	8.9	14.4	15.7	16.1	17.1

TABLE 2.3. Index of Change in Faculty Size and Percentage of New
            Hires (Based on Assumption of Constant Compensation
            Budget For Different Retirement Patterns)

	1979	1982	1987	1992	1997	2002
Base Case--Retirement at Age 65						
1. Faculty size	100.0	97.9	99.3	100.4	101.1	102.9
2. New hires	16.5	6.9	18.9	18.1	16.7	19.3
Retirement Based on Age 70 MRA Patterns						
3. Faculty size	100.0	97.9	99.1	100.0	100.9	102.6
4. New hires	16.5	6.9	18.5	17.8	17.0	19.0
Retirement Based on Worst Case--Age 70 MRA						
5. Faculty size	100.0	97.9	95.6	96.4	98.0	100.4
6. New hires	16.5	6.9	10.9	16.5	17.2	18.8
Retirement Based on Faculty Expectations						
7. Faculty size	100.0	97.6	96.9	97.6	99.0	101.2
8. New hires	16.5	6.9	13.7	16.7	17.2	19.1

faculty members age 60–64 continue to age 65–69; of course, this is less arbitrary than assuming that they all continue to age 70!

The results based on faculty expectations (lines 7–8) seem most plausible, resting on the answers faculty provided in their questionnaires. (Henceforth, our comparisons are confined to the base case, representing a continuation of the age 65 MRA, and to the last case, which assumes that with the lifting of the exemption faculty expectations are the all-important determinant of retirement patterns.) Thus, the effect of allowing the exemption to expire is, under the constant faculty size constraint, to raise the compensation costs of affected institutions by about 2 percent on average, with this additional cost decreasing slowly over time. New hires would initially drop by about 20 percent below the level prevailing in the absence of a change in the MRA, but then begin a slow rise back to near but not quite their old levels. It is important to point out that not all faculty and institutions will be affected. As of early 1980, the proportion of all faculty members likely to be affected had fallen from two-thirds to one-third because of changes in state law or institutional practices. Nevertheless, among those institutions affected there will be a range of effects, from little or no effect to the worst case results just described.

What is the effect of these various changes on the age distribution of faculty members? For the two key situations in Table 2.2, Table 2.4 shows the median age of faculty members and also the percentages of faculty members age 60 + and age 50 + . We see that under the base case the percentages of faculty age 50 + and age 60 + stabilize after 1982. The median age, however, slowly declines back toward its original level. With the change to an age 70 MRA, the percentages above age 60 and age 50, for example, are considerably higher by 1992. Moreover, the median age rises more sharply and over a more sustained period. Thus, expiration of the exemption clearly will increase the proportions of older faculty members.

DIFFERENCES IN AGE STRUCTURE

All of these results are for an "average" institution, or for an average of all affected institutions. Yet we know that institutions are not all alike, certainly with respect to their age distributions. Some faculties are older than others; some have more rigid tenure standards than do others; some have grown rapidly and are necessarily quite young. To illustrate the significance of age, it became necessary to rerun the simulations for different faculty age structures.

The age distributions used for this exercise and shown in Table 2.5 are not actual age structures so much as renditions of them, representing an effort to portray the several general patterns. Distribution I is the average, as

TABLE 2.4. Effects of Simulations on Age Structure of Faculty
           (Based on Constant Faculty Size Case of Table 2.2)

	1979	1982	1987	1992	1997	2002
Base Case--Retirement at Age 65						
Median age	40.8	43.4	43.4	43.2	41.1	40.2
Percent 60+	7.0	10.4	10.6	10.0	11.0	10.8
Percent 50+	26.5	33.3	33.5	33.7	33.3	33.2
Retirement Based on Faculty Expectations						
Median age	40.8	43.4	44.7	45.0	44.6	41.6
Percent 60+	7.0	10.4	13.1	14.8	15.0	14.8
Percent 50+	26.5	33.3	36.6	38.1	37.9	36.8

TABLE 2.5. Alternative Age Distributions of Faculty Members for
           Simulations

Age	I	II	III	IV	V
<30	165	165	165	20	60
30-34	165	135	135	60	80
35-39	150	95	110	150	150
40-44	130	95	110	150	150
45-49	125	95	110	150	150
50-54	115	95	110	150	150
55-59	80	180	150	180	150
60-64	60	120	90	120	90
65-69	10	20	20	20	20
Totals	1,000	1,000	1,000	1,000	1,000
Median Age	40.8	45.5	44.1	49.0	48.0
Percent Above 50	26.5	41.5	37.0	47.0	41.0
Percent Above 60	7.0	14.0	11.0	14.0	11.0

of early 1980, across all institutions with an age 65 MRA. Distribution II represents an older age distribution, with 41.5 rather than 26.5 percent of the faculty age 50 and above. Distribution III has the same proportion of older faculty and additionally preserves the same distribution (as in distribution I) of younger faculty under age 35; as a result, the distribution is "thinner" in the middle age ranges from 35 to 54. Distribution IV has an even larger proportion of faculty age 50 and above, namely 47 percent, and it has a heavy distribution in the middle age range. Distribution V is similar to IV except that it maintains the same proportion of younger faculty (under age 35) as distribution I.

The impact of these different age distributions on budget costs and new hires is shown in Table 2.6 based on the constant faculty size assumption. By 1987 cost increases range from 1.7 to 3.7 percent higher than they would be in the absence of a change; the increase for distribution I, already discussed, is mild by comparison with the increases for other distributions. By 1992 there is a considerable narrowing of the cost increases, with a range from 1.5 to 2.7 percent; the additional costs drop for all distributions except I. By 1997 the costs decline further and continue to do so thereafter. This is the result, of course, of a one-time change in the age of retirement from 65 to 70. In general, however, the magnitude of the additional costs varies with age structure, a finding that is not too surprising.

The impact on new hiring patterns is shown in Table 2.7, again under the assumption of constant faculty size. Hirings are from 3 to well over 6 percent lower when the exemption expires, depending upon the age distribution of the faculty. Again, the effect is most severe in 1987 but quickly diminishes, and for some distributions the effect is reversed.

These results indicate that differences in age structures can easily magnify the effects of changes in retirement ages on budget costs and new hires. The effects of later retirements are even greater on faculty size and new hires under a constant budget rather than a constant faculty size constraint.

DIFFERENCES IN AGE-SALARY PROFILES

The shape of the age-salary profile is also important in affecting budget costs. Thus far, all the simulations utilized the overall salary profile derived from our survey data and linked to other faculty salary data so as to provide the full age-salary profile. A number of institutions, however, offer salaries such that the cross-section pattern of salaries at the upper age range is not horizontal but rising. Consequently, it seemed advisable to test the sensitivity of our simulations of total costs for different age distributions to the introduction of a steeper salary profile, one that has salary at age 65–69 reaching $32,000, double that at the entry age of under 30 and about $3,000 higher than the average salary at that age for members of our sample.

A comparison of the results in Table 2.8 with those in Table 2.7 shows

TABLE 2.6. Impact of Change to Age 70 MRA on Total Budget Costs
            (Based on Different Age Distributions and Assumption of
            Constant Faculty Size)

Age Distribution	1979	1982	1987	1992	1997	2002
I	0	0	1.7	2.2	2.0	1.7
II	0	0	3.6	1.5	1.1	1.1
III	0	0	3.0	1.9	1.5	1.4
IV	0	0	3.7	2.7	2.0	1.6
V	0	0	3.0	2.7	2.2	1.7

Note: Results assume shift in 1982 to faculty expectations about
retirement age.

TABLE 2.7. Percentage Point Reduction in New Hires
            from Change to Age 70 MRA (Based on Different Age
            Distributions and Assumption of Constant Faculty Size)

Age Distribution	1979	1982	1987	1992	1997	2002
I	0	0	-3.1	-1.5	-0.4	-0.7
II	0	0	-6.2	+2.4	-0.3	-0.7
III	0	0	-5.3	+0.9	-0.1	-0.8
IV	0	0	-6.6	+0.7	-0.2	-0.4
V	0	0	-5.5	-0.4	-0.1	-0.5

Note: Results assume shift in 1982 to faculty expectations about
retirement age.

TABLE 2.8. Impact of Change to Age 70 MRA on Total Budget Costs
            (Based on Different Salary and Age Distributions and
            Assumption of Constant Faculty Size)

Age Distribution	1979	1982	1987	1992	1997	2002
I	0	0	2.1	2.8	2.6	2.4
II	0	0	4.2	1.8	1.6	1.4
III	0	0	3.6	2.3	1.9	1.8
IV	0	0	4.1	3.0	2.4	1.9
V	0	0	3.5	3.1	2.6	2.1

quite clearly that the steeper age-salary profile produces bigger increases in
costs as retirement age rises; the increases are about 0.5 percent greater. Put
another way, the costs shown in Table 2.8 are about 15 to 20 percent higher
because of the difference in the salary profile. There is also an impact on
new hires, as shown by comparing Tables 2.9 and 2.7. New hires are about 3
percent lower by 1987 but soon begin to reapproach their old levels again.

ENROLLMENT CHANGES

What happens if enrollments begin to fall? These effects are shown in Table
2.10 where we assume that the binding constraint is the existence of a constant faculty–student ratio. This means that our analysis focuses on budget
costs, new hires, and per student costs. Enrollment declines of 30 and 10
percent are examined; declines of these magnitudes seem quite possible. To
facilitate the comparisons, simulation results for the constant enrollment
case are also presented. For purposes of these simulations we assume that
institutional revenues are contingent on enrollments. The results are presented in Table 2.10.

   If enrollment drops by 30 percent after 1982 and the faculty–student
ratio remains constant, the budget drops 21.2 percent below its 1979 level
(line 7) by 1987 with the result that costs per student rise by almost 13 percent above their 1979 level (line 9). However, these costs begin to drop
rapidly thereafter, as might be expected. The precipitous decline in enrollments produces a sharp one-time drop in new hires by 1987 (line 8). The increase in student costs also might have some negative effect on enrollments;
however, the results of a 10 percent enrollment cut are not quite so dramatic
(lines 13–15). What we see here, as contrasted to the steady-state enrollment
of lines 1–3, is a seniority-based reduction in faculty size and its attendant
impact on budget costs.

TABLE 2.9. Percentage Point Reductions in New Hires from Change
            to Age 70 MRA (Based on Different Salary and Age
            Distributions and Assumption of Constant Faculty Size)

Age Distribution	1979	1982	1987	1992	1997	2002
I	0	0	−3.1	−1.5	−0.4	−0.7
II	0	0	−6.2	+2.4	−0.3	−0.7
III	0	0	−5.3	+0.9	−0.1	−0.8
IV	0	0	−6.6	+0.7	−0.2	−0.4
V	0	0	−5.5	−0.4	−0.1	−0.5

TABLE 2.10.   Impact of Enrollment Declines on Indexes of Budget Size
and of Cost per Student, and on Percentages of New Hires
(Based on Assumption of Constant Faculty-Student Ratio
for Different Retirement Rates)

	1979	1982	1987	1992	1997	2002

ENROLLMENT--NO CHANGE

Base Case--Retirement
at Age 65

	1979	1982	1987	1992	1997	2002
1. Index of budget size	100.0	104.0	103.2	102.5	101.8	100.6
2. Percentage of new hires	16.5	8.9	17.5	17.2	16.5	17.8
3. Index of cost per student	100.0	104.0	103.2	102.5	101.8	100.6

Retirement Based on Faculty
Expectations

4. Index of budget size	100.0	104.0	104.9	104.7	103.8	102.3
5. Percentage of new hires	16.5	8.9	14.4	15.7	16.1	17.1
6. Index of cost per student	100.0	104.0	104.9	104.7	103.8	102.3

ENROLLMENT--30% DECLINE, 1982-87

Base Case--Retirement
at Age 65

7. Index of budget size	100.0	104.0	78.8	76.1	72.9	69.6
8. Percentage of new hires	16.5	8.9	5.4	20.0	20.6	20.6
9. Index of cost per student	100.0	104.0	112.6	108.7	104.1	99.4

Retirement Based on Faculty
Expectations

10. Index of budget size	100.0	104.0	80.3	78.1	74.7	71.0
11. Percentage of new hires	16.5	8.9	3.6	17.6	19.6	20.1
12. Index of cost per student	100.0	104.0	114.8	111.6	106.7	101.5

ENROLLMENT--10% DECLINE, 1982-87

Base Case--Retirement
at Age 65

13. Index of budget size	100.4	104.0	95.9	94.3	92.9	91.2
14. Percentage of new hires	16.5	8.9	8.3	18.6	17.8	17.7
15. Index of cost per student	100.0	104.0	106.6	104.8	103.2	101.3

Retirement Based on Faculty
Expectations

16. Index of budget size	100.0	104.0	97.7	96.6	94.8	92.9
17. Percentage of new hires	16.5	8.9	4.9	16.9	17.3	17.0
18. Index of cost per student	100.0	104.0	108.5	107.3	105.4	103.3

If in addition to the 30 percent enrollment drop by 1987 there is a sharp rise in retirement age, we observe much the same kind of relative effect as shown by our earlier steady-state comparison and analysis of a shift to a retirement age of 70. Costs are higher than they would have been otherwise, 80.3 percent of the 1979 level as contrasted to 78.8 percent of the 1979 level in the absence of a shift in the MRA (lines 10 and 7). New hires drop even lower (line 11 versus line 8), and costs per students are almost 2 percent higher (line 12 versus line 9). Again, the effects of a 10 percent enrollment decline are considerably smaller but no less significant.

The intent of these last simulations has been to dramatize the magnitudes of the adjustments to changing the MRA at the same time that enrollments are likely to be declining in higher education. The effects of the MRA change with constant enrollments are substantial. While the proportionate effects drop steadily as enrollment decline accelerates, the adjustments that institutions will be forced to make to these simultaneous and related changes are going to tax them severely.

The effects of enrollment declines on the graying of the faculty is vividly illustrated by comparing our age distribution measures for the situations depicted in Table 2.10 where the MRA 65 exemption continues; with enrollment held constant, there is a 10 percent enrollment decline in 1982–87, and a 30 percent enrollment decline in 1982–87. The results are presented in Table 2.11. With an enrollment drop of 10 percent, the median age rises by five years in 1987 and then falls off a bit; with an enrollment drop of 30 percent, the median jumps by 6.1 years in 1992 and then drops off again. The percentages of faculty over age 50 average about one-third with constant enrollments; if enrollment drops by one-third, the percentage of older faculty above age 50 approaches 50 percent in the late 1980s and early 1990s.

To the degree that funding per student is guaranteed, the task of adjusting will be difficult enough. If, however, average-cost funding of students goes out of fashion among state legislatures and formulas carrying reduced funding are introduced, the problems of adjusting will be much worse. And to the degree that private institutions experience difficulty raising funds to continue subsidizing students who already pay substantially higher tuitions, their problems of adjusting to the MRA change will be severe. Thus, it appears that the large short-run effects of the change in the MRA combined with the impact of other externally determined changes will place higher education institutions under enormously greater financial pressures as the 1980s unfold.

One way to minimize some of these difficulties is to reduce the faculty–student ratio. Simply put, try to reduce costs. Table 2.12 shows the result of reducing the faculty–student ratio by 10 percent. It cuts budget

TABLE 2.11. Effect of Simulations on Age Structure
of Faculty for Base Case--Retirement at Age 65
(Based on Declining Enrollments of Table 2.10)

	1979	1982	1987	1992	1997	2002
ENROLLMENT--NO CHANGE						
Median age	40.8	43.4	43.4	43.2	41.1	40.2
Percent 60+	7.0	10.4	10.6	10.0	11.0	10.8
Percent 50+	26.5	33.3	33.5	33.7	33.3	33.2
ENROLLMENT--10% DECLINE, 1982-87						
Median age	40.8	43.4	45.8	45.4	45.0	44.6
Percent 60+	7.0	10.4	11.8	12.2	12.2	12.0
Percent 50+	26.5	33.3	37.2	37.0	36.0	35.8
ENROLLMENT--30% DECLINE, 1982-87						
Median age	40.8	43.4	49.0	49.5	47.0	39.3
Percent 60+	7.0	10.4	15.1	15.7	15.7	15.4
Percent 50+	26.5	33.3	47.8	48.1	47.6	34.1

costs by 10 percent, and it also reduces the average cost per student and makes higher education more attractive financially to prospective students. But, it further reduces new hires in the short run.

These various results apply to the average institution with an average age distribution (I) and the average age-salary profile (A). However, institutions and faculties that differ in their characteristics will experience more or less severe effects. Anything less severe will make the adjustment process less difficult. Anything more severe will produce serious financial strains, strains that may be great enough to force some institutions to cease operations or greatly curtail the quality of the educational services they provide.

OTHER BEHAVIORAL RESPONSES

This analysis fails to incorporate various behavioral responses by either individual and potential faculty members or institutions, both to the general forces affecting the labor market for academics and to the particular effects of altering retirement. A few examples will help to illustrate the wide range of possibilities.

The substantial imbalance between new PhDs supplied and those to be employed is assumed to have no effect on the number of future/new PhDs

TABLE 2.12. Impact of Enrollment Declines on Indexes of Budget Size
             and of Cost per Student, and on Percentages of New Hires
             (Based on Assumption of 10 Percent Decline in Faculty-
             Student Ratio 1982-87, for Different Retirement Rates)

	1979	1982	1987	1992	1997	2002
ENROLLMENT--NO CHANGE						
Base Case--Retirement at Age 65						
1. Index of budget size	100.0	104.0	96.6	95.1	93.7	92.1
2. Percentage of new hires	16.5	8.9	9.2	18.4	17.6	17.7
3. Index of cost per student	100.0	104.0	96.6	95.1	93.7	92.1
Retirement Based on Faculty Expectations						
4. Index of budget size	100.0	104.0	98.3	97.3	95.6	93.8
5. Percentage of new hires	16.5	8.9	5.8	16.8	17.3	16.9
6. Index of cost per student	100.0	104.0	98.3	97.3	95.6	93.8
ENROLLMENT--30% DECLINE, 1982-87						
Base Case--Retirement at Age 65						
7. Index of budget size	100.0	104.0	73.6	70.4	66.7	62.9
8. Percentage of new hires	16.5	8.9	2.5	21.1	21.7	21.9
9. Index of cost per student	100.0	104.0	105.2	100.6	95.3	89.8
Retirement Based on Faculty Expectations						
10. Index of budget size	100.0	104.0	75.1	72.5	68.5	64.4
11. Percentage of new hires	16.5	8.9	0.8	18.4	20.6	21.2
12. Index of cost per student	100.0	104.0	107.3	103.5	97.9	92.0
ENROLLMENT--10% DECLINE, 1982-87						
Base Case--Retirement at Age 65						
13. Index of budget size	100.0	104.0	89.5	87.2	85.3	83.0
14. Percentage of new hires	16.5	8.9	4.8	19.9	18.2	18.5
15. Index of cost per student	100.0	104.0	99.5	96.9	94.8	92.2
Retirement Based on Faculty Expectations						
16. Index of budget size	100.0	104.0	91.1	89.4	87.2	84.6
17. Percentage of new hires	16.5	8.9	2.8	18.1	17.5	17.8
18. Index of cost per student	100.0	104.0	101.3	99.3	96.9	94.0

or on the relative salaries of younger faculty members. Both would be expected to decline in view of the generally weak market and the even greater weakening of the market as the transitional effects of the mandatory retirement change are felt.

Nor is any attention given to the possibility that faculty members in their middle professional years may leave for other, more attractive positions in the private sector of the economy because of declining relative salaries. The result would be to ameliorate somewhat the aging effect that would otherwise occur. Neither is attention given to the likelihood that institutions will search more aggressively for early retirement incentives to minimize the aging of the professoriate or for methods of weakening the age-salary-tenure link. Finally, the impact of inflation has been ignored. We did attempt, however, to pick up the effect of some of the more obvious responses of individual faculty members to early retirement inducements and to the effects of inflation. The alternatives we explored are not exhaustive; they were limited by the number of possibilities we could pose in the already long questionnaire used in our retirement effects study.

EARLY RETIREMENT OPTIONS

The impact of early retirement options can be approximated by incorporating the retention rates developed from the responses of faculty members to the several questions asked in our faculty survey. In that special survey, faculty members were asked whether they might retire sooner and if so how much sooner, if (a) upon early retirement their retirement benefits were fully indexed and (b) they could reduce their teaching activity with commensurate reduction in pay. The impact of (a) is represented in lines 5 and 6 of Table 2.13, with the effect of this option reflected by the differences from lines 3 and 4. By 1987 costs are only 0.6 percent lower (104.3 versus 104.9 — lines 5 and 3, respectively) but they drop by much more in 1992 and beyond. Similarly, new hires are slightly higher. Because the indexing of retirement benefits would entail additional costs, it is unlikely that any net gain would accrue to institutions of higher education. The impact of (b) (lines 7 and 8) is considerably larger, reducing costs by 2 percentage points (compare lines 7 and 3) in 1987 and by 2.5 percent in 1992. New hires increase somewhat — by about 20 percent in 1987 — but then taper off quickly once again. These results fail to take account of the, say, half-time salary that would be paid to a professor in a "phased" retirement program and thereby overstate the number of new hires that could occur. Despite these shortcomings, the phased or partial retirement approach may be useful; certainly there is considerable interest in it.

INFLATION RESPONSES

The effect of faculty responses to different inflation rates can also be simulated, as shown in Table 2.14. Lines 5 and 6 show how expected retirement age would be changed if inflation were to rise to a 20 percent annual rate. The rapid erosion of faculty salaries and retirement assets would cause faculty members to continue teaching as long as they could. With a 20 percent inflation rate, rather than the 12–16 percent rate prevailing at the time of the faculty survey, costs would jump by 1.5 percent by 1987 (line 5 minus line 3) and rise even higher until well into the twentieth century. New hires would drop somewhat (line 6 versus line 4) in 1987 but then closely resume their original level.

ALTERNATIVES TO ALTER FACULTY DEMOGRAPHY

Those concerned about faculty demography and all that it implies have several options available that could potentially alter the projections provided here. These alternatives and the direction of their effects are discussed below. It should be noted that all of them cost money.

Early Retirement Incentives

Methods of stimulating faculty members to retire early vary enormously, but all of them represent an attempt to increase the present value of a faculty member's stream of retirement benefits relative to the flow of earnings until retirement, plus the subsequent stream of retirement benefits. This can be accomplished by reducing actuarial reductions in benefit levels, buying faculty members additional annuities, and the like. No early retirement plan will ever make an individual financially "whole" but a sweetening of the benefit levels combined with the earlier release from work activity is likely to be attractive to large numbers of faculty members.

Midcareer Changes

Whereas early retirement incentives might come into play beginning at, say, age 55–60, midcareer change programs are designed to help individuals move out of academic positions and into other sectors of the economy beginning at, say, age 45–50 (Patton, 1979). The motivation for such programs is twofold. One is that some individuals find their jobs unsatisfying, but without special incentives would continue to hold their academic positions. Another is that some faculty members become less essential to their institutions, either because of weak performance or because of program

TABLE 2.13. Impact of Early Retirement Options on Index
of Budget Size and on Percentage of New Hires
(Assumes Constant Faculty Size)

	1979	1982	1987	1992	1997	2002
Base Case--Retirement at Age 65						
1. Index of budget size	100.0	104.0	103.2	102.5	101.8	100.6
2. Percentage of new hires	16.5	8.9	17.5	17.2	16.5	17.8
Retirement Based on Age 70 MRA						
3. Index of budget size	100.0	104.0	104.9	104.7	103.8	102.3
4. Percentage of new hires	16.5	8.9	14.4	15.7	16.1	17.1
Retirement Based on Option CPI Adjusted Benefit Option						
5. Index of budget size	100.0	104.0	104.3	103.5	102.8	101.6
6. Percentage of new hires	16.5	8.9	15.6	16.8	16.2	17.2
Retirement Based on Retirement Phased Option						
7. Index of budget size	100.0	104.0	102.9	102.2	101.6	100.5
8. Percentage of new hires	16.5	8.9	18.0	17.3	16.5	17.6

TABLE 2.14. Impact of Inflation Expectations on Index
of Budget Size and on Percentage of New Hires
(Assumes Constant Faculty Size)

	1979	1982	1987	1992	1997	2002
Base Case--Retirement at Age 65						
1. Index of budget size	100.0	104.0	103.2	102.5	101.8	100.6
2. Percentage of new hires	16.5	8.9	17.5	17.2	16.5	17.8
Retirement Based on Age 70 MRA Pattern						
3. Index of budget size	100.0	104.0	104.9	104.7	103.8	102.3
4. Percentage of new hires	16.5	8.9	14.4	15.7	16.1	17.1
Retirement Based on 20% Inflation Expectations						
5. Index of budget size	100.0	104.0	106.4	106.5	105.6	103.9
6. Percentage of new hires	16.5	8.9	11.9	14.5	15.5	16.5
Retirement Based on 7 to 10% Inflation Expectations						
7. Index of budget size	100.0	104.0	104.9	104.6	103.7	102.2
8. Percentage of new hires	16.5	8.9	14.5	15.8	16.1	17.2

retrenchment. To facilitate the movement of these individuals out of academe, midcareer programs can be established. These might range from offering severance pay to paying for the retraining of individuals for other types of employment.

Salary Policy

While these two alternatives might provide positive inducements for faculty members to leave their positions earlier than they had intended, there is the possibility of using negative rather than positive incentives. This refers to a policy of no salary increases or perhaps even salary reductions for faculty members whose services are no longer effective or needed. Such a policy would force down the real salaries of individuals and might be expected to cause at least some of them to leave for other jobs. Of course, if their employment alternatives outside academe are poor, these individuals might feel compelled to remain. If so, then some combination of positive and negative inducements might be used with good effect.

Creation of Research Positions

Two recent proposals would alter faculty demography less directly by creating a near-academic class of professionals (Commission on Human Resources, 1979). One of these calls for federal funding of senior research faculty members whose movement to full-time research positions would open up new positions for young PhDs. These senior individuals would continue doing the kind of research they have done in their customary university settings. The resulting salary relief to their institutions would permit hiring either the same number of younger faculty members, leaving some unused compensation funds unused, or a larger number of younger faculty members so that the institution's compensation budget would be unchanged. Another proposal calls for funding a number of junior research positions for new PhDs who would operate in university settings and be viewed much like faculty members. This plan would have no direct effect on institutional compensation budgets but would augment the nation's research capability.

Stimulation of Demand for Higher Education

A quite different approach is to try to live with faculty demography by stimulating the demand for higher education. This can be done through such devices as cultivating older people beyond age 25 who might have an interest in college, stimulating more undergraduates to go on for advanced training, and encouraging more high school graduates to attend college.

All of these demand-raising approaches could be tried; at the same time they raise questions about possible conflicts of interest if we subscribe to the view that consideration be given to market forces in determining how many individuals should be enrolled in colleges and universities.

CONCLUSIONS

What conclusions emerge from this exercise? There are many, but we focus on those most closely linked to our interest in faculty vitality and development:

1. The economic conditions surrounding higher education for the rest of the 1980s and the early 1990s are bleak, with the result that there will be relatively little hiring of new PhDs even though the supply of new PhD holders will be more than adequate.
2. The faculties of institutions will "age," and larger proportions of faculty members will push beyond age 50 and beyond age 60. This situation has become marginally worse with the expiration in 1982 of the exemption for tenured faculty members from the 1978 amendments to the Age Discrimination in Employment Act of 1967. If the age of mandatory retirement is eliminated, aging will take place at an even more rapid rate, but its exact extent cannot be pinpointed because we know little about how faculty members would respond to such a situation.
3. The effect of this aging will be to raise salary and hence institutional costs faster than would otherwise have been the case, thereby increasing the already intense financial pressures on the higher education sector.
4. The "graying" of college faculties can be offset, at least potentially by developing effective early retirement incentive programs and midcareer change programs, by recasting the salary structure, and by invoking more rigorous tenure quotas. The creation of new federally subsidized research positions seems rather unlikely. And the stimulation of new demand will require considerable effort.

The ease of altering faculty demography should not be overestimated, however, and here we venture beyond the content of this chapter. First, colleges and universities are not completely free to develop effective measures for altering faculty demography because of various constraints they face. They may lack funds or, for public institutions, authorization to establish more attractive early retirement programs. They may be ill equipped to establish midcareer change programs. They may be precluded by collective bargaining contracts or state compensation policies from awarding salary increases in a more selective way. It is only with respect to tenure quotas that institutions have much scope for taking action. Second, even if these measures could be developed and implemented, it is necessary to determine whether and by how much these measures can indeed reduce the increases in costs associated with the demography of college and university teaching staffs. More attractive early retirement schemes and midcareer change programs are not costless to implement. How much a more selective salary policy might yield in reducing costs is not at all clear. And while enlarging or holding constant the size of the nontenure staff, money savings may result but at the expense of other new problems. It would be helpful to have a careful evaluation of both the feasibility and the economic costs and benefits of these several measures — but that is a major task, one beyond the scope of this chapter.

Chapter 3 | # Faculty Career Development: Theory and Practice

Robert T. Blackburn

THE PROBLEM, ITS IMPORTANCE, AND THIS INQUIRY

One need not extensively document the factors and circumstances that justify how important the problem of faculty career development is. Citizen disaffection with education in general, financial shortfall, program reduction and closure, the demographics of declining 18-year-old cohorts, and more newly recruited PhDs than there are vacancies constitute but a few agreed upon items on the typical disaster litany introducing today's discussion of higher education. Indeed these are times of uncertain futures for most academics irrespective of their age. How faculty careers can be enhanced *is* a critical issue — for the sake of the students who seek the best education possible, for the sake of the institution which has societal obligations for the production of knowledge, for the transmission of culture and the education of future experts, for service to its many communities, and for the sake of the professors themselves.

Colleges and universities are concerned about the healthy development of their staffs for more than practical and humane reasons, however. After all, for the most part, faculty are productive and satisfied, neither discontented nor dying. What faculty do, though, is to subscribe to a norm of improvement. As effective as faculty are — and by most every standard they receive an "A" grade — they strive to be even better. Functioning at some level lower than the highest possible is not acceptable over the long run. Like Jonathan Livingston Seagull, the academics' raison d'etre is to be the best at what they are called to do. Solving problems is the professor's sky diving.

Although faculty career development is not a new problem (see, e.g., Pellino et al., 1981a for a brief history of sabbaticals and other strategies institutions have used to assure faculty vitality), it has an intensified urgency

55

today. Furthermore, the growth of studies on faculty and the development of a theoretical literature on adults makes this a favorable time to examine both theory and practice from new perspectives.

This chapter has aims that extend beyond the reduction of faculty stress resulting from fewer options; aims that are more comprehensive than simpler improving the operations of an already humane and effective organization; and aims that are more inclusive than the political pacification of critics—as important as each of these considerations is. This inquiry aims to create *a theory of career development,* one that will not only encompass academics but also ultimately include the careers of those in a wide range of occupations.

First, we will examine the ingredients of a good theory so that criteria for judging what is developed here are available. Then, we will look at a number of existing theories—adult development, career stages, demography, and socialization—for their strengths, weaknesses, and the consequences which follow from each. The empirical evidence is then introduced. Its general quality and limitations are discussed before specific data on research productivity, teaching, service, personality, and career stages are placed against the theories. Because of the inadequacies of the existing theories, a new conceptual framework is introduced. Additional, needed research is indicated, and consequences for policy and practice are briefly pointed out.

THE INGREDIENTS OF A THEORY AND ITS FUNCTIONS

First, some clarifications are in order so that the conceptual framework developed can be judged. The approach used here is closest to the logical positivists. It makes the same kind of assumptions Carnap, Frank, and others—most visibly Kuhn (1970)—have made. Briefly, their review of theory includes some undefined terms and a set of definitions followed by axioms from which theorems and corollaries are deduced. [By way of illustration, Newton's *Principia* begins with eight definitions (leaving undefined distance, time, and density or mass), is followed by three axioms (his laws of motion), and leads to theorems and corollaries—e.g., the conservation of momentum.] Theory brings order to a wide assortment of phenomena. It simplifies matters, illuminates the subject, makes us believe we better understand events, and leads to predictions of new relationships. In this latter function, it both guides research and informs decision making.

Such is the logical positivist's view of theory, the natural science model. Its aims are warranted assertions, statements expressing universal truths about the natural (especially the physical) world. The approach taken here is less ambitious, although the scientific aims are not discarded. Rather, the emphasis is on the principal aim of the social sciences as the more appropriate one, because the discovery of universal truths is not possible for relationships that are in part determined by specific and differing social contexts and cultures. The more limited goals are close to the grounded theory approach of Glaser and Strauss (1967) as exemplified by Conrad (1978) in higher education. With these understandings of aims and limitations, some existing relevant theories are advanced.

SOME THEORIES

Adult Development

This popular notion has many proponents and an equal number of variations. Fortunately, several writers have collected the most frequently advanced models of adult development, displayed their similarities and differences, and in some cases included critiques. Chickering and Havighurst (1981), Rice (1980), Van West (1982), Weathersby and Tarule (1980), and Wortley and Amatea (1982) are current sources with collected references. They cite Gould, Levinson, Neugarten, and Super, among others. The purposes sought here can be served by using any of these references. For many reasons, including the opportunity to make comparisons with other studies, Levinson et al. (1978) is selected (see Figure 3.1).

A principal strength of this model is the rich longitudinal data from which its inferences are drawn. In addition, it apparently touches the personal experiences of many people. Hodgkinson (1974) was certain it fit his career perfectly and believed it was appropriate for most everyone in higher education. Blackburn and Fox (1983) made some sense out of apparently random career data on physicians using Levinson's set of concepts. Boberg (1982) has data on faculty expressed stress that fit "fairly well" with Levinson's age stages. (How good a fit is required for corroboration or rejection is a point that is returned to later.)

The theory has limitations, as do all. Four occupational sets of ten males over a limited period of time and not extending past midyears is hardly an adequate sample. Second, its "that describes me" attractiveness is simultaneously dangerous. The theory has a seductive quality; we are tempted to bend the evidence to fit the theory, to ignore or suppress the exceptions that exist.

The theory does lead to predictions, however. For example, we expect moves to other institutions or in or out of administrative posts during Levinson's transition periods rather than during settling-down stages. Data on faculty behavior will be put up against such deductions (see Figure 3.2).

FIGURE 3.1.   Developmental Periods According to Levinson et al.
              (1978)

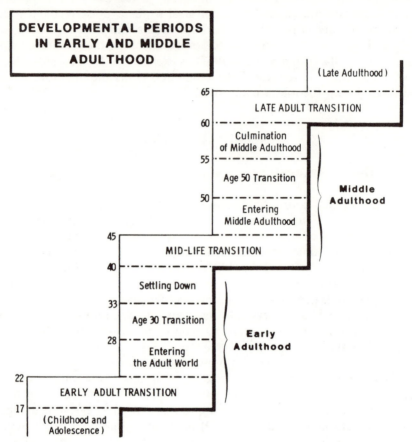

Note: From D. J. Levinson, C. M. Darrow, E. B. Klein, M. H.
Levinson, and B. McKee, The Seasons of a Man's Life (New York:
Knopf, 1978), p. 57. Reprinted with permission.

Career Development

Spilerman (1977) serves as a spokesperson for this model. His approach
differs from the adult developmentalists principally in its attention to decision points rather than to inevitable, invariable chronological occurrences. Its argot is one of entry portals and job changes out of a set of alternatives, which result in models that resemble Markov chains. It is the
focus on events that is the particular contribution of this perspective.

Grid with World Events at the Time Professors Launched Their Careers (Borrowing from Bess, 1973)

Chronological Age

NOTE: In the above wave pattern, "transitional periods" are represented by high amplitude waves and "stable periods" are represented by lower amplitude, longer waves.

Its limitation is its nonspecificity. With no time dimension, it cannot predict when an event will occur nor why it occurred later rather than earlier. The theory is not without any predictive power, however. For example, it would expect the initial position a new PhD takes to determine to a great degree future positions, a phenomenon in accord with data on faculty.

Demographic Theory

Among others, Pfeffer (1983) has increased our understanding of institutional behavior by his analyses of the demographic characteristics of organizational members. Socioeconomic status, sex ratios, and simple age patterns can account for some events. A new leader is likely to select chief officers from her or his cohort excluding those older and younger. Furthermore, successive cohort norms can well be significantly different from another.

By way of illustration (and borrowing from Bess, 1973a), Figure 3.2 overlays Levinson's transitional (high amplitude waves) and stable (lower amplitude and longer wave length) stages on an age grid with world events that can be expected to shape the values of those who are undergoing preparation for the academic professions. Cohorts entering colleges and universities circa Sputnik versus those beginning their careers when Vietnam was a key social issue (as well as a war) are not likely to value the importance of science in the same way.

Demographic theory's deficiencies are similar to those of need theory in motivation psychology. It makes the past understandable, but its predictive powers are limited. It does direct attention to the dangers of cross-sectional data, for changing successive cohort norms may be the proper explanation for what otherwise are frequently interpreted as age-related changes.

Socialization Theory

Sherlock (1967) and Sherlock and Morris (1972) are singled out from many because one of their ideas is utilized in this paper's newly created conceptual framework. (Their study was conducted with dental students over four years in two nonrandomly selected settings.) Generally, socialization theory focuses upon a number of external forces acting upon individuals, processes which shape their careers and their lives. For example, professional societies set requirements for curricula and hence act upon those passing through the program.

Socialization theory's strengths, then, are the attention they bring to the external forces affecting behavior. Its limitations are its failures to recognize individual differences, and hence to predict on other than large samples. The theory does suggest that mentoring and networking will impact on academic careers, findings that are substantiated in the literature (Blackburn, Chapman, & Cameron, 1981; Cameron & Blackburn, 1981).

Other social scientific theories might be inserted at this juncture (e.g., Katz & Kahn, 1978); however, this is not a theory review. Rather, it is a confrontation of evidence with theory, and the chapter now turns to this engagement.

SOME EVIDENCE

This section first discusses the nature of existing evidence on faculty and their careers. It then presents data on selected faculty roles—research, teaching, and service—and on their personal characteristics. Special attention is given to age-related studies.

The Nature of the Evidence on Faculty

To begin with, twenty years ago there indeed was scant literature on professors at work. Research on important issues ranged from none to few. The past decade has witnessed a veritable publication explosion—some 1,500 studies alone on student ratings of teaching, a not unimportant topic, but one whose consequences on the future of higher education is not pivotal. Furthermore, there is an appreciable increase in the quality of the research. Journal editors today would not send out for review most of what was published in their own leading magazines twenty years ago.

Nonetheless, limitations persist even with the quantitative and qualitative increase in research in academics. One vexing problem arises from the noncomparability of most studies. Investigators create a new measure for each inquiry—what is accepted as a publication, for example—but the correlations of similar appearing dependent variables is frequently unknown.

A second shortcoming is sample selection. There are few national studies. The vast majority select a discipline and a college or university type. But higher education is pocketed with distinct subcultures and generalizations are impossible under these conditions. The community college English teacher and the research university microbiologist lead very different lives.

Other flaws in the literature frustrate the investigator who seeks to construct a general theory—of career development or anything else. The data are overwhelmingly on males, frequently because of their preponderances in the occupation. But when women are included, too often analyses have not controlled for sex and/or have not oversampled females so as to acquire an adequate number for analysis. Also, studies are disproportionately set in research universities even though there are fewer of them than there are, say, traditionally black institutions, a segment of higher education about which we know precious little. And then there are major gaps in the research. For example, little is known about consulting, a function that about 50 percent of the faculty engage in and yet one that is surrounded with taboos.

In addition, there is the ever-haunting fact that nearly all of the age-related data are cross-sectional, not longitudinal. Among others, Riley et al. (1972) and Rynder and Westhoff (1971) have delineated the pitfalls of attributing sequential changes on the basis of snapshot evidence. (Recall also the remarks on demography when Pfeffer's notions were introduced earlier.)

By way of illustration, Bayer and Dutton's (1977) publication rate data (see Figure 3.3) are plotted against age. They are cross-sectional data. The inference nearly everyone draws (see [h] in Figure 3.3, total for all fields) from this curve is that as retirement approaches, article publication rate goes down, the "tapering off in old age" stereotype that people accept. But all that is really known is that 65-year-olds are publishing less than 55-year-olds, when these data are collected. Maybe the older cohort always published at this rate. Maybe the 55-year-olds will continue at their current rate (the norms were different when they entered) — or increase their rate over the decade (pressure is increasing). The curve could have a quite altered shape tomorrow. (Cohort and cross-sectional data on mathematicians are shown in the next section. The data are not in perfect accord.)

This very serious limitation will not go away in the analyses about to be advanced. Caution has to be exercised at every step. Despite these deficiencies, the evidence is now examined in detail. It displays many more studies of faculty scholarship expressed as published research than it does on any other faculty role, principally because this research dimension is the only one with data banks that also have age information. Faculty believe teaching is, in addition, a creative endeavor, as are some consultantships when they are problem-solving situations (Pellino et al., 1981b). Studies on these roles are discussed briefly.

Faculty Age and Career Data

Research Productivity.   Figure 3.4 contains a plot of two of Bayer and Dutton's five disciplines — earth sciences and experimental psychology (see Figure 3.3). These plots of cross-sectional data show a rapid early rise peaking just at the end of the 28–33 transition period, as is predicted. A similar fit with Levinson occurs at the conclusion of the age 50–54 transition period. However, the data are not in accord with expectations for those in their early 40s and 60s. (On Figure 3.4 and following figures, original curves have been redrawn so as to give each a comparable time spread and identical

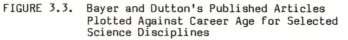

FIGURE 3.3. Bayer and Dutton's Published Articles Plotted Against Career Age for Selected Science Disciplines

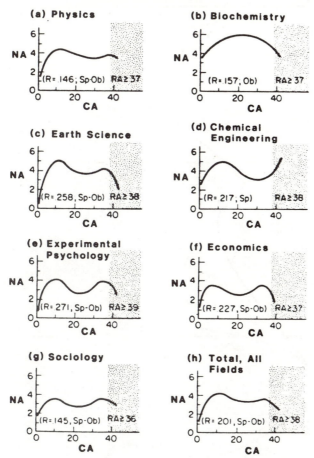

Notes: These are plots of best-fit model of career age with number of published articles in last two years, by field. NA is number of articles published in last two years, CA is career age, and RA is career age at which retirement is expected.

From Allan E. Bayer and Jeffrey E. Dutton, "Career Age and Research-Professional Activities of Academic Scientists," _Journal of Higher Education_, May/June 1977, <u>48</u>(3), p. 273. Reprinted with permission.

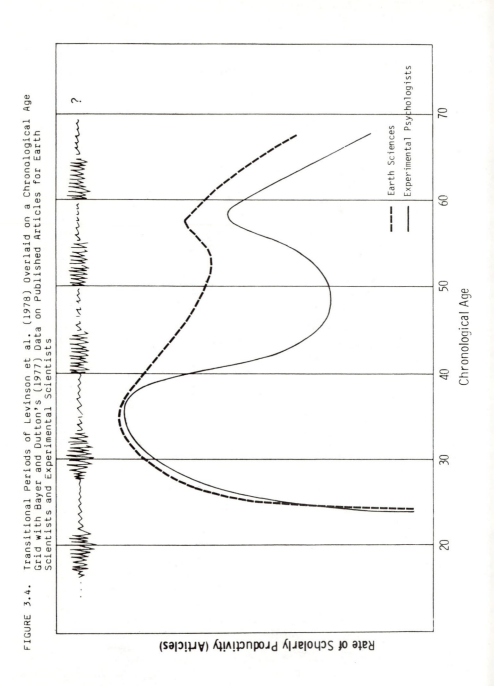

FIGURE 3.4.   Transitional Periods of Levinson et al. (1978) Overlaid on a Chronological Age Grid with Bayer and Dutton's (1977) Data on Published Articles for Earth Scientists and Experimental Scientists

maximum and minimum. Hence, the shapes have been distorted, especially the slopes—rates of change. However, it is the crests and troughs that will receive attention in the analysis and their location on the age axis has not been altered. Furthermore, the production scales on the vertical axis are arbitrary in the originals.)

These two Bayer and Dutton disciplines are the "best fit" with Levinson. For example, Figure 3.5 shows sociology and the total curve for all fields. Peaks and valleys, up-slopes and down-slopes have no consistent pattern for this large national sample of professors. Before setting aside either theory or data, or both, one notes that Bayer and Dutton show principally "hard" data disciplines and nothing from the humanities (English and philosophy, for example). So the conclusions are temporarily held in abeyance until more evidence is examined.

Allison and Stewart (1974, p. 600) and Cole (1979, pp. 962, 964–965) report data on three studies of mathematicians. Allison and Stewart have both article rates and citation rates (Science Citation Index, SCI) for their cross-sectional population. The latter indicator is often championed as the better measure of scholarly quality, for it recognizes how frequently other scientists use the author's contribution, not just how many pieces have been published. The two measures correlate highly, about 0.7. In this instance, however, three of the six rates are changing in the opposite direction over an age interval, a point that will be returned to shortly.

On the other hand, the Cole data on a small cohort have article and SCI changes perfectly synchronized. At the same time, their cross-sectional data are out of phase in two of the six age intervals. Furthermore, the specific age spans differ in the two studies as to when they are in and out of phase.

Despite the unexplained shortcomings of the curves included to demonstrate in part the difficulty of the analysis, three of the six curves are plotted against age and Levinson and others' transition periods in Figure 3.6—Allison and Stewart's cross-sectional citation data, Cole's cross-sectional article data, and his cohort article data. In addition to showing the conflicts, only the Cole cross-sectional data has some congruence with the Levinson theory. These discrepancies will be returned to later.

Next, Pelz and Andrews (1966, 1976) have longitudinal data on scientists in industry. One set is PhDs in research laboratories. Figure 3.7 shows the number of scientific contributions for those who are strongly motivated from within (p. 192). These data fit well with Levinson. However, the time frame is restricted and most of their subjects were not in universities.

The final data displayed come from Blackburn, Behymer, and Hall (1978, p. 137). These cross-sectional publication rates are for faculty in

(continued on page 69)

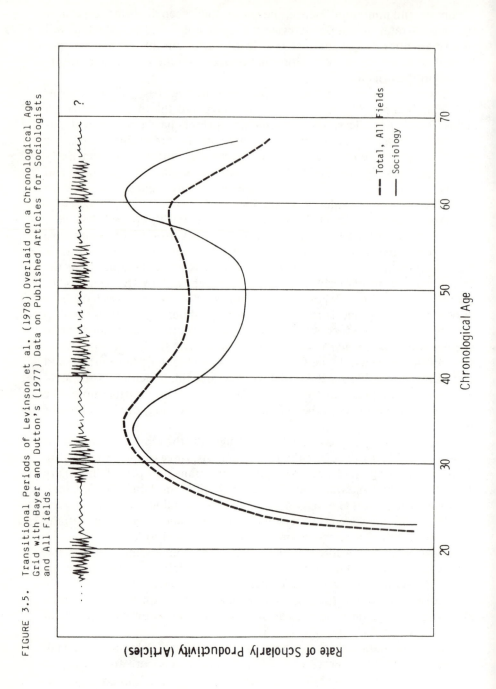

FIGURE 3.5. Transitional Periods of Levinson et al. (1978) Overlaid on a Chronological Age Grid with Bayer and Dutton's (1977) Data on Published Articles for Sociologists and All Fields

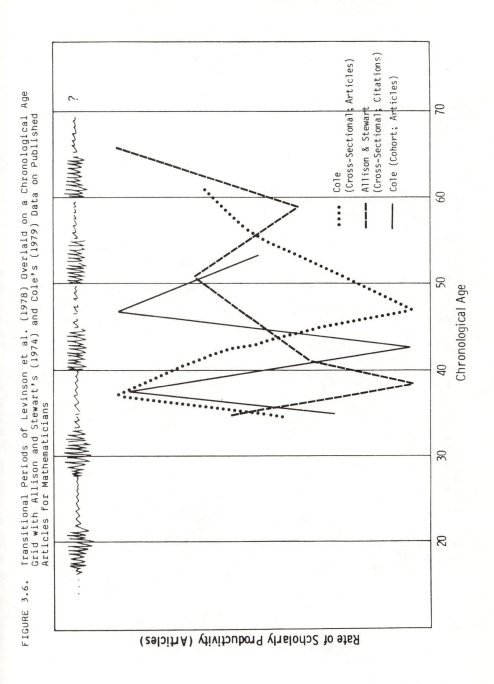

FIGURE 3.6. Transitional Periods of Levinson et al. (1978) Overlaid on a Chronological Age Grid with Allison and Stewart's (1974) and Cole's (1979) Data on Published Articles for Mathematicians

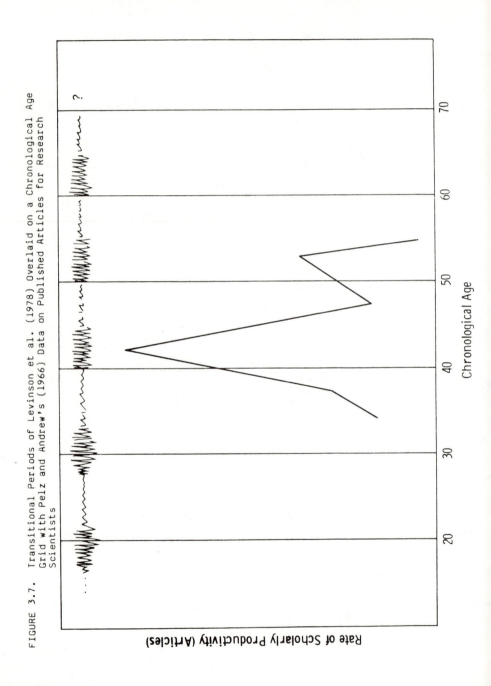

FIGURE 3.7. Transitional Periods of Levinson et al. (1978) Overlaid on a Chronological Age Grid with Pelz and Andrew's (1966) Data on Published Articles for Research Scientists

"high prestige" institutions (Carnegie Council, 1976). (Curves for professors in Carnegie's other classes are similar but less pronounced as the rates are lower.) They are from the same national sample Bayer and Dutton used, but include all fields of knowledge. Figure 3.8 is an almost perfect nonfit with expectations, a result which is at once so devastating as to dictate the abandonment of further analysis and yet so intriguing by its complete incongruence that we are persuaded not to scuttle the effort at this juncture. Other data of this nature could be introduced here but would not change the principal inference to be drawn.[1]

What emerges from this protracted and, at times, labored inquiry is the irregularity of productivity over time. Whether the data are cross-sectional or longitudinal, from one discipline or many combined, productivity seems cyclical rather than either linear or single peaked. There is, in most instances, more than one rise and one fall. Something reoccurring is going on, and that in itself supports adult developmental theorists' contentions. In fact, if we arbitrarily shift curves for Allison and Stewart, Cole, Pelz and Andrews, and Blackburn, Behymer, and Hall (Figure 3.9), what previously had been seen predominantly as misfits becomes nearly the opposite, so that we have a possible confirmation of adult development theory.

A more tempered claim than confirmation is that fluctuations are taking place, but they are not occurring at specific chronological times. The fact that the data do not mesh perfectly is not surprising—after all, citations lag article appearance. Career advancement differs across disciplines and even within subspecialities in the same field. Either one or both facts might account for the contradictions. The fluctuations—"saddle shapes" Pelz and Andrews called them as they more graphically appear in smoothed data—do suggest something is affecting behavior, occurrences perhaps more related to career events than to chronological age.

Figure 3.10 overlays on the Levinson and the age grids used previously some common yet significant career events, namely, the receipt of the AB, AM, and PhD, the last of which occurs more than five years later for humanists than it does for natural scientists.[2] The awarding of the doctorate is taken as congruent with official career launching, the accepting of a full-time position. Then there are two promotions, the first to associate professors and the awarding of tenure, an act symbolizing full acceptance by one's colleagues, and the second to full professor, the last recognition accorded to all before an emeritus title upon retirement (now officially at age 70, but still practiced at age 65).[3] These phenomena are mentioned frequently when retired academics list the most important events that shaped their careers (Blackburn & Havighurst, 1979).[4] Figure 3.10 shows adult development transitions with appointment, promotion to full professor, and preretirement, all periods of intense faculty activity. Levinson and

(*continued on page 73*)

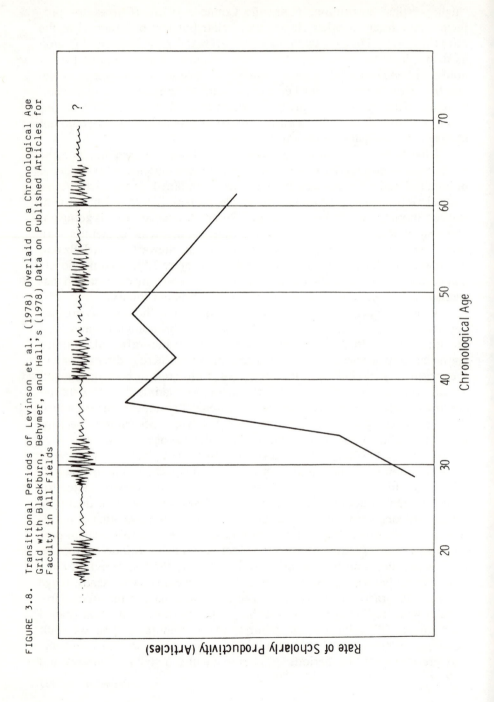

FIGURE 3.8.   Transitional Periods of Levinson et al. (1978) Overlaid on a Chronological Age Grid with Blackburn, Behymer, and Hall's (1978) Data on Published Articles for Faculty in All Fields

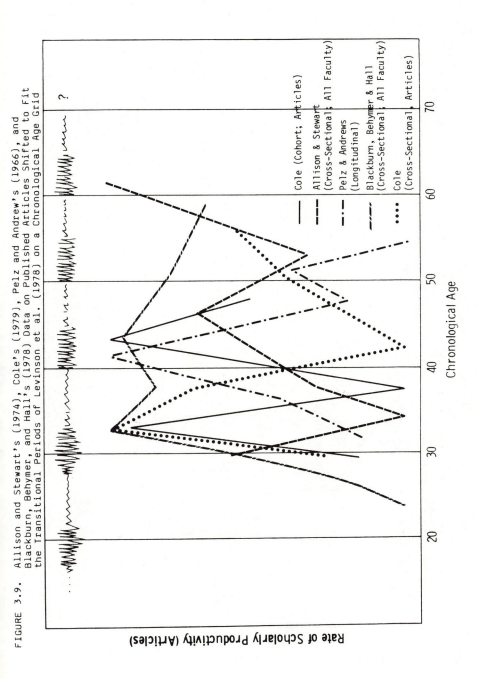

FIGURE 3.9. Allison and Stewart's (1974), Cole's (1979), Pelz and Andrew's (1966), and Blackburn, Behymer, and Hall's (1978) Data on Published Articles Shifted to Fit the Transitional Periods of Levinson et al. (1978) on a Chronological Age Grid

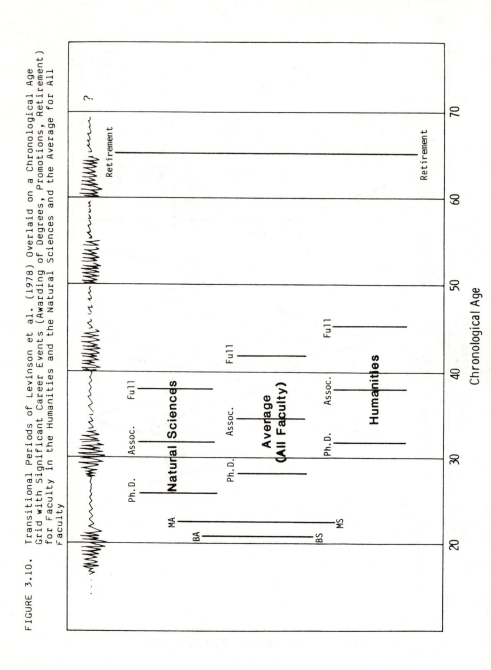

FIGURE 3.10. Transitional Periods of Levinson et al. (1978) Overlaid on a Chronological Age Grid with Significant Career Events (Awarding of Degrees, Promotions, Retirement) for Faculty in the Humanities and the Natural Sciences and the Average for All Faculty

others' age 50–54 transition period fits little of the data, a fact that will receive greater attention later in this discussion.

One sign that a career event grid better accounts for the phenomena, that is, contains the ingredients for career theory, is that data seen earlier to have little or no relationship to fixed-time stages now have a better "fit." Figure 3.11 displays the productivity data for Bayer and Dutton's sociologists and the total curve for all faculty. While the middle Levinson transition periods remain out of phase, the early and late career ones are in phase.

Figure 3.12 replots the Allison and Stewart, Cole, Blackburn, Behymer, and Hall, and the Pelz and Andrews data on the career event grid. Now the fits are remarkably "good."

However, lest we suppress the negative evidence, there are data that also fail to fit the advance made by switching career development from fixed-age stages to unpredictable but significant career events (see Figure 3.13).

Before examining the event theory more fully, we will consider evidence on faculty in the teaching and service roles and what is known about personal characteristics and general career development.

Teaching.   Every time-related study on faculty teaching employs student ratings as the measure of effectiveness. Furthermore, the research focuses on the stability of student ratings over time. (The concerns are reliability, especially if decisions regarding tenure and promotion are involved.) Most often the time intervals are short. The longest longitudinal study is on faculty in one institution over six terms teaching the same course (Felder & Blackburn, 1981). The results are the same in every case. Ratings are stable. Over the short run, then, if there are career stages in relation to teaching, no longitudinal data exist to support this possibility.

Blackburn (1972) and Hitch (1980) have some cross-sectional data on student ratings of faculty teaching effectiveness, the former on a liberal arts college and the latter on an engineering school within a research university. Neither one of the sets of data shows any age- or career-related pattern other than that the variance seems to increase with time. Cycles do not appear. Blackburn (1982) found no evidence to support age- or career-related stages with respect to faculty motivation to teach.

In summary, the data here are not what we wish. What little data do exist contribute nothing positive to a theory of either career stage or adult development.

Service.   The faculty service role has escaped systematic investigation. When service is identified with institutional activities, committees, and especially governance, older faculty spend more time at it than do their

(*continued on page 77*)

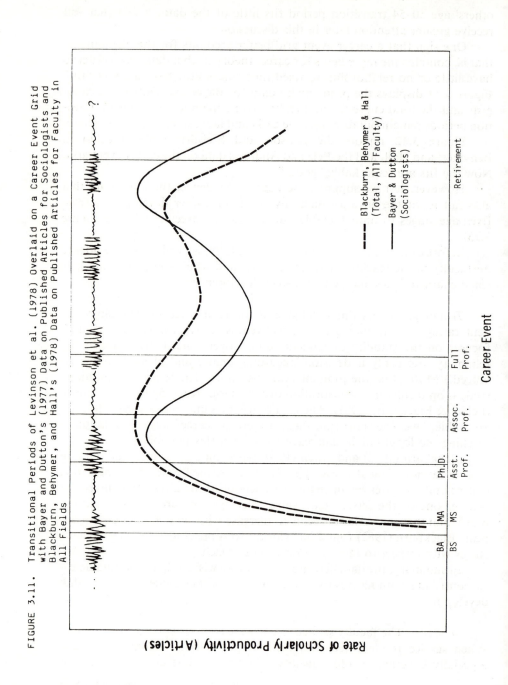

FIGURE 3.11.   Transitional Periods of Levinson et al. (1978) Overlaid on a Career Event Grid with Bayer and Dutton's (1977) Data on Published Articles for Sociologists and Blackburn, Behymer, and Hall's (1978) Data on Published Articles for Faculty in All Fields

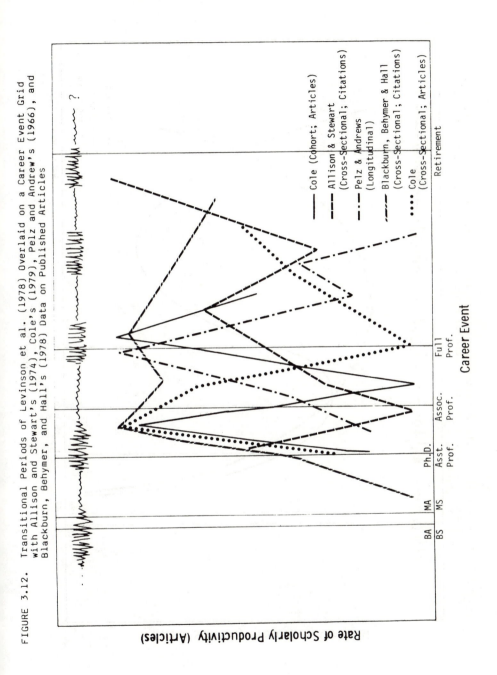

FIGURE 3.12. Transitional Periods of Levinson et al. (1978) Overlaid on a Career Event Grid with Allison and Stewart's (1974), Cole's (1979), Pelz and Andrew's (1966), and Blackburn, Behymer, and Hall's (1978) Data on Published Articles

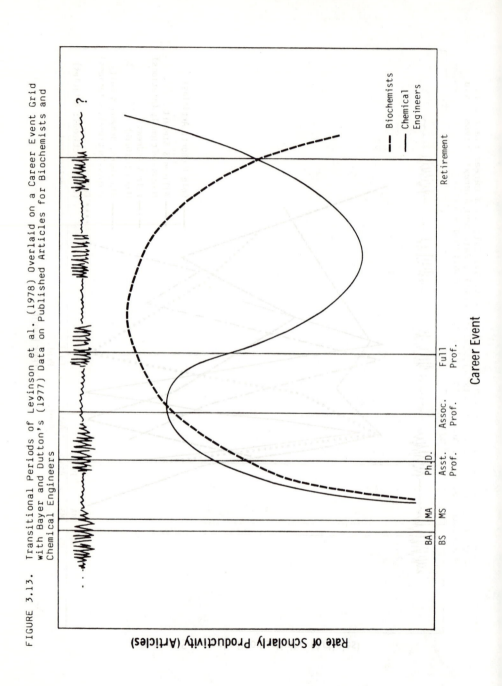

FIGURE 3.13. Transitional Periods of Levinson et al. (1978) Overlaid on a Career Event Grid with Bayer and Dutton's (1977) Data on Published Articles for Biochemists and Chemical Engineers

younger peers (Mortimer, 1969). When service is external, consulting is most often the activity. Only one study has age and discipline data on this phenomenon (Lanning, 1977).

In both kinds of service, data are inadequate either to corroborate or to refute adult- or career-stage development theory.

Personal Characteristics.   In general, adult behavioral characteristics hold constant for most individuals (much to the disappointment of those championing change). The limited evidence on faculty, all cross-sectional, is no exception. Some data show a trend toward "conservatism" (e.g., voting Republican), while other indicate the outcomes are context specific (older people favor medicare, a "liberal" program, for example). On "openness to change" at a liberal arts college (Blackburn, 1972) and on a war-related issue (Schuman & Lauman, 1967) in a research university, rank (career stage) differences were noted. The more "liberal" are the assistant and full professors (transition periods); the more "conservative" are the associate professors (settling down periods).

The research on this dimension is sparse, and no inferences can be drawn to support or refute career- or adult-development theory on the basis of personal characteristics.

General.   Three studies, one completed (Braskamp, Fowler, & Ory, 1982) and two in progress (Van West, 1982, and Clark & Corcoran, 1982) have conducted external, in-depth interviews with faculty at different career stages. Despite sampling problems that limit the generalizability of these studies, they are highly important inquiries. First, they reconstruct longitudinal data, even though somewhat distorted by selective memories. Second, they identify contexts and situations that directly affect careers. And third, they are likely to uncover information cross-sectional surveys seldom touch. While it is too early to draw general inferences, Braskamp, Fowler, and Ory support Levinson. Van West does not. Clark and Corcoran's analyses are not completed at this time.

Two completed studies, Baldwin and Blackburn (1981) and Blackburn and Havighurst (1979) enforce the career event rather than age-stage notion as critical. Their ideas are developed in the final section on results.

RESULTS

The Model

Figure 3.14 depicts events of different kinds that affect the academic career. Some are sequential while others clearly have no necessary chrono-

FIGURE 3.14. Transitional Periods of Levinson, et al. (1978) Overlaid on a Career Event Grid with Major Changes in Activities, New Ideas, Recognitions, and Accomplishments

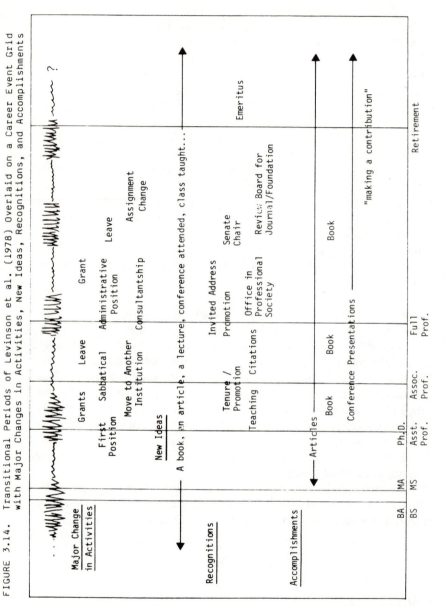

logical order. For example, a changed assignment can occur early when a young assistant professor is singled out to serve a stint in a dean's office or much later to assist in the development of a new program. Baldwin and Blackburn (1981) learned that such an event significantly affected recently promoted full professors in liberal arts colleges. It seemed to reinvigorate some who otherwise looked ahead to twenty more years of the same routine by seriously considering a career change. Blackburn and Havighurst's (1979) data show that those who take on an administrative post, especially if it is accompanied by a move from a research to a regional university, are much less likely to maintain their scholarly productivity and more likely to report retirement, a more dramatic event, than those professors who are never selected or decide not to enter administration.

New ideas, recognitions, and accomplishments also have genuine impacts on a career. Their occurrence is not predictable. As they are talked about by Blackburn and Havighurst's respondents, they do not cluster at the chronological time intervals that Levinson (or the other adult developmentalists) identify. Perhaps these psycho/biological stages alter the significance of an event or affect the decisions we make. Perhaps a transition phase is more likely to have professors relocate than decide not to seek and/or accept positions at other colleges or universities. The hypothetical possibilities are many and there is no evidence to support or refute any of them. To overlook critical occurrences, however, would be to keep career development in the dark.[5]

Figure 3.15 synthesizes the evidence examined in the inquiry. It is advanced as a theory of academic-career development. It utilizes the event rather than the chronological grid, and hence it has a time line that can be adjusted for the different disciplines. It does not include an adult development component, although that could be overlayed as was done in some of the figures in this chapter.

Down the left-hand column are nine socialization processes that act on individuals to shape their career development. Alongside each are two bars that begin and terminate at different career points in the chart. In each instance, the upper bar represents the actions of the graduate school on the individual. The lower bar stands for the actions of the college or university at which the individual works. The intensity of the socialization process is shown by the vertical lines. A dense cluster of vertical lines means the process is stronger at that stage of an individual's career.

Selection/attrition means those forces which act to pull one into a career or drive one out. As the undergraduate approaches the BA, some of her or his professors transmit signals that he or she ought to go on to graduate school. The talented individual is singled out and has an opportunity to see the professorial life from a closer vantage point. (Most studies

FIGURE 3.15. A Career Development Conceptual Framework

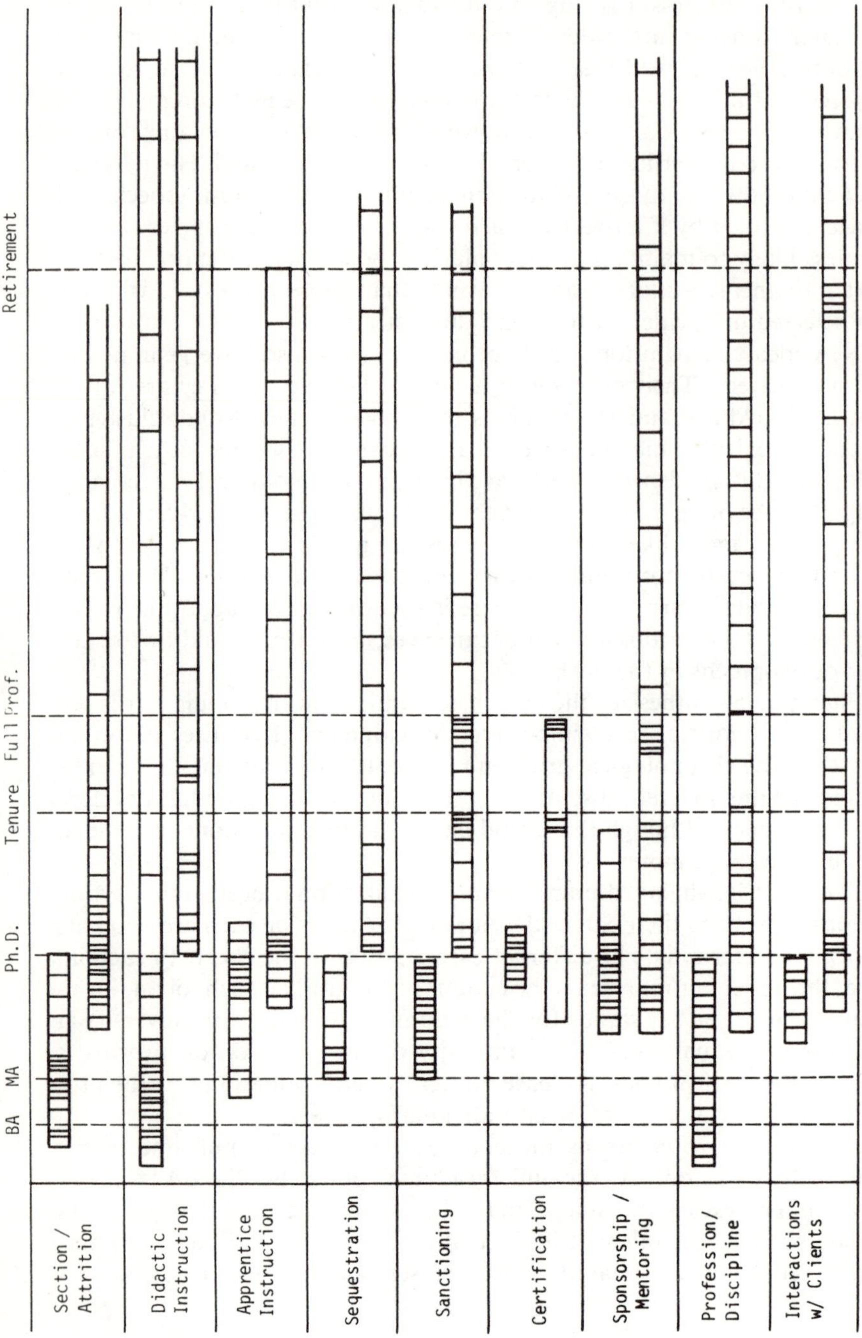

Note: For each career event on the left, the top bar represents graduate school actions and the lower bar represents the actions of the college or university where the individual is employed.

cover people back into their academic careers; Gustad, 1960). For the most part, they do not announce that they are going to go to college in order to become professors as do those who want to become doctors or engineers.

As they approach the MA, the process is repeated, for a fewer number to be sure, and continues as they start formal doctoral studies; usually by then the career decision is made. Then the employing institution has the greater impact on selection and attrition. A job before the PhD is completed puts one in the environment that will act on the individual to tell her or him that a right (selection) or wrong (attrition) decision has been made. After the degree is earned and the assistant professorship is attained, a critical 6 to 7 year interval begins. The promotion/tenure decision is a climactic one, an act by colleagues to take the person into the fold forever. After that, attrition is low (where the lines are far apart), although there does seem to be a period after full professorship when alternate careers are seriously considered. The theory shows very little attrition after that point.

Didactic instruction is just that — formal preparation almost exclusively in the gaining of knowledge and scholarly (but not instructional) skills. After the PhD, formal instructional situations are fewer, although one might return to graduate school for postdoctoral work or on a sabbatical. At the place of work, one might sit in on classes, attend a lecture series, be involved in a symposium, or go to a workshop, for example. The lines for didactic instruction are thin, but always present over the career in both the graduate institution and in the college or university.

Apprentice instruction is most likely to be in the form of a teaching assistantship in the graduate school (or as a postdoc) and in a faculty development office at work. Just how these socialization processes shape the professor has not been well studied. Teaching fellows receive mixed messages. They are honored by being selected for the position and yet simultaneously are told not to give the role too much attention for it will interfere with their scholarship and the career they are about to enter. Yet many TAs report great personal rewards from the experience. This is their first chance to do what many wanted to do, namely, to teach, to transmit ideas, affect others.

Sequestration is not nearly as great for the academic career as it is, say, for medicine, the ministry, or the military, where a class is well sheltered from the outside world, the norms of the profession are induced, and questions of the occupation's legitimacy are rarely heard or entertained. A new class of arts and science doctoral students can form a cohort for their classwork and psychologically (although not physically) shut out the rest of the world. The new assistant professor also is so fully immersed in the job that indoctrination is a strong process at that career point. And then there is continual (and even if weak) sequestering in the occupation — the ivy tower that the nonreal academics are said to live in, especially when in a college or university town.

Sanctioning is intense in the PhD program. There are grades, fellowships, projects one is selected (or not selected) for, best dissertation awards, departmental prizes, and the like. They tell the about-to-be academic how good he or she is, whether or not this is the right career, what kind of a position can be reasonably expected. There is less sanctioning on the job (other than two promotions and raises). The young assistant professor does receive indirect sanctions of what to do and what not to do (go to the chair's open house and do not flunk the entire class). The rewards are less visible, however — the assignment of an advanced class, a public recognition of an article published.

The graduate school *certifies* with the awarding of the PhD (and in the natural sciences with a postdoctoral fellowship). The employing institution gives recognition by (two) promotions. As infrequent as the certification processes are, they are critical events. As the evidence above showed, these are what faculty most frequently mention when highlighting their careers. The certification process legitimizes the individual.

Sponsoring/mentoring has been receiving increased attention and scholarly investigation. Evidence from this research was cited above. The dissertation chairperson is the critical individual and socialization through that process may be the single strongest force at career launching time. The opportunity to present a paper, coauthorship of research, active job search, placement advice (the first position is one of the most critical events that affects a career), introductions to important persons, these and other sponsoring activities are in the hands of the chair. The impact can continue to a second position if the first one does not work out. Beyond then, however, the chair's influence essentially ends as far as direct sponsorship goes. (Coauthorship, projects, and the like can continue throughout a career, but then in a collegial rather than a sponsoring way.) The dissertation chair cannot acquire tenure for a protégé.

Mentoring can also occur in the place of employment. A senior professor may take on the new assistant professor and shepherd her or his career. The impacts will be most intense at promotion times, but take place over the entire span. The shadings in Figure 3.15 represent these more and less intense times. The discipline, that is, the *professional organization* (e.g., the American Chemical Society) has a strong socializing influence on both the preparation for the career and on individual conduct. It can specify the degree requirements, accredit a curriculum, and set standards for staff. It exerts a wide range of power over the events an academic novitiate encounters.

The profession is equally powerful in its effects on the individual's career once on the job. Besides embodying the tradition of the discipline and the norms that have developed over time, it controls the entry portals to many career awards, even more than the institution at which a person works. It puts on the national conferences, endorses the distinguished journals, and in general controls national visibility. Its effects go beyond retirement.

Interaction with clients principally means what happens to faculty because of students they teach and work with. The evidence here is minimal. The teaching fellow phase was mentioned and is represented by the upper rectangle for this socialization process. As for on the job interacting, we have mostly anecdotal accounts. The vast research on college students has been almost exclusively from the perspective of what happens to them, not what the consequences are for the professor. We suspect students are sources of satisfaction and ideas. Young assistant professors sometimes are close to students, but then a distance sets in which is rarely recaptured by most faculty. The heavier shading just before retirement comes from Baldwin and Blackburn, when this age group expresses the satisfactions they receive from students at this career point. For the most part, however, little is known about how clients affect professorial careers.

In summary, these nine socialization processes acting in two different settings and with different intensity at different career stages are advanced as a model for understanding academic-career development. The next task is to critique the model on the basis of the criteria set forth earlier in the manuscript.

The Model's Strengths and Weaknesses

To begin with, the model recognizes the complexity and scope of the phenomena under consideration. While it has not reduced the data to a small set of undefined terms and propositions, it has managed to synthesize a large amount of information for many subcultures within an occupation having 500,000 members.

Second, it is able to adjust to differences between disciplines and institutional type, and hence for the career variations that exist in higher education in the United States. However, it has not been examined for its fit with faculty in community colleges, for there is almost no age-related data on this large subgroup. It is to be expected that modifications will need to be introduced, since the model has been built on the PhD as a certification point and as a critical event. Less than 10 percent of two-year college faculty hold this degree, one not required for career entry to this institution.

Next, the model has no provisions for psychological variables that will be related to individual differences. Its predictive powers are statistical — what is likely to happen to a group but not a particular individual. As was noted, the data are overwhelmingly on males and the model cannot be expected to be fully applicable for females, especially women who enter the profession later than normal and/or who work in it less than full-time.

Fourth, the model does not meet another principal criterion of a good theory. It produces "understanding," it "explains"; for example, it makes clear why the first years on the job are critical ones. Also, it shows that the long interval between full professor and retirement has few processes going on with a high degree of intensity. At the same time, the adult-development literature predicts a major transition phase for those in their early 50s. We now understand why this is a trying time for faculty. This a period at which mentoring and interactions with students, two processes which might provide needed support, are weak. The model suggests that administrators might intervene for the sake of the individual as well as for the good of the organization.

Fifth, the model cannot resolve the contradictions within the evidence (nor can any theory). It can, however, suggest which reported research needs to be examined for possible methodological flaws.

Last, and closely related, the model does fulfill the criterion of suggesting research. The gaps in age data on other faculty roles have already been pointed out. It shows the need for longitudinal studies, the kind of research which unfortunately is expensive in dollars and in time, but necessary for providing crucial information to improve the model. Other gaps are identifiable, and the model directs attention to the variables that need to be examined and/or controlled.

In summary, the model has met some of the criteria but not all. It has accomplished some of its aims but still has flaws.

Some Consequences for Policy and Practice

In addition to the general faculty development literature (e.g., Palmer & Patton, 1981; Pellino et al., 1981a) with its heavy emphasis on improving teaching, the role with which most faculty are already comfortable (Blackburn, 1979), the conceptual framework informs administration on what policies and practices are most likely to have desired consequences. It tells them to recognize disciplinary and sexual differences. It indicates the critical nature of the early years (the heavy shading in Figure 3.15; also see Clemente, 1973). It shows that the times of teaching concern correspond with faculty need for knowledge regarding student development (e.g., Parker & Lawson, 1978). The long recognition gap from full professorship to retirement suggests the greater importance of internal over external rewards (McKeachie, 1979). The already cited literature (Pelz & Andrews, 1976; Baldwin & Blackburn, 1981) support the advantages of changed assignments and work groups for keeping faculty active over their entire career.[6]

Times change and administrators need to alter their responses accordingly. Today, grants are difficult to acquire. The external support many faculty have lived on to give themselves flexibility and options has disappeared or diminished. Fewer graduate students mean less research assistance and increased pressures on senior faculty to staff introductory courses they have not taught for many years. Reduced numbers of graduate students can lead to increased faculty competition for them — for the status a doctoral candidate accords and the personal rewards they gain through cloning.

The organization cannot supply what it cannot obtain. It can, however, be sensitive to what forces are acting on its faculty and can be creative in introducing alternatives that professors will find rewarding. The model does indicate where the more critical career stages will occur. In this way, it aids practice and policy as well as understanding and research.

NOTES

1. For example, Parsons and Platt (1968) had national cross-sectional data, but biased toward high status research universities. Roe (1965) has the most extended longitudinal data, but limited to a small, distinguished set of scientists. Ladd and Lipset (1975) and Blau (1973) have large cross-sectional samples across disciplines. Raymond (1967) has good data on productivity rates of economists. Fulton and Trow (1974) tap the same data bank as did Bayer and Dutton and Blackburn, Behymer, and Hall. Long (1978) and Reskin (1979a) have the best longitudinal data on scientists (biochemists and chemists, respectively), albeit for a rather limited time period vis à vis the concerns of this analysis.

Last, there is another set of productivity studies exemplified by Lehman (1958) and Dennis (1956b). They deal with the age at which a scholar's outstanding contribution was made. They refer to a single event from a small, atypical set of scholars. As interesting and as important as they are, they have but a minor bearing on this inquiry. Their findings that a historian's major contribution occurs later in life than a mathematician's, however, does.

2. There are individual variations on the timing of all these events and those differences are not incorporated in the model being developed.

3. Time in rank differs but slightly across disciplines. When it does, natural scientists are advanced more rapidly than humanists (again with social scientists in between).

4. The remaining figures will use the "average" ages at which appointments and promotions occur. They will also no longer indicate chronological ages. The model, then, is developed for career events rather than strict age occurrences.

5. McCormmach's (1982) *Night Thoughts of a Classical Physicist* is a marvelous fictional reconstruction of a German professor from 1870 to 1918. The hero, Jakob, is a composite of actual scientists. As he looks back on his career, he notes his nonaccomplishments — the book he never wrote, the honor he did not receive — as well as his successes.

6. The theory, however, does not deal with academic leadership. Little empirical data exist with regard to it. That which does (e.g., Elmore & Blackburn, 1983; Blackburn & Schluckebier, 1982) shows how important it is.

Chapter 4

Aging and Productivity: Careers and Results

Barbara F. Reskin

For almost half a century, students of science have been interested in whether scientists' age affects the quality or quantity of their scientific contributions. More recently, with the increasing focus on and concerns about aging and faculty vitality in higher education (see Hansen, Chapter 2 in this volume), the issue has taken on increased importance. Because almost all of the empirical studies of this question have been flawed methodologically, unequivocal evidence on the existence, strength, and form of the relationship between age and scientific productivity is still lacking. In this review, several methodological problems that vitiate most of the work on the impact of age on scientists' productivity are discussed. Some general findings on the relationship between age and scientific productivity based on data that are aggregated across scientific disciplines are then summarized and several possible theoretical models of the form of the relationship are presented. Finally, results for several scientific disciplines are reviewed, and some tentative conclusions are presented regarding the probable impact of scientists' age on their scientific productivity.

METHODOLOGICAL PROBLEMS

Early work by Lehman (1936, 1944, 1953) supported the commonly held belief that scientific performance declines as scientists age. However, Lehman's work has been criticized on methodological grounds (Dennis, 1956a,

This chapter is adapted with permission from "A Review of the Literature on the Relationship Between Age and Scientific Productivity," Appendix C in National Research Council (Commission on Human Resources), *Research Excellence Through the Year 2000: The Importance of Maintaining a Flow of New Faculty into Academic Research* (Washington, DC: National Academy Press, 1979).

1956b, 1958, 1966; Cole, 1979). Rather than comparing the proportions of scientists in each of his age groups who made important discoveries to see whether they diminish over time, Lehman asked what proportion of important discoveries was made by scientists of different ages. Thus he implicitly and erroneously assumed an equal proportion of scientists in each age group. In fact, the growth of science over the last two centuries means that scientists are disproportionately young, so proportionately more discoveries should be made by young scientists even if age has no effect. A second problem with Lehman's work is the effect of life span on the distribution of the achievements of scientists at various ages. Accomplishments by scientists who die young are necessarily made by young scientists. Had they survived, some of them probably would have produced additional important work at older ages as well. Thus, if all scientists were equally long-lived, Lehman would presumably have observed more scientific achievements by older scientists.

Several other methodological problems characterize most empirical work in this area. First, many studies used measures of association that assume a linear relationship when in fact evidence indicates that the relationship is nonlinear. Second, most studies have considered only the bivariate relationship between age and productivity, ignoring other variables (e.g., organizational context) that undoubtedly affect the form of the relationship. Discipline is often ignored, and recent research by Bayer and Dutton (1977) demonstrates the existence of disciplinary differences. Third, in the absence of true longitudinal data, distinguishing between age and generation (cohort) effects is problematic, since both could produce the same pattern of declining productivity among older cohorts of scientists.

Fourth, difficulties involved in measuring scientific performance are often ignored. Neither of the most common measures — recent article and citation counts — may wholly capture the phenomenon of interest. On the one hand, article production may decline over time as scientists change their publication patterns without any decline in the quality of their scientific contributions. Citation counts, on the other hand, presumably reflect both the calibre of scientists' work and their professional visibility, which is partly a function of factors that are not performance related such as the prestige of their academic department. Other measures of scientific performance such as lifetime contributions are more seriously flawed. Bayer and Dutton (1977) show the dependence of age-performance curves on the criterion selected.

Fifth, many studies of the relationship between age and scientific performance fail to assess the amount of variance in productivity that is uniquely attributable to age. Where this feature is reported, age accounts for an inconsequential proportion of the variation in productivity. Although this variation can be caused by misspecification of the prediction model (either improper specification of the form of the relationship or failure to include all appropriate predictors), more likely it reflects the unimportance of age relative to other factors such as the calibre of scientists' training, their propensity to publish, their early research experience, their place of employment, and the availability of resources and rewards for research that affect whether or not scientists continue to carry out and publish research as they age (Reskin, 1977, 1978).

Finally, the generalizability of even the most robust findings is dubious, in view of the omitted intervening variables that might account for any association between age and productivity. If, for example, older scientists publish less because they are disproportionately recruited for administrative responsibilities, as the number of older scientists increases, a smaller proportion of them would be subject to competing administrative obligations, and the association would be attenuated. Taking into account primary activity during the period performance is observed is obviously essential.

STUDIES BASED ON AGGREGATED DATA

In their study of doctoral scientists employed in research and development laboratories, Pelz and Andrews (1966, rev. ed. 1976) found two peaks in several measures of scientific performance (including "scientific contributions" and published and unpublished papers), although the slump occurred earlier for those in research (ages 45–49) than in development (ages 50–54). The authors believed that motivational changes were more likely to be responsible for the midcareer slump than the assumption of administrative responsibilities. Elsewhere in the study they showed that at least moderate administrative loads did not interfere with scientists' output.

Blackburn, Beyhmer, and Hall (1978) examined the association among PhD holders who were faculty members at four-year colleges and universities. Among those in high-prestige institutions, they observed the "spurt-obsolescence" pattern (Bayer & Dutton, 1977) — a bimodal "saddle-shaped" curve which Lehman also reported much earlier. Productivity was highest for scientists in their late 30s and late 40s, with a slump in the intervening years. However, the bimodal pattern did not occur among scientists at lower-prestige institutions.

Although this review excludes studies restricted to eminent scientists (e.g., Roe, 1965), data presented by Zuckerman (1977) on age-specific annual productivity rates for Nobel Laureates and a matched sample of non-Laureates are of interest. Both groups showed the biomodal pattern described above, although the peaks for the Laureates are half a decade later than those for the members of the matched sample (and, of course, the Laureates outproduced the matched sample at every age).

MODELS OF THE RELATIONSHIP BETWEEN AGE AND PRODUCTIVITY

Perhaps the most sophisticated research on the relationship between age and scientific performance is that of Bayer and Dutton (1977). It uses 1972–73 American Council on Education data for over 5,000 doctoral teaching faculty from seven scientific fields to assess six alternative models of the relationship for eight measures of productivity: recent articles, lifetime articles, books, number of works cited in the 1973 *Science Citation Index,* pure research orientation, time spent in research, number of journal subscriptions, and time spent consulting. Reasoning that the linear model might misspecify and hence underestimate the strength of the actual relationship, the authors test the linear model and five alternative models for goodness of fit to the data. The six models, shown in Figure 4.1, are as follows:

1. Linear or cumulative growth: $Y = a + bX$ (where Y equals the productivity measure and X equals age).
2. Declining rate of increase which reflects the "aging" hypothesis that performance tapers off over time, such that $Y = a + b \log X$.
3. Leveling out function, which also reflects the "aging" hypothesis, but with a plateauing effect of age such that $Y = a - b (1/X)$.
4. Obsolescence function, a parabolic function in which performance peaks and then declines, either because scientists lose their "vigor" or because the declining returns for performance reduce scientists' incentive to do research. Here, $Y = a + b_1 x - b_2 x^2$.
5. Spurt function, a bimodal distribution that overlays the expected effects of the academic reward system on the direct aging effects to yield two peaks—one during the early creative years and a second ten to fifteen years later. Here, $Y = a + b_1 x - b_2 x^2 + b_3 x^3$.
6. Spurt-obsolescence function bimodal distribution, in which the second peak is followed by a decline in performance such that $Y = a + b_1 x - b_2 x^2 + b_3 x^3 - b_4 x^4$.

Although the authors present analyses for both aggregated data for all seven fields as well as data disaggregated by field, for none of their eight productivity measures did the same model provide the best fit for each of the seven fields. Hence, generalizing from the results for one discipline to another may often be inappropriate.

FIGURE 4.1.   Alternative Models of Aging Functions

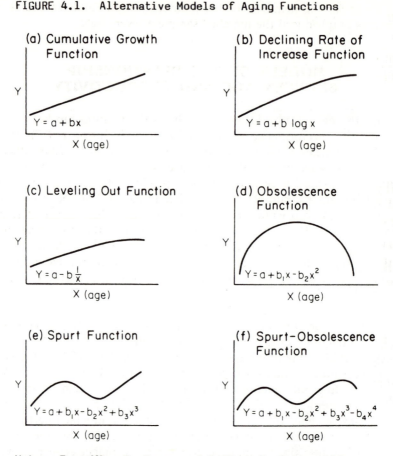

(a) Cumulative Growth Function — $Y = a + bx$

(b) Declining Rate of Increase Function — $Y = a + b \log x$

(c) Leveling Out Function — $Y = a - b\frac{1}{x}$

(d) Obsolescence Function — $Y = a + b_1 x - b_2 x^2$

(e) Spurt Function — $Y = a + b_1 x - b_2 x^2 + b_3 x^3$

(f) Spurt–Obsolescence Function — $Y = a + b_1 x - b_2 x^2 + b_3 x^3 - b_4 x^4$

X (age)

Note: From Allan E. Bayer and Jeffrey E. Dutton, "Career Age and Research–Professional Activities of Academic Scientists," Journal of Higher Education, May/June 1977, 48(3), p. 262. Reprinted with permission.

THE RELATIONSHIP BETWEEN AGE AND PRODUCTIVITY WITHIN SELECTED DISCIPLINES

There are several reasons to expect field differences in the relationship between age and scientific productivity. Fields differ in the length of doctoral training and hence in the age at which students typically complete their PhDs, they differ in the extent to which research is a collaborative enterprise, in journal acceptance rates and publication time, and in the form in which publications typically appear. They also differ in their degree of codification (Zuckerman & Merton, 1973, p. 303), that is, the extent to which empirical knowledge is consolidated into succinct theoretical formulations or the degree to which practitioners share consensus on what the important questions are and how they can be solved. Zuckerman and Merton hypothesize that the degree of codification in a field should affect the ease with which young scientists learn research questions and appropriate techniques and hence the extent to which they do not need long experience to become competent practitioners.[1] Finally, fields differ in the extent to which techniques learned in graduate school are subject to technological obsolescence.

Physics

Bayer and Dutton (1977) report a weak spurt-obsolescence pattern for recent publications among a sample of PhD-holding college and university teaching faculty (see Figure 4.2) with age accounting for less than 2 percent of the variance in recent output. On a sample of physicists from PhD-granting departments, Cole's (1979) results from a study of academic scientists in six fields employed in PhD-granting institutions show an obsolescence pattern among the physicists with mean article productivity peaking between the ages of 40 and 44, and then declining steadily to 55 percent of its peak level among older cohorts.

Physicists' mean number of citations did not show the same obsolescence pattern. Rather, they were about equally high—about three per year—for physicists aged 35–39 and those over 60, but less than half as high for physicists between 45 and 49, thus displaying a spurt pattern.

Differences in the results for article productivity in the compositions of the two samples might account for the discrepancy for physicists nearing the end of their careers, since the less productive, older scientists in Bayer and Dutton's more heterogeneous sample might have been more likely to abandon teaching and research positions earlier than more productive researchers. If so, those faculty remaining would show an apparent upsurge toward the ends of their careers. As Bayer and Dutton showed, the patterns for articles and citations typically differ.

Allison and Stewart's (1974) aggregate analysis of data for faculty at PhD-granting departments showed increasing inequality in the distribution of scientific productivity among older cohorts of physicists. This result is consistent with sociologists for the "accumulative-advantage" hypothesis that holds that maintaining scientists' productivity over time is primarily a function of the availability of resources and other professional rewards that are distributed more unequally as cohorts age (Cole & Cole, 1973).

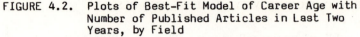

FIGURE 4.2. Plots of Best-Fit Model of Career Age with Number of Published Articles in Last Two Years, by Field

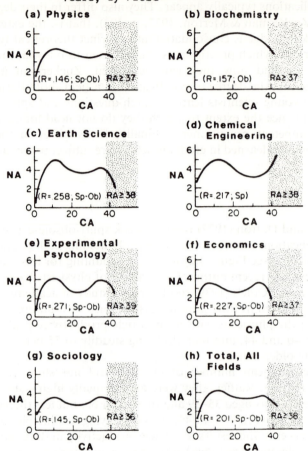

Notes: These are plots of best-fit model of career age with number of published articles in last two years, by field. NA is number of articles published in last two years, CA is career age, and RA is career age at which retirement is expected.

From Allan E. Bayer and Jeffrey E. Dutton, "Career Age and Research-Professional Activities of Academic Scientists," _Journal of Higher Education_, May/June 1977, _48_(3), p. 273. Reprinted with permission.

Astronomy

As part of a larger study on peer review, the National Science Board (1977) identified 85 significant advances ("innovations") made by four disciplines during the past twenty years (as judged by nonrandom samples of scientists selected from the four fields). In addition to exploring funding patterns that led to the innovative work, they considered the characteristics of the investigators credited with the work. Of the 21 innovators in astronomy, 52 percent were under 35 years old, although in 1973 only 32 percent of doctoral astronomers were under 35. While the proportions are not strictly comparable since the 52 percent refers to the investigator's age at the time of the innovation (up to 20 years earlier), the basis is a conservative one because fields have been growing younger rather than older for most of this period. This finding and those for the other three fields (chemistry, earth sciences, and mathematics) reported here lend some support to the belief that the most creative work is done disproportionately by young scientists.

Mathematics

Stern's (1978) analysis of data on 43 distributed university-based mathematicians and on mathematicians elected to the National Academy of Sciences showed a spurt function among the university mathematicians, with the peaks for both single and coauthored papers between the ages of 35 and 39 and after age 60, and the nadir between 45 and 49. Analysis of citations showed a spurt-obsolescence function, with declines for mathematicians between the ages of 45 and 49 and over 60. Stern suggests that administrative obligations assumed by scientists in their 40s may account for their productivity slump during that period.

Cole's (1979) analysis of longitudinal data for a 25-year period for about 500 university mathematicians who received their PhDs in the late 1940s showed a slight spurt-obsolescence pattern, with peaks 5–10 and 15–20 years after the PhD, although Cole concluded that "productivity does not differ significantly with age." He found that the proportion of mathematicians who published at least one paper and received at least two citations over each five-year period was quite stable over the 25 years (14–17 percent), while the proportion who published nothing increased over time from 38 to 61 percent. Hence, correlations between the number of publications in various five-year periods were moderate, ranging from 0.6 to 0.8 depending on the amount of intervening time. Analysis of ages at which mathematicians published papers that elicited at least five citations suggests that the ability to produce highly cited work, while uncommon among sample members, was probably unrelated to age, although the data for university mathematicians who are over 60 are not reliable.

A study of scientific innovations conducted by the National Science Board (1977), on the other hand, showed that 10 (55 percent) of 18 "innovations" in mathematics over a 20-year period were by scientists under age 35, a group that included only 39 percent of all mathematicians. This finding offers some support for the widely held belief that creative work in mathematics is done disproportionately by younger scientists.

Consistent with their hypothesis that productivity is closely tied to the scientific reward structure, which itself generates increasing inequality over time, Allison and Stewart (1974) found increasing inequality in article productivity among older cohorts of mathematicians.

Chemistry

Cole's (1979) data showed an obsolescence pattern in mean article productivity with peak productivity between the ages of 40 and 49. Mean number of citations showed a spurt pattern: chemists in their early 40s and over 50 received the most citations (an average of at least one per year) while those 35–39 and 45–49 received less than 0.7 citations on the average. The National Science Board (1977) study of innovations found that young chemists made a disproportionate number of the 17 innovations judges reported in the field of chemistry over the past 20 years (53 percent compared to their representation as 33 percent of practitioners).

Allison and Stewart (1974) observed the same pattern of increasing inequality among their synthetic cohorts of chemists that they found for physicists and mathematicians.

Chemical Engineering

Unlike most of the disciplines they examined, the relationship between age and article production in Bayer and Dutton's (1977) sample of chemical engineers was of the spurt form, peaking about ten years after the PhD and at the end of the career (see Figure 4.2). However, age accounted for only 4 percent of the variance in productivity.

Biochemistry

The biochemistry faculty Bayer and Dutton (1977) studied were the only group whose publication patterns showed a simple obsolescence curve, consistent with a deleterious effect of aging on productivity. Their peak was slightly later than that for the other six disciplines, occurring at about the middle of the career (see Figure 4.2). However, age was a poor predictor of article productivity ($R = -0.157$), accounting for only 2 percent of the variance.

Biology

No individual-level analyses on the relationship between age and productivity among biologists could be located. The pattern for biologists in Allison and Stewart's (1974) aggregate-level analysis differed from those for physics, chemistry, and mathematics, in that it showed only a very slight increase in article inequality as the synthetic cohorts "aged." The authors suggest that this may be accounted for by lower consensus among biologists on important research questions and poorer communication among practitioners, which could inhibit an efficient allocation of rewards according to merit, so that scientists best able to convert resources into future performance do not accumulate them.

Earth Sciences

The age-productivity association among the earth scientists Bayer and Dutton (1977) studied was of the spurt-obsolescence form, with the first peak slightly more pronounced than the second (see Figure 4.2). The data fit the curve better for earth scientists than for most of the other fields they examined; but age still accounted for only 7 percent of the variance in article productivity. The National Science Board study of innovations mentioned previously found that young researchers were overrepresented among those who had made important innovations in the earth sciences. Although researchers under age 35 constituted only one-quarter of the discipline, they were credited for 37 percent of the innovations.

Geology

According to Cole (1979), both the mean numbers of articles and citations of geologists showed an obsolescence curve. Both peaked for geologists between 40 and 44 years old, and declined sharply after age 50.

Psychology

The psychologists whom Cole (1979) studied showed a similar pattern to that of the geologists, except that the peak productivity period began earlier, extending from age 35 to 45. On the other hand, the *experimental* psychologists in the Bayer and Dutton (1977) study showed a spurt-obsolescence pattern for articles published in the past two years, with a fairly strong decline among those who had had their PhDs about twenty to twenty-five years (see Figure 4.2). The difference in specialty distributions or institutional locations of members of the two samples could account for the discrepancy in their results.

Economics

The results for Bayer and Dutton's (1977) economists were quite similar to those for the experimental psychologists, except that the first peak appeared among slightly younger scientists and the length of time between the two peaks was correspondingly greater (see Figure 4.2). The data for the experimental psychologists fit the curve marginally better than did those for the economists ($R = 0.271$ and 0.277, respectively). Thus, in neither field did age account for more than 7 percent of the variance.

Sociology

The curve for the sociologists Bayer and Dutton (1977) analyzed was the flattest and yielded the poorest fit to the data. Nevertheless, the data suggest a slight spurt-obsolescence pattern (see Figure 4.2). Cole's (1979) results, on the other hand, showed an obsolescence function for both articles and citations—as did almost all of his disciplines—with peaks between the ages of 45 and 49. Again, the greater heterogeneity of Bayer and Dutton's (1977) sample may account for the discrepancy if less productive researchers tended to retire earlier than more productive individuals.

Clemente and Sturgis's (1974) study of sociologists reported a very weak negative relationship between age and article counts, but the obvious misspecification of the form of the relationship renders this result of little value.

CONCLUSIONS

Some regularities across disciplines occurred in the discipline-specific analyses. First, in no case did productivity show a simple, negative relationship with age, and in almost all cases the simple linear model of cumulative growth was inadequate. The failure of the "declining" and "leveling out" models to fit the data well is inconsistent with the existence of simple aging effects, and it seems safe to rule out the hypothesis that increased age necessarily leads to lower productivity. Second, the results broken down by discipline suggest that linear models are inadequate to describe the relationship between age and at least certain measures of scientific performance. This is not to say that articles (or citations) do not decline among older scientists at certain ages. The spurt-obsolescence model offered the best fit for most fields (but in biochemistry the obsolescence model was superior, and the spurt model fit the data for chemical engineering better than the alternatives assessed; see Figure 4.2). Among the groups studied, the first of the two peaks tended to occur about ten years after the PhD and the second as scientists neared retirement age. These patterns are consistent with market effects or selective attrition, where scientists whose productivity does not recover from a midcareer slump tend to shift into nonresearch positions or to retire early (although early retirements are uncommon among doctoral scientists). Bayer and Dutton (1977) concluded that market, generational, and selective attrition effects on performance may all be overlaid with any effects of aging.

Finally, regardless of their forms, any simple effects of aging appear to be small. Although Cole did not provide information on the strength of the associations for the data he examined, the nonlinear models Bayer and Dutton assessed never accounted for more than 7 percent of the total variance in productivity and usually explained substantially less. Moreover, the small zero-order effects of age would presumably be further attenuated in more properly specified models that included demonstrated determinants of productivity such as primary activity, institutional setting, and research resources, which are usually correlated with age. Multivariate analyses for specific scientific disciplines that permit nonlinear effects of age are necessary to learn whether age per se has any independent effect on scientists' performance.

NOTE

Cole (1979) points out that codification should also affect the extent to which there is consensus in a field on what findings are important and that significant discoveries can be readily identified as such, but although this may affect the relationship between age and professional recognition, it should not influence the relationship between age and productivity.

Chapter 5 | **Aging and Productivity: The Case Of Older Faculty**

Robert J. Havighurst

The purpose of this chapter is to describe our knowledge of the productivity of university faculty members as they grow older, and specifically as they grow through their 60s. What happens to faculty members as they grow through their 60s and on into their 70s? What about their ability to teach complex subjects? To what extent do they carry on research? What about their desire to retire as compared to their drive to go on teaching and working on research? In brief, what are the likely effects of aging, especially with older faculty, in regard to concerns of faculty vitality?

RETIREMENT OPTIONS IN THE 1980s

We know in general that most faculty members retire sometime in their 60s or early 70s. But what causes their retirement? It is obviously a combination of two factors: First, it is clearly a function of the individual's wishes. His or her attitudes toward work are very important. How important is the job in the individual's life style? What about his or her health? Does the individual have financial needs that would not be satisfied by a retirement pension or social security benefits or savings and investments? Second, it results from rules and expectations of employers and of government. The college or university may have a rule mandating retirement at a specific age. Historically, this rule was at age 65, 68, or 70.

The federal government in 1967 established the Age Discrimination in Employment Act, which made it illegal to force an employee to retire before the age of 65, unless his or her health or other conditions made it impossible for the individual to carry on. As noted by Hansen in Chapter 2, the 1978 Amendments to the Age Discrimination in Employment Act pushed the age permitting mandatory retirement up to 70 years. At the same time, the federal government abolished compulsory retirement on the basis of age for federal government employees. There is now serious discussion of passage of a federal government law which would eliminate all mandatory retirement on the basis of age. Social Security rules also have been recently liberalized, allowing older workers to earn a limited amount of money while they draw Social Security benefit payments.

Thus the options for retirement that are open to individual faculty members during the decade of the 1980s might be summarized as follows: retirement chosen by the individual sometime in his or her 60s, continued employment into their 70s for faculty members in some universities, a variety of part-time positions at reduced salary for faculty members in their 60s or 70s.

The decade of the 1980s will probably be one of considerable readjustment of retirement ages and practices in relation to (1) enrollment trends in colleges and universities, which will affect the demand for faculty members and for faculty time, and (2) the large number of well-trained young adults who are seeking employment in college teaching. The baby boom of 1955–65 will produce a very large age cohort from 25 to 35 in the 1985–95 period who will need employment, thus exerting pressure on workers in their 60s to retire or to move to part-time employment.

EFFECTS OF AGE ON INTELLECTUAL PERFORMANCE

Recognizing that age of retirement is becoming more optional for college and university faculty members, we want to know how productive they probably will be in teaching and research, as they grow past the age of 60.

There is a variety of opinion and a variety of research (see Reskin, Chapter 4 in this volume) bearing on the possible effects of age on the intellectual performance of people working in academe. One school of thought and research is concerned with the relations between age and creativity in the various academic disciplines. Studies of the age at which outstanding scientists and scholars have done their most creative or path-breaking work have tended to conclude that people working in the natural sciences have done their best work in their 30s, while philosophers and historians have been most productive in their 50s and 60s. There is also an area of research on adult intelligence that may have some bearing on the performance of faculty members.

There appear to be two broad categories of intellectual performance, one which increases during adulthood, while the other decreases. Horn and Cattell (1966, 1967) studied the performance of adults of various ages over about 50, on a battery of some thirty mental ability tests. They found one set of skills or abilities that did not decline with age in the 50–75 age range, and another set that decreased with age.

The two groups of abilities, which they categorized either as *crystallized* or as *fluid intelligence,* included the following:

CRYSTALLIZED INTELLIGENCE	FLUID INTELLIGENCE
Word meanings	Inductive reasoning
Mechanical knowledge	Figure matching
Fluency of ideas	Perceptual speed
General information	
Arithmetic ability	

In more general language, crystallized intelligence is the collective intelligence of a society, which is passed on from one generation to the next by means of schooling, the parental word, and personal example or instruction from older to younger persons or by learning from experience. It grows rapidly during childhood and adolescence, and continues to grow more slowly during the adult years. It varies among persons of equal potential for learning in relation to the amount and quality of learning experience. After about age 60, crystallized intelligence only increases in people who are intellectually active. Fluid intelligence consists of the abilities that depend most directly on the physiological structure of the organism, and especially on the central nervous system. It declines with age after about age 30. The neural structures of the central nervous system grow during infancy and childhood, and thereafter may decline. For example, the speed of reaction to a touch on the back or to a light signal decreases. The decline becomes marked after about 50 years of age.

However, some recent research at Pennsylvania State University raises some questions about age changes in fluid intelligence. It was suggested that at least a part of the decline with age in tests of fluid intelligence is caused by the slowing down of processes within the central nervous system, to which people become accustomed. When they are faced with a set of items on a test of fluid intelligence, they work deliberately; if there is a time limit for the test, they do not complete as many of the items as younger people do. Also, if the test items are difficult, they take more time than they really need, just to be sure of their performance.

A STUDY OF MALE FACULTY MEMBERS IN THEIR SIXTIES

The author directed a research project in 1975–76 that was aimed at finding out how faculty members use their time during their 60s. Special attention was paid to male social scientists whose careers were in sociology and psychology departments of universities and colleges.

The men in this study were born between 1893 and 1903. They were nearly all members of the American Sociological Association or the American Psychological Association at about 1960, when they were aged 57–67. Their names, birth years, and academic positions were copied from the directories of these associations and placed on cards. A few additional names were secured from *American Men of Science: Social and Behavioral Sciences,* 1962 edition. All the names that were retained referred to men with a career emphasis that had been primarily academic. Those whose primary vocation had been college or university administration were excluded. Similarly, those were excluded whose primary work for the fifteen to twenty years prior to their reaching age 60 had been in government service, clinical practice, church service, or industrial or military service. This procedure produced 779 names.

Once this basic list had been made, the names were looked up for publications in *Psychological Abstracts, Sociological Abstracts,* and the Library of Congress *National Union Catalog.* In order to qualify for the "productive" group, a nominee needed to have at least one publication dated when he was in the age range 59–63. After this process was completed, there were 343 names in the "productive" group. These names were looked up in the latest directories of the psychological and sociological associations, so as to obtain current mailing addresses. Some had died since 1960, and others had dropped their membership. Letters with a return postcard were sent to the latest available addresses for those not in the more recent directory and not known to be deceased. These letters brought current addresses from 16 percent of those to whom the letters were addressed. Eventually, current or recent addresses were obtained for 292 of the 343 names in the original "productive" group.

There were 436 of the 779 men who had not published during their 59–63 age period. Of these nonpublished, a random sample of 117 was drawn, on a stratified proportional basis to be comparable in age and discipline to the published.

A substantial questionnaire was mailed to the 409 men whose names appeared on the list of 292 in the "productive" group or on the list of 117 nonpublished. This questionnaire consisted of the following: part A, concentrating on the person's experience since about age 60; part B, asking questions about the person's youth, career, and current activities; and a specially designed personality inventory, containing adapted items from the Omnibus Personality Inventory (OPI) (Heist & Yonge, 1968) and the Cattell 16 PF Inventory (Cattell et al., 1970). The respondents were encouraged to write freely concerning their retirement experiences and their careers, to supplement their responses to the questionnaire items.

Of the 409 questionnaires sent out, 91 were returned with reports that the men were deceased or too ill to respond (40), or returned by the Post Office as not deliverable (51), which meant that the men were deceased or had moved from the addresses we had and could not be located by the Post Office. This meant that 318 men probably received the questionnaire, of whom 166, or 52 percent, responded by answering the questionnaire.

Table 5.1 reports the numbers of responses to the AB Packet by psychologists and sociologists separately, and by published and non-published. It can be noted that men who published were more likely to respond than men who did not publish, and younger men were more likely to respond. Also, publishing sociologists responded in a greater proportion than did publishing psychologists.

Measurement of Productivity During the 60-75 Age Period

Productivity of the study group was studied in the following four main aspects: (1) amount and type of publications output; (2) citations of the respondents' works in the published works of other authors; (3) research grant monies received; and (4) academic activities after formal retirement such as advising graduate students or serving on faculty committees.

Publications were scored as follows: sole author of a book = 50; senior author of a book = 40; junior author of a book = 30; revised edition of a book = 25; editor of a book = 25; monograph = 30; chapter in a book =

TABLE 5.1. Responses by Male Social Scientists to AB Packet

Year of Birth	Psychologists		Sociologists	
	Number	Percent Responding	Number	Percent Responding
Publishing				
1901-03	68	49	47	53
1897-1900	66	41	40	58
1893-96	43	28	19	37
Totals	177	41	106	52
Nonpublishing				
1901-03	28	29	20	25
1897-1900	28	39	15	33
1893-96	18	28	8	25
Totals	74	32	43	28

Note: These percentages do not take account of reasons for no response (e.g., cases where individuals were ill, deceased, or where the packet was returned as "not deliverable").

15; an article reporting original research = 15; and literature review, discussion of concepts or selected studies = 15.

Citation data were collected from the *Social Sciences Citation Index* volume covering the year 1974 with credit given to works that fell in the period when the respondents were 60 through 71 years old.

The questionnaire asked about the receipt of grants to do research since age 60 for five age intervals: 60–64; 65–67; 68–69; 70–72; and 73 plus. Approximate amounts of money received were requested and scored.

Experience After Age Sixty

The study group gradually decreased in proportion with full-time paid employment (79 percent at age 65–66 to 9 percent at age 73–74). Mandatory retirement came for some at age 65, some at age 68, and many at age 70. Even at age 73–74, 45 percent of the group had part-time or full-time paid employment, though some of this was not at regular faculty salary.

Publication Groups

The men were divided into three publication groups. The "high" group had maximum publication scores for three or four of the age periods: 59–61; 62–64; 65–67; 68–70. The "low" group did not publish at all between 59 and 70 years of age, or at the most one research article or chapter in a book. The "middle" group had some publications, spread over the four age intervals. In terms of the size of the three groups, we should remember that these academic male social scientists were born between 1893 and 1903 and living in 1975. Of this "universe" of approximately 700 men, 20 percent were in the "high" group, 25 percent were in the "middle" group, and 55 percent were in the "low" group of nonpublished.

Other Forms of Productivity

It should be noted that the study group was not analyzed for the quality and quantity of their teaching. This analysis could not be done through a questionnaire, although it is important to recognize that teaching is a form of productivity. The questionnaire did ask the respondent how much time he had given to nonclassroom and nonpublishing academic activities during the latest two years. As is shown in Table 5.2, this outcome has a fairly high correlation with publication scores.

Personality, Life-Style, and Productivity

In our study of productive male social scientists, the men were asked to respond to some parts of the Omnibus Personality Inventory (social ex-

TABLE 5.2. Correlates with Productivity Variables

| | Productivity Variables | | |
General Variables	Publications Ages 59–70	Citations Ages 60–71	Grants Ages 60–72
Total academic activities, last two years	.36*	.23*	.44*
Access to college facilities, ages 60–65	.29*	.09	.26*
Total proportion of time given to paid employment, ages 65–72	.19*	.20*	.23*
Publications, ages 59–70	–	.35*	.46*
Citations, ages 60–71	.35*	–	.33*
Grants, ages 60–72	.45*	.33*	–
Social extroversion	.06	-.04	.09
Complexity	-.03	.06	.00
Practical outlook	.08	-.09	.02
Theoretical orientation	.11	.11	.16*
Competitiveness	.12	-.03	.09
Emotional stability	-.13	.06	.13
Warmth and sociability	-.03	-.05	.00
Self-sufficiency	.23*	.24*	.20*
Life satisfaction inventory	.00	-.14	.11

*p less than .05.

troversion, complexity, practical outlook, theoretical orientation) and of the Cattell 16PF Inventory (competitiveness, emotional stability, warmth and sociability, self-sufficiency). Correlations of the productivity variables with these personality variables are shown in Table 5.2. Those marked with an asterisk are reliable at better than the 5 percent level.

The one personality variable which is reliably related to productivity is "self-sufficiency" from the Cattell Inventory. On this factor high scorers are said to have a preference for working alone; they are independent and introspective. Low scorers are gregarious, outgoing, tactful, and sensitive to the needs of others.

It should be noted in Table 5.2 that there was no reliable difference between high and low productive men on the life satisfaction inventory, a widely used measure of morale, or social-personal adjustment.

Some research studies have looked for personality differences among scientists and scholars in various fields and found a few significant differences. A study by Chambers (1964) comparing personality characteristics of "creative" and "average" psychologists found only one significant trait difference between the two groups.

Sources of Self-Esteem

An item on the questionnaire asked respondents to indicate, from a list of possibilities, three main sources of their self-esteem. Table 5.3 compares the responses of the high published with those of the low published.

The high published pay significantly more attention to the approval of their national colleagues (70 percent versus 27 percent), whereas the low published are more oriented to a local reference group (48 percent versus 11 percent) for approval by local colleagues and (35 percent versus 4 percent) for approval by the local community. High published are much more likely to view their research and writing (70 percent versus 43 percent) as an important source of self-esteem, together with "my books and speeches" (66 percent versus 18 percent). It is interesting that "my leadership experience" is favored by the low published (40 percent to 6 percent), probably because they are local leaders in a variety of situations.

To summarize these varied types of evidence, it appears that the low published are more aware of, and sensitive to, the immediate social environment in which they live and work, with a stronger orientation toward a local reference group. The high published, on the other hand, are driven by more internal and even abstract motivations; they search for creativity and new experience, but are not dependent on the support of their immediate personal environment.

TABLE 5.3.   Sources of Self-Esteem for High and Low Published Faculty

	Percent in Each Subgroup of Published Faculty	
	High	Low
Approval by colleagues nationwide	70	27
Approval by local colleagues	11	48
Approval by local community	4	35
My research and writing	70	43
My leadership experience	6	40
Attention given my books and speeches	66	18
Awards and prizes	6	5
Approval of my family	28	50
My financial status	9	22
Number of persons in group	(47)	(59)

Note: Respondents were asked to indicate 3 sources of self-esteem.

The Continuity Principle

A striking feature that emerges from this examination of life-styles may be called the *continuity principle*. There is continuity or stability of life-style from middle age through the age period from 60–75, with little or no change caused by retirement, mandatory or voluntary. The high published continued to make writing and research their principal concern. The low published exhibited more diversity as they had done before age 60. Some of them continued a concentration on teaching and academic activities; and others carried on a variety of service activities in the communities where they lived. Some, but not many, focused their time and energy on leisure activities and hobbies.

The continuity principle can almost certainly be extended to apply to the entire career. It is true that we do not have a lifetime publication score for the study group members; but a preliminary exploration of publication records of members of our high and low published (age 59–70) showed that there was a very high correlation between lifetime publication and publication from age 59–70.

By applying these findings to the total age cohort of male social scientists, we may conclude that: approximately 20 percent have devoted themselves to research and teaching during their entire career, and beyond their formal retirement; approximately 55 percent have teaching with administration and other service activities with little research or writing during their career and beyond their formal retirement; and 25 percent have combined some research with a major emphasis on teaching and service activities.

Social Scientists Then and Now

The group we have been studying, born between 1893 and 1903, became 25 years old between 1918 and 1928. To what extent are their careers and life-styles similar to the age cohort born in 1920–30, who became 25 years old between 1945 and 1955? When the 1920–30 birth cohort is studied in the year 2000, when they have passed through the 60–75 age period, may we expect to find life-styles similar to the life-styles we observe in the present study group?

This is an "academic question" we might say, but some light is thrown on it by the research study of the Carnegie Commission on Higher Education, directed by Martin Trow and published in 1975. A questionnaire was sent to the faculty in a sample of universities and colleges in 1968–69. The colleges and universities covered the entire status range, from junior or community colleges to universities with the highest prestige doctoral and professional programs. We may confine our attention to faculty in the highest four of the seven institutional "quality levels" defined by the commission and also used by us in selecting members of our study group. The Trow (1975) research asked faculty members to tell whether their interests lie primarily in research or in teaching, and to report on their "current publication" output.

The Trow research asked the faculty members to describe their orientation toward teaching and toward research in three categories, and reported the following results: Primarily or exclusively teaching, 48 percent; both teaching and research, 31 percent; or strongly research 21 percent. These percentages are strikingly similar to our findings of 55, 25, and 20 percent for low, medium, and high published.

In general, we are led to expect that the life-styles and working characteristics of our 1893–1903 cohort are similar to what we may expect in the cohorts that reach retirement during the remainder of this century.

Status of Colleges and Universities Where the Study Group Worked

It was necessary to have a basic measure of the academic status and prestige of the colleges and universities in which our respondents worked, as a means of describing the environment in which the person worked, and also to serve as a measure of the status of the job held by the person. Accordingly, we have rated the several hundred colleges and universities on a 5-point rating scale which stems from work of the Carnegie Commission on Higher Education. We expect the respondents to be located mainly in institutions at the top 3 points of the scale.

Sources of the Rating Scale. We have used two sources of ideas and data for the rating scale. One is the Carnegie Commission on Higher Education (1973a). The other is the work of Astin on "selectivity of colleges" for admission of students. The Carnegie categories have a basis in the prestige of the institution as a place to work and to study, with special emphasis on the amount and quality of graduate work supported by the school. We have assigned scores to the Carnegie categories on a scale from 5 (high) to 1 (low).

LEVEL	TYPE OF UNIVERSITY OR COLLEGE
5	*Research Universities I.* These have the largest programs of research and doctoral study. There are 52 in the Carnegie category, and they are all given a rating of 5. No others are rated at this level.
4	*Research Universities II.* These are also research-oriented universities, but slightly less so than those in the top category. There are 40, and all of them are ranked 4.
4 or 3	*Doctorate-Granting Universities I.* These have produced fewer doctorates, but they have an active graduate program, with a good

many MA candidates. The number totaled 53. They are divided about evenly between levels 4 and 3, according to their selectivity in admitting students.

3   *Doctorate-Granting Universities II.* These have relatively small doctoral programs, but they have large MA programs. Here we identified 48. They are placed mainly on level 3, but some are on level 4.

4 or 3   *Liberal Arts Colleges I.* These are the high status, selective liberal arts colleges. Most of them offer the master's degree, but their emphasis is on high level work with selected students. The number totaled 146. About half of this group are ranked 4, and the other half are given a 3.

4 or 3   *Comprehensive Universities and Colleges I.* These are middle-sized and middle-level institutions, generally with a master's degree program and with one or more professional schools, such as education, engineering, commerce, nursing. There are 321 of them, and they are rated 4 or 3, the majority in category 3. This category contains most of the former state teachers colleges, most of which have now become state universities with a liberal arts degree program added to the earlier teacher education program.

3   *Comprehensive Universities and Colleges II.* These are less well-financed and less selective institutions of the comprehensive type. The number totaled 132. They are all ranked 3.

2   *Liberal Arts Colleges II.* There are 573 four-year colleges in this group, many of them church related. Their students have lower scholastic aptitude scores, on the average, and are less likely to pursue graduate work. They are ranked 3 and 2, with the majority at level 2.

1   *Two-Year Colleges.* There are 1,061 two-year institutions, mainly public. They vary among themselves in selectivity and in program emphasis. We have ranked them all 1, even though they have a wide range of student ability and student career aspirations. Relatively few of their faculty or administrators will qualify as more than average in publication or in leadership roles.

There is another category consisting of special schools, usually focused on a particular occupational area, but sometimes specializing in provisions for students with special needs. Very few of our respondents were attached to schools in this category.

Selectivity as a factor in rating institutions.   For ratings of 2, 3, or 4, the Carnegie category is not sufficient, since some categories contain too wide a range of quality to permit assignment of one of these ratings without more information. One index of quality or nature of an institution is the academic ability level of its students. In general, the school with very able students is likely to have a faculty and administration of superior academic qualifications. (However, there are other things to be considered. A school with open admissions may have attracted an unusually creative and problem-oriented faculty.) It is generally of some value to use the ability level of the students as an index of the quality of the faculty. Alexander Astin has collected data on scholastic aptitude and similar ability tests of students in 2,300 colleges (1971). He has used these data as a basis for a *Selectivity Index* ranging from a high of 7 to a low of 1. These data are published for accredited institutions. However, a number of these schools either did not possess such data or did not share them with Astin. Still, the *Selectivity Index* is available for general reading, and it is likely that the more selective schools were the most likely to share their data with Astin.

Consequently, we have noted those schools with Selectivity Indices of 5 to 7, and generally given them the higher of the two rating points available in their category. One problem here lies in the fact that most state universities admit any applicant who has a high school diploma in that state. Thus, the entrants are likely to cover a wide range of test scores, and the selectivity index for this kind of school is likely to be a 4 or a 5, and sometimes a 3. However, the larger state universities are generally in one of the research or doctorate-granting categories, where the selectivity index is not needed for rating purposes. The *Selectivity Index* as a source is most useful in sorting out the liberal arts colleges, category I, with ratings of 4 or 3. It is also used with comprehensive universities and colleges, category I, which contains 321 institutions that can be given ratings of 4 or 3.

Table 5.4 shows how the study group of male social scientists are distributed among the various status levels of universities and colleges. It is clear that the members of the study group were located predominantly in the high status institutions, which would naturally attract the more productive faculty members.

TABLE 5.4.   Status of Universities and Colleges Served by Members of the Study Group of Male Social Scientists

Status		Percent of Group
1	Low	0
2		6
3		25
4		25
5	High	44

SUMMARY

The decade of the 1980s will see major changes in procedures for retirement of faculty members. The 1978 Amendments to the Age Discrimination in Employment Act will force a number of colleges and universities to postpone mandatory retirement to the age of 70. At the same time, there will be substantial pressure for the employment of qualified young men and women, in view of the fact that unusually large cohorts of 25–30-year-olds will be completing graduate study and seeking faculty jobs.

College administrators will seek procedures which offer options to senior faculty members to move into part-time appointments and to take leaves of absence that will permit them to travel and to take work assignments that will assist their scholarly output.

Our survey of the careers of male social science professors after they reach the age of 60 tells us that they fall into three groups with respect to their activity during their 60s and early 70s. One group has a record of productive research and publication. This group, which we will call the A-group, numbers about 20 percent of the total. Members of a second group, called B group, have a medium quantity of publication and continue to be active and effective teachers until they retire; they are 25 percent of the total. Those in a third group, the C group, have no publications and are active in teaching as well as in a variety of administrative and service roles that are essential for the maintenance of the college or university; they are 55 percent of the total. With respect to retirement, 48 percent of the total group retired at the mandatory age of 67–70. A few, 8 percent, retired at 71 or over, and the other 44 percent retired voluntarily at 70 or under, including 32 percent who were 66 or younger.

Formal retirement was not a decisive event in the life-styles of these men. In general, age 65–72 was a rather stable period during which the men maintained their already established life-styles. Most of the men had built up a satisfactory set of habits and skills by the age of 60, and they simply made use of the momentum they had built up to continue their academic life pattern on beyond age 70, as far as their physical vigor and the demand for their services would carry them.

A study by Alan Rowe (1976) entitled "Retired Academics and Research Activity" reports similar findings on continuation of professional activity after formal retirement.

It is important to recognize that the actual date and age of retirement is not apparently of great concern to the individual professor, provided that his income is protected by his TIAA (Teachers Insurance Annuity Association) and his Social Security benefits and his savings.

Flexible Retirement Programs

From our survey of the experience of social science professors during their 60s, it appears that the colleges and universities will work toward *flexibility* in their retirement programs — a kind of flexibility that takes advantage of the variety of life-styles actually exhibited by faculty members during the 1960–75 period.

We might envisage a retirement program operating during the 60–70 age period for faculty members of a university with an enrollment of 10,000 and a faculty numbering about 800, including about 200 over the age of 60. The university program of courses given in the various departments would have a stable structure, with most of the instruction given by full-time faculty members under the age of 60. The program for faculty over the age of 60 might operate in a somewhat different manner. A general practice, allowing for many alternatives, might be a half-time appointment at half of the person's full-time salary. The individual professor would work out his program in consultation with his department head and with the dean of his college so as to be in residence half of the college year, or sometimes more or less to fit a program covering a two- or three-year period. In exceptional cases, the professor might take an appointment in another university for a period of time, or possibly travel, or work in a research institute. He would work out the arrangements in his own university through negotiation with his department head and the administration, with salary appropriate for the service he performs.

Obviously, there would be a wide variety of individual programs, as was seen in the actual programs of the men in our study of social science professors in their 60s.

Chapter 6

Individual and Organizational Contributions to Faculty Vitality: An Institutional Case Study

Shirley M. Clark and *Mary Corcoran*

In these times of constrained resources, it is widely held that faculty and institutional vitality are affected adversely. The study reported here has been stimulated by present concerns with faculty vitality in the university setting. This exploratory investigation uses an institutional case study approach to examine individual and institutional contributions to faculty vitality. Objectives of the study include the identification of patterns, themes, relationships, similarities, and differences in faculty career experience in the university as these factors relate to dimensions of vitality and productivity.

One response to the present and anticipated future conditions of steady state if not decline in the growth of higher education has been the recent enthusiasm for programs of faculty development or faculty renewal. (John Centra discusses this more fully and critically in Chapter 7 of this volume.) A faculty development movement seems to be in process, with a new professional subspecialty employed to conduct it — "faculty developers" are emerging on campuses across the country. Concern is growing for the general welfare, professional growth, and productivity of faculty members who will be the institutions' greatest asset in the next two decades. In this same context, there is concern also about the university as employer and as workplace, and about the organizational qualities that shape careers, aspirations, performance, and morale. The efficacy of policies and programs of faculty development, career interventions, and assistance may be enhanced by the results of faculty vitality studies.

STUDY BACKGROUND AND SIGNIFICANCE

Concerns about the continued vitality of faculties and institutions that pre-occupy many of us in higher education today should be considered in the context of widespread societal concerns for the vitality and health of America's economy and way of life. As we move toward the mid-1980s, Americans are reminded that our growth rate of economic productivity has slowed even while Japan and Germany, our closest competitors, have increased theirs (Margolis, 1979). Politicians urge us to revitalize or reindustrialize our technological base, while analysts ponder the balancing of choices: quality of life versus economic development (White, 1982). The character of the national work force has been changing; it includes more female representation, it is aging, and it is better educated. These various shifts bring changes in patterns of consumption, in income, and in social attitudes and values about work (as interpreted by Daniel Yankelovich, in his best seller of 1981, *New Rules*). If under these conditions there is concern with vitality in the larger society, it follows that concerns would be intensified for the status and condition of higher education, which is primarily responsible for enhancing and disseminating the knowledge base critical to societal productivity and quality. Communities of highly prepared professionals, the faculties, are among the few who are entrusted by society with responsibilities for systems of science and scholarship (Smith, 1978). It is to issues of faculty vitality that this inquiry is addressed.

In the 1970s, the prospect of a steady state and even decline became the reality for higher education as enrollments leveled off or shrank. It became clear that the period of unprecedented expansion had come to an end. Enrollment projections and associated faculty position forecasts share a common pessimistic outlook that predicts declining faculty demand in the 1980s and for most of the 1990s. Couple the present and predicted relative lack of faculty openings for more recently trained and usually younger doctorates with immobile, aging, and increasingly tenured faculties and the concern with faculty vitality becomes one of the most significant issues in American higher education of our times (Carnegie Council on Policy Studies in Higher Education, 1980; National Science Foundation Advisory Council, 1978; National Research Council, 1979).

Problems and Prior Studies

As noted throughout this book, a set of present and near future circumstances seems likely to affect faculty and institutional vitality adversely. Briefly, these circumstances include: continuation of the status quo or shrinkage in faculty size, increasing proportions of faculty who hold tenure, extension of mandatory retirement age by federal and state laws, and changing salary structures as a result of higher rank, tenure, and increased age combined. These conditions are also interactive and interrelated; for example, the increase in the mandatory retirement age coupled with high tenure rates and the declining market, which depresses mobility, means that individuals in many departments will grow old together in a community whose membership is closed.

A number of interesting assumptions and conditions combine to produce a scenario that might be described as follows:

- Renewal will not be accomplished by the pattern of the recent past where faculty members (at least a significant portion of them) "played the market" and moved to institutions that provided better matches for their needs and characteristics, and where the expansion of the professoriate enabled many newly trained doctorates to find their places and refresh or rejuvenate the academic specialties of departments, or even to establish new specialties of recent origin.
- Promising young and/or recently trained doctorates will not find the opportunity structure open to them and they will either choose to accept marginal faculty roles in the nonladder and nontenure ranks in which the new doctorate faculty will "churn" in and out of academe or they will seek alternative nonacademic employment. A "lost generation" of scholars may result in a loss in scientific discoveries which may have broad social and possibly economic impact (Radner & Kuh, 1978; Linnell, 1979).
- Promising female and/or minority doctorates will find the opportunity structure nearly impenetrable at a time when, ironically, a national policy is in place to encourage affirmative action and equal employment opportunity for heretofore excluded sex, racial and ethnic categories (Newman, 1979; Sandler, 1979).
- Although there are creative and productive faculty in their 60s, 70s, and 80s, the prevailing view and much of the research evidence (cross-sectional rather than longitudinal, however) suggests that older faculty members, especially those who are beyond 60 or 65, are less productive in their research output and therefore, less "vital" than younger ones (Bayer & Dutton, 1977; Reskin, 1979).
- Generational differences between faculty and students will be exacerbated as average age discrepancies increase. These may be associated with problems of effectiveness as teachers and as research mentors, for the life experiences of the different age cohorts in the historical dimension of the social process are bound to be different (Bess, 1973b).
- The opportunity structure for faculty, consisting of a very short ladder of statuses, a relatively flat salary curve, and limited possibilities of obtaining significant administrative positions may result in feelings of being "stuck" versus feelings of "moving" or "progressing" in their careers.

Responses to "stuckness" may be lowered self-esteem, disengagement from work, resistance to change and innovation, and disposition to unionize (Kanter, 1979).

• As resources become scarce, as job security becomes an issue even for tenured faculty, and as centralization of power in institutions continues, organizationally powerless people will reflect a demoralized atmosphere in which risk taking and distinguished performance will be discouraged (Kanter, 1979).

Scenarios such as this one are derived from research, observations, idiosyncratic experience, and personal beliefs. Popular notions and even much of the literature about faculty vitality and performance are a mixture of the tested and the untested, intuitive hunches, logical deductions, facts and stereotypes. Furthermore, faculty vitality issues are often presented as though the faculty could be conceived as an undifferentiated number of professionals pursuing identical roles in institutions with identical societal missions. Obviously, this is not the case. Faculty members at two-year community colleges may be faced with a set of vitality issues different from those of faculty members at research and graduate training-oriented multiversities, for example, and undoubtedly there are great intrainstitutional differences as well.

Another problem with the overgeneralization of the issues seems to be that we are only in the early stages of the creation of a theory of faculty career development, which includes organizational as well as individual dimensions. Robert Blackburn's analysis in this book carries this activity significantly forward with a socialization model. Perhaps there are linkages between the occupational socialization of faculty members for their roles and vitality issues relative to teaching performance, research productivity, and service orientations. Dan C. Lortie's seminal ethnography *Schoolteacher* (1975) suggests ideas that might be pursued in this regard. We know little of variations in role behavior and preferences of faculty members over the career life span, by institutional type, by sex, and by discipline. Institutional "management" of faculty careers in the form of interventions such as mentoring and sponsorship of research activities to boost productivity, consultation relative to the improvements of teaching, midcareer assessment and transition assistance, and preretirement planning would benefit from a broader knowledge base.

The Idea of Faculty Vitality

The concept of faculty and institutional vitality is discussed in the opening chapter and within other contributions in this collection, particularly in John Centra's analysis of faculty development programs. We shall highlight here issues that have affected our present study. We have focused on the institutional context for vitality concerns, and on identifying problems, conditions, and assumptions that seem to underlie vitality issues. What, specifically, are the problems? In what context do they occur? Who and what are affected? Do proposed solutions have a clear knowledge base?

Since our research focus is individual and organizational conditions relating to faculty vitality, we have found it stimulating and useful to consider more general discussions of vitality (including synonyms and related terms) as well as those which are specific to certain institutional types. Of the former, John W. Gardner in his writings *Morale* (1978) and *Self-Renewal* (1963) suggests the themes of human growth, equilibrium, risk and renewal:

> A society concerned for its own continued vitality will be interested in the growth and fulfillment of individual human beings—the release of human potentialities. (Gardner, 1978, p. 73)

> In a vital society, the forces making for disintegration and death are balanced—or more than balanced—by new life, growth, and health. (Gardner, 1978, p. 144)

> People with the vitality to gamble on their future, whatever the odds. . . . Men and women of vitality have always been prepared to bet their futures, even their lives, on ventures of unknown outcome. (Gardner, 1978, p. 152)

> Continuous renewal depends upon conditions that encourage fulfillment of the individual. . . . A society decays when its institutions and individuals lose their vitality. (Gardner, 1963, p. 2)

> In the ever-renewing society what matures is a system or framework within which continuous innovation, renewal and rebirth can occur. (Gardner, 1963, p. 5)

Gardner also recognizes that human vitality is a product of the interaction between the individual and the environment/organization:

> The development of abilities is at least in part a dialogue between the individual and his environment. (Gardner, 1963, p. 11)

> Too often in the past we have designed systems to meet all kinds of exacting requirements except the requirement that they contribute to the fulfillment and growth of the participants. . . . It is essential that in the years ahead we undertake intensive analysis of the impact of the organization on the individual. (Gardner, 1963, pp. 63–64)

The roughly 3,000 institutions of higher education in the United States are extraordinarily diverse in the functions that they perform for our society. In a large-scale national study sponsored by the Carnegie Commission, Fulton and Trow (1974) have spelled out the division of labor within American education relative to research activities. They have suggested that in the "leading" universities, the faculty role includes the expectation of continuing research activity. In some other universities and colleges, there is no expectation and acceptance that the role may or may not include active research. In still others, research is not normally expected of the faculty member (Fulton & Trow, 1974, p. 68). This reinforces an obvious point advanced earlier: consideration of faculty vitality cannot and should not be separated from the mission(s) of the institution. It suggests that institutions with different functions or emphases will have different ideas about faculty vitality and, to carry it a step further, different ideal types of faculty role performance will emerge.[1] In some institutions, vitality concerns may affix to undergraduate teaching quite exclusively; at the other extreme, vitality concerns may affix to research productivity and graduate training, with enormous variation in patternings in between.

The University of Minnesota, Twin Cities campus, is described as a large, research-oriented, land grant multiversity, notwithstanding substantial internal variations by college and by department. The implications for faculty vitality drawn from the typology that fits Minnesota generally are that the several missions of the institution will be reflected in the assignments, expectations, performance, and vitality of the faculty. Thus, it was not surprising that university's planning council included the following definition of faculty vitality in a memorandum to President Magrath:

> A faculty is vital if it exhibits sustained productivity in its teaching, its research, and its service activities. Productivity is characterized not by quantity of output but by quality of these outputs as judged by faculty peers. A faculty is vital if it is continually creating important, new knowledge and expanding our understanding of the world in which we live. A faculty is vital if there is a balance between innovative and traditional approaches to teaching and research. The University faculty is vital if it is responding to the needs of the state, the nation, and the world for new knowledge. On occasions, this vitality is recognized through awards and prizes for scholarship. Perhaps most important a faculty is vital if its members find their work stimulating, enjoyable and satisfying. (Planning Council, 1980, p. 4)

It is from the core of this definition of vitality, "sustained productivity in its teaching, its research, and its service activities," and the knowledge that this definition has been expected (and accepted) as the primary criterion in promotion and tenure, as well as salary adjustment policies in the university as far back as its founding documents, that we settled upon an operational assumption for an exploratory study of faculty careers.

PLAN OF STUDY AND PRELIMINARY FINDINGS

Why an Institutional Case Study?

As Fulton and Trow (1974) in their mapping of research activities of faculty in higher education institutions have established and as numerous other students of the demography of American higher education have shown, the range of institutional types is great and the academic profession is not unified. Rather, there is differential emphasis upon assignments and qualitative/quantitative expectations for the teaching of undergraduates, the training of graduate students, the preparation of professionals, research and creative activities, contributions to problem-solving in society, and administrative services. In the complex university type of which Minnesota is an exemplar, faculty vitality may find more than one appropriate model. These models most likely include sustained productivity both of a qualitative and quantitative sort in the domains of instruction, research/scholarly/creative work, and associated professional service. However, the models may emphasize the faculty performance domains differentially at different stages of the career life cycle, and the performance domains may be emphasized differently in individual faculty careers as a whole. Thus, we expected that in this context an institutional case study approach would provide a rich source of information and insights about various dimensions of vitality.

Notwithstanding the conflicts and dysfunctions of the research-oriented, land grant multiversity, there is plenty of evidence that American colleges and universities judge each other and themselves against a standard of research preeminence (Trow, 1975) in their intense competition for institutional prestige (Light, 1974). Considerations of vitality, including the way the issue is framed, and ideal types of faculty careers do take this professional and institutional norm into account. For this and other reasons, we decided to begin our exploratory study of individual and organizational conditions related to faculty vitality by investigating highly productive and vital faculty careers.

Study Phase I – The Highly Active Ideal Type

Funds from the Graduate School and from the College of Education of the University of Minnesota, which we gratefully acknowledge, enabled us to undertake the inquiry from 1980–82.[2] The focus of the inquiry is the convergence of the organizational and individual in careers, the structural determinants of behavior in organizations, and the interactive aspects of the person-organization relationships.

We used a reputational, two-step nominations process for samples of faculty members who met the criteria for inclusion into the highly active ideal type—those who continuously publish, teach, and perform administrative and/or professional services at highly productive levels; these faculty members were identified by broadly knowledgeable faculty and administrative colleagues in the sample sites: the College of Biological Sciences, the physical sciences and mathematics departments of the Institute of Technology, and the traditional social sciences and humanities of the College of Liberal Arts.[3] At least two judges recommended each tenured associate or full professor nominated for inclusion. We recognized that this is simply *one* ideal type model of faculty vitality, but it is a strongly positive one about which there is widespread consensus in a large research-oriented university.

During summer of 1980, an interview guide was developed, pilot tested, and subsequently used with faculty respondents in the samples from the three colleges. The plan and procedures for the exploratory study design were discussed with a project advisory group. After the fall quarter of 1980 began, faculty nominees were contacted by letters which invited their participation in a lengthy, tape-recorded interview. The letter of invitation was followed up with telephone calls. The response and cooperation was excellent. Only four of the total number contacted expressed unwillingness to be interviewed and at the end of February, 1981, scheduled interviews for a total of 63 were completed. One or the other of us conducted each interview, since our involvement seemed to facilitate full and open responses from colleagues. On average, interviews extended over a two-hour period or longer.

It is from preliminary analysis of selected data from Phase 1—the highly active, ideal type—that we will be drawing later (see "Report of Phase I Findings" in this chapter).

Interview Guide Development

The interview guide consists of approximately fifty questions, some of which contain subparts and probes, and almost all of which are open-ended. In a few instances, questions were adapted from those used in other studies. For example, questions concerning research and teaching interests and orientations were adapted from Trow's Carnegie Commission on Higher Education study of faculty activities (1975); questions concerning some aspects of professional socialization, career and work rewards, and the relevance of collegiality to performance were adapted from studies of teachers done by Lortie (1975). In several instances, a scholar's conceptualization, for example, the "one life–one career" imperative and the psychological sense of community (Sarason, 1977) or the ideas of opportunity and power structures (Kanter, 1979), stimulated eventual development of questions.

In order to achieve a quasi-longitudinal perspective, the questions and their sequencing were planned to explore retrospective, present, and future aspects of the faculty member's career in the organization. Specifically, question areas included:

1. *The decision to pursue an academic career.* When did it occur; what were the circumstances; who influenced it; were alternatives considered; what was the attraction to it; and what were the personal qualities which fit well with it?

2. *Graduate school dimensions of career socialization.* How the graduate school was chosen, opportunities for role learning, relationships with advisers and others, expectations of performance, career assistance and sponsorship, assistance after achieving entry level position, peer relationships related to professional success.

3. *Career stages and socialization as a faculty member.* How the career entry position was obtained, expectations of performance from early probationary years to the present on the part of colleagues, students, faculty, self; how performance is assessed by self and others, solo or collaborative work style/preference, involvement in interdisciplinary/ multidisciplinary work/new fields, encouragement of colleagues and reward structure to explore and take risks in work, balance of "inside/ outside" orientations to colleagues in career.

4. *Work interests and preference orientations.* Weight of interests in research and/or teaching time committed to work-related activities, teaching load, perceptions of time commitments as compared to colleagues, involvements with students, research patterns relative to involvement of others, research administrative aspect, personal importance of various activities relative to college activities, impact of relative career maturity on energy level, stamina, attitudes, morale; outside interests and activities.

5. *Dimensions of productivity and success.* Descriptive criteria for outstanding faculty member, comparative perception of success at various career stages, attribution of basis for success, organizational conditions, situations or factors that facilitated or interfered with success, experience of being blocked or stuck in career, differential needs by career stage.

6. *Morale, satisfaction, and perceptions of change.* Satisfactions and dissatisfactions with career, changes in career expectations, consideration of midcareer change, choice of faculty career if starting over, advice to others about entering academic careers today, why new people are attracted to the faculty under present conditions, why people stay.

7. *Appraisals and future considerations.* Professional/career ambitions projected, assessment of academic career today, aspects of "ideal" organizational environment relative to career productivity at different stages.

Approaches to Analysis

Because it was considered premature to approach this research problem through traditional theory testing and verification procedures, the research strategy and methodology were based primarily upon a qualitative paradigm that emphasizes discovery or generation of theories.[4] However, we assumed that quantitative methods could be used also, to enable us to triangulate on the underlying facts and offer some perspective on the relative frequency with which certain events and assessments were reported. We sought to translate the data obtained from the interviews into numbers and subsequently into patterns through the coding process, and we preferred to record the interviews verbatim in order to capture and preserve the richness of the language and meaning systems of the articulate faculty respondents.

Thus, in formulating these strategies, we hope to find out what explanatory schemes are used by the respondents in the study to make sense of their social realities, and what theories, concepts, and categories are suggested by the data themselves. The insistence upon closeness to the real worlds of the respondents and to comprehending their actions in situ gives strong support to the explanations that the research eventually constructs (Filstead, 1979, p. 38). In developing explanations of phenomena, use is made of sensitizing concepts rather than operational definitions. Also, the selection of particular faculty members for the study may change based on (1) what data are being collected and (2) the direction such information suggests with respect to who can provide additional information to answer emerging questions. Glaser and Strauss (1967) call this "theoretical sampling." A substantial body of literature, primarily in anthropology and sociology, has accumulated on the assumptions, techniques, and strategies in the approach and use of qualitative methods.

As applied to the study at hand, the qualitative paradigm seemed to fit best the generalized nature of the research problem, the ambiguities and complexities of the concept of faculty vitality that forestall easy operationalization, and the relative accessibility of thoughtful and cooperative "expert" respondents. Thus, we proceeded with the methodology of in-depth interviewing of both specialized (highly active, ideal type) and representative samples, and with preliminary data analysis, both of a qualitative and quantitative nature.

In order to facilitate data analysis, the interview tapes were transcribed into verbatim typescript. Coding of both the interviews and the respondent vitae was completed using an inductively derived survey code, which we developed to accomplish the empirical categorization of the responses. Interrater agreement exercises were undertaken to assure that the procedure met adequate standards of reliability.

In addition to the descriptive analysis facilitated by the coding of data for processing to obtain numerically based patterns of response, prospective content analysis of each interview is aimed at discovery of themes, patterns, and relationships in the data. Quotations that best illustrate patterns of response are included in the research findings reported here. We turn now to presentation of selected research results.

Report of Phase I Findings

The analysis that follows is based on our examination of coded responses to selected interview questions and initial reading of the transcripts. Subsequent analyses will draw more fully on the transcripts. We also are focusing at this time on those sections of the interview that deal with work interests and preferences, opinions about productivity and success, and satisfactions or dissatisfactions with organizational conditions as these relate to faculty work.

The report begins with selected descriptive information about the Phase I group, which as noted earlier was identified by judges as productive in the full range of faculty work, teaching, research, and service. The total group of 63 interviewees was drawn from four academic areas: humanities, social sciences, biological sciences, and physical sciences and mathematics, with numbers roughly proportional to the relative size of these groups in the faculty of the University of Minnesota. All were tenured faculty, about two-thirds at full professor rank and one-third at the associate professor rank. Three aspects of our analysis are presented: First, what have we learned about the nature and the quality of faculty vitality in this select group? Second, what motivates these faculty? And third, in what ways is the university environment most supportive of their work? In what ways does it hinder them?

Characteristics of a highly productive faculty group. There are several background characteristics that describe the sample in which readers may have an interest. Eleven percent of the sample were women, and they were distributed across the four areas. The ages of respondents ranged from the early 30s into the 60s, with a median age in the 40s in all four fields; most were born between 1925 and 1945. The social science group had somewhat fewer younger people than the other groups.

While a sizable number (43 percent) of the physical scientists and mathematicians made their career decisions while still in high school, or in a few cases even before, others, particularly among the social and biological scientists (45 percent and 50 percent, respectively) did not reach a decision until they were in graduate school. These field differences reportedly represent shifts in majors and in the biological sciences, awareness of emerging fields of inquiry. Of the total group, their doctoral years span three decades with most of the concentration in the 1950s, 1960s and, to a lesser extent, the 1970s.

These faculty members who were regarded by knowledgeable peers as meeting criteria for inclusion into the highly active, ideal type who "does everything"—research and publish, teach and contribute services—were asked midway through the interview for their own comparative view of their success at various career stages. As if to acknowledge or reaffirm the estimation made by others, some 70 percent of the total sample responded that they have been either "more successful" or "much more successful" than their peers. Most of the others, as can be seen in Table 6.1, regarded themselves to be at least as successful as their peers.

They also typically think that they work harder than most of their colleagues. According to Table 6.2, 68 percent hold this view. Among those 30 percent who, perhaps with some modesty, stated that they were average in this respect, a number went on to say that they thought their colleagues were, in general, a hard-working group.

Parsons and Platt in *The American University* (1968, p. 144) assert that academic values center on the pattern of cognitive rationality and that research is the activity most central to the core, all other functions of higher education ranking below research. This core-periphery image "like so much research in this area, brilliantly illuminates the research professor at the center and leaves most of American higher education in the shadows" (Light, 1974, p. 6). Trow (1975, pp. 32–33) found that of the total national sample of faculty members surveyed by the Carnegie Commission in 1969, 77 percent indicated their interests lay either "very heavily in teaching" or in "both but leaning to teaching." However, in that subgroup of faculty drawn from high quality universities into the Carnegie Commission survey, the responses divided quite evenly between preferences for research and for teaching (Trow, 1975, p. 44). Thus, in our study of highly productive faculty, we would expect either a relatively even division of interests and orientations between teaching and research, or a skewing toward preference for research on the basis of the Carnegie Commission study and as suggested in the ideas about elites in American higher education. As shown in Table 6.3, the preference for research is a decided one, particularly among the biological and physical scientists. Of the total group, 51 percent selected "both, but leaning to research" and 29 percent selected "very heavily in research/scholarly work."

In summary, the Phase I faculty group see themselves as a high achieving, hard-working group, who enjoy the balance of teaching and research with the weighting toward research and scholarly work that their careers afford. Their ages span a three-decade range, but they are typically over 40. Their post-doctoral experience ranges from 5–35 years with 15–20 years most typical. They are predominantly male, as is true of this faculty group generally.

Assessment of vitality. A number of the interview questions were

TABLE 6.1. Self-Ratings of Success Compared to Peers

Response Categories	Humanities (N=10)		Social Sciences (N=22)		Biological Sciences (N=10)		Physical Sciences and Math (N=21)		Total Group (N=63)	
	N	%	N	%	N	%	N	%	N	%
Much more successful	1	10	3	15	–	–	1	6	5	9
More successful	5	50	13	65	6	60	10	63	34	61
About the same	4	40	3	15	3	30	4	25	14	25
More in some ways, less in others	–	–	–	–	1	10	1	6	2	3
Less successful	–	–	1	5	–	–	–	–	1	2
No data or non-scorable response	–		(2)		–		(5)		(7)	

Note: Percentages are based on the number of individuals, by group, who have a codable response.

TABLE 6.2. How Hard Do You Work Compared to Colleagues?

Response Categories	Humanities (N=10)		Social Sciences (N=22)		Biological Sciences (N=10)		Physical Sciences and Math (N=21)		Total Group (N=63)	
	N	%	N	%	N	%	N	%	N	%
Harder than most	7	78	14	67	7	70	13	65	41	68
About average	2	22	7	33	3	30	6	30	18	30
Less than average	–	–	–	–	–	–	1	5	1	2
No data or non-scorable response	(1)		(1)		–		(1)		(3)	

Note: Percentages are based on the number of individuals, by group, who have a codable response.

TABLE 6.3.   Interest Priorities: Research Versus Teaching

Response Categories	Humanities (N=10)		Social Sciences (N=22)		Biological Sciences (N=10)		Physical Sciences and Math (N=21)		Total Group (N=63)	
	N	%	N	%	N	%	N	%	N	%
Lean heavily to research	1	10	7	32	5	50	5	26	18	29
Both, but lean to research	6	60	10	45	4	40	11	58	31	51
Both, but lean to teaching	2	20	5	23	1	10	1	5	9	15
Lean heavily to teaching	-	-	-	-	-	-	-	-	-	-
Other	1	10	-	-	-	-	2	11	3	5
No data or non-scorable response	-		-		-		(2)		(2)	

Note: Percentages are based on the number of individuals, by group, who gave a codable response.

designed to assess various dimensions of faculty vitality. This assessment will require considerably more investigation of the individual interview transcripts before it can be definitive, but our initial examination of responses suggests that certain items are potentially useful in arriving at such an assessment. Remembering that the Phase I group selected was a highly active group, the expectation would be that typically they would stand out in our assessment of these items.

By self-report, these faculty members consider themselves to be among the "moving" rather than the "stuck," to borrow Kanter's terms (1977). They have aspirations, they have high esteem and value their competence and accomplishment, and for them work is a central life interest that demands energy and engagement. When asked, "Do you have professional or career ambitions that you hope to achieve in the next 5-10 years?", over 80 percent of the group were able to indicate specifically what they hoped to do. When asked "Have you ever felt that you reached a certain level and became blocked or stuck in your career, that you lacked opportunity or were unable to take advantage of opportunity to move ahead?" (and related probes), over half responded that they never felt that way. In short, they are "high in opportunity" as mobility and growth are structured in complex organizations (Kanter, 1977, pp. 246-247).

In a similar vein, 82 percent of the highly active group report perceiving no decline in their performance productivity over different career stages. However, according to Table 6.4, some differences by field are suggested in the responses with 38 percent of the physical scientists and mathematicians claiming that their performance has decreased. Whether this finding may be explained by age differences in productivity in different disciplines, or by other theories, will be interesting to pursue.

While productivity seems to be holding its own, some changes in energy level were noted as reported by field in Table 6.5. About half of the total group report a decrease in energy level over that attributed to earlier career stages, and the other half report no change or an increase. Respondents did express some age-associated explanations with their personal assessment, coupled sometimes with the comment that they had learned how the system works and how to use work time and energies better than in earlier years, thus becoming more efficient.

This group responded in the affirmative to the question, "If you were starting over today, would you choose again the career of faculty member?" In spite of the well-publicized decline in the conditions of academe and the problems of faculty relative to the tight market, declines in real faculty income, changes in public confidence in higher education and others, 42 percent of the total group indicated that they would choose this career again *now* without hesitation, and another 49 percent indicated that they would follow suit, with qualifications, as noted in Table 6.6. These responses will require further examination before they can be directly interpreted as in-

TABLE 6.4.   Change in Productivity in the Course of the Career

Response Categories	Humanities (N=10)		Social Sciences (N=22)		Biological Sciences (N=10)		Physical Sciences and Math (N=21)		Total Group (N=63)	
	N	%	N	%	N	%	N	%	N	%
Increased	5	56	3	14	4	40	5	31	17	30
Ups and downs	2	22	11	52	3	30	3	19	19	34
No change	2	22	3	14	3	30	2	12	10	18
Decreased	–	–	4	19	–	–	6	38	10	18
No data or non-scorable response	(1)		(1)		–		(5)		(7)	

Note: Percentages are based on the number of individuals, by group, who gave a codable response.

TABLE 6.5. Change in Energy Level

Response Categories	Humanities (N=10)		Social Sciences (N=22)		Biological Sciences (N=10)		Physical Sciences and Math (N=21)		Total Group (N=63)	
	N	%	N	%	N	%	N	%	N	%
Increased	1	10	–	–	3	43	2	11	6	11
No change	7	70	7	37	1	14	8	42	23	42
Decreased	2	20	12	63	3	43	9	47	26	47
No data or non-scorable response	–		(3)		(3)		(2)		(8)	

Note: Percentages are based on the number of individuals, by group, who gave a codable response.

TABLE 6.6. Would You Choose an Academic Career Today?

Response Categories	Humanities (N=10)		Social Sciences (N=22)		Biological Sciences (N=10)		Physical Sciences and Math (N=21)		Total Group (N=63)	
	N	%	N	%	N	%	N	%	N	%
Yes, unqualified	4	45	9	45	1	10	11	55	25	42
Qualified yes or maybe	3	33	11	55	7	70	8	40	29	49
No	2	22	–	–	2	20	1	5	5	9
No data or non-scorable responses	(1)		(2)		–		(1)		(4)	

Note: Percentages are based on the number of individuals, by group, who gave a codable response.

dications of general morale or vitality because of the nature and range of qualifications given.

Our preliminary conclusion is that this Phase I sample in general would be described as a vital group of faculty members with a high level of morale. In subsequent analysis it will be important to differentiate those who seem to be outstanding in respect to those who seem less so and determine, if possible, from the interview content what some of the distinctions are. If this analysis yields suggestions, then some useful criterion measures of vitality may be developed to assess this quality in other faculty groups.

Motivational characteristics of a productive faculty group. Studies of faculty have frequently emphasized the importance of motivational factors intrinsic to a faculty member's work in contrast to extrinsic rewards such as salaries. For example, in the series of studies of Minnesota college teachers initiated by Ruth Eckert and John Stecklein (1961), the most frequently identified sources of satisfaction have been those intrinsic to the career, including opportunity to work with college age students, stimulating colleagues and associates, the intellectual atmosphere of the campus, and freedom to plan one's own time (1961). On the other hand, the most frequently mentioned dissatisfactions were such working conditions as numbers of meetings, salary, and administrative attitudes. Citing the Eckert and Stecklein study and several others, Wilbert J. McKeachie describes conditions that lend themselves to motivating faculty:

> Peer support, a feeling of autonomy and control over one's work, a sense of stimulation from one's students and colleagues, and an administration that encourages rather than restricts faculty initiative — all of these contribute to higher levels of motivation and investment on the part of faculty members. (1982, p. 462)

The responses to two questions in our study with respect to satisfactions and dissatisfactions of career followed a similar pattern with frequent mention of intrinsic aspects of academic work such as the intellectual play of ideas and the attractions of research and teaching and of the academic life-style, notably, its freedom as satisfactions. Similarly, dissatisfactions focused on salary and administrative attitudes. In addition, there were concerns regarding funding possibilities and institutional support of the academic life generally.

Two other questions also yielded reactions about the interplay of internal and external considerations for these faculty members. The first of these concerned reasons for success. This question followed the question reported earlier with respect to self-appraisal of relative degree of success. It can be seen in Table 6.7 that most responses focused on individual qualities and

TABLE 6.7. Reasons for Success

Response Categories	Humanities (N=10)		Social Sciences (N=22)		Biological Sciences (N=10)		Physical Sciences and Math (N=21)		Total Group (N=63)	
	N	%	N	%	N	%	N	%	N	%
Hard work	3	43	13	81	3	43	6	55	25	61
Personal qualities	1	14	5	31	–	–	6	55	12	29
"Luck"	3	43	9	56	2	29	6	55	20	49
Chose right field	–	–	1	6	3	43	–	–	4	10
Availability of funding	1	14	3	19	2	29	1	9	7	17
Institutional support	1	14	2	12	1	14	2	18	6	15
Other	3	43	4	25	2	29	1	9	10	24
No data or non-scorable responses	(3)		(6)		(3)		(10)		(22)	

Note: Percentages are based on the number of individuals, by group, who gave at least 1 codable response. Up to 3 responses were coded. Therefore, the percentages in any column may add to more than 100.

hard work, that is, aspects of the self, while others (but fewer) focused on externals such as availability of funding and institutional support. One that was often given first and then modified was "luck." When respondents were pressed to describe it, luck was seen to involve a mixture of matters, including being in the right place at the right time and choosing the right field. Luck has something of an external aspect to it, but is also internal in part as well, in the sense that the person was capable of recognizing and making use of opportunity.

Similarly, a mixture of internal and external explanations was given in response to the question, "How do you judge how well you are doing?" As displayed in Table 6.8, there was strong evidence of reliance on external recognitions (whether formal or informal) by many, but there was also a sizable group in most fields for whom their own self-assessments were most important. Still further insights into the factors that faculty members consider important are given in the next section, where we focus on institutional and environmental forces.

Environmental factors contributing to faculty vitality in a selected group. Responses to two questions regarding organizational conditions, situations or factors supportive of faculty productivity and success, and

TABLE 6.8. Bases for Judging "How Well You Are Doing"

Response Categories	Humanities (N=10)		Social Sciences (N=22)		Biological Sciences (N=10)		Physical Sciences and Math (N=21)		Total Group (N=63)	
	N	%	N	%	N	%	N	%	N	%
Formal external recognition	4	40	12	57	5	56	12	71	33	58
Informal recognition by peers	3	30	4	19	5	56	9	53	21	37
Student achievement and feedback	2	20	9	43	1	11	4	24	16	24
Self-evaluation	5	50	7	33	–	–	5	29	17	30
Promotion and tenure	1	10	4	19	1	11	2	12	8	14
Uncertain	2	20	2	10	2	22	3	18	9	16
Other	–	–	1	5	2	22	–	–	3	5
No data or non-scorable response	–		(1)		(1)		(4)		(6)	

Note: Percentages are based on the number of individuals, by group,
who gave at least 1 codable response. Up to 3 responses were coded.
Therefore, the percentages in any column may add to more than 100.

those that interfere with it or hinder it, shed light on environmental factors contributing to faculty vitality. In their open-ended answers, interviewees could present any number of responses and up to three responses were coded. It is useful to summarize these two sets of responses in terms of two major categories, those that concern the general environmental support of scholarship, and then specific support for faculty research. As can be seen in Table 6.9, the supportive aspects of the environment, which included stimulating colleagues, strong academically oriented administration, and recognition by administrators and colleagues, were reported as positive factors by 51 percent of the respondents, and research funding availability was discussed by 46 percent of the total group.

Faculty development resources such as single-quarter leave and sabbaticals were seen as positive element by some, but others were concerned about lack of free time that can be distinctly dedicated to research. Similarly, quality of graduate students is mentioned both positively and negatively, though our Phase II cross-sectional interviews suggest that this may be more often negative than suggested here.

Specific support for faculty research is the area in which faculty feel very strongly with respect to the freedom aspect. The ability for faculty to

TABLE 6.9.   Institutional Conditions Supporting Success

Response Categories	Humanities (N=10)		Social Sciences (N=22)		Biological Sciences (N=10)		Physical Sciences and Math (N=21)		Total Group (N=63)	
	N	%	N	%	N	%	N	%	N	%
Supporting university environment	5	50	11	58	4	40	10	50	30	51
Funding availability	5	50	10	53	4	40	8	40	27	46
"Freedom"	6	60	6	32	3	30	3	15	18	31
Good teaching load	–	–	2	11	5	50	5	25	12	20
Single quarter leaves; sabbaticals	2	20	6	32	1	10	1	5	10	17
Good graduate students	1	10	–	–	1	10	2	10	4	7
Expanding field	–	–	1	5	1	10	2	10	4	7
Good facilities	1	10	–	–	1	10	–	–	2	3
Other	1	10	1	5	–	–	4	20	6	10
No data or non-scorable response	–		(3)		–		(1)		(4)	

Note: Percentages are based on the number of individuals, by group, who gave at least 1 codable response. Up to 3 responses were coded. Therefore, the percentages in any column may add to more than 100.

direct their own scholarly activities is one of the most frequently mentioned attractions of an academic career. Also stressed is the availability of time for research because they are not burdened by heavy teaching or administrative responsibilities. As shown in Table 6.10, however, others find problems in both the lack of funding and burdensome teaching responsibilities, and also with the quality of library and laboratory facilities. In summary, the institutional factors that emerge as most critical in the assessments of this group focus on the nature of the environment in support of scholarship and research, the availability of funds for scholarship and research, and the relative weight of the assigned teaching responsibilities vis à vis other expectations.

One other consideration that may indeed be a source of concern for both faculty and institutional vitality arises from responses to the question, "In your experience as a faculty member, do you feel that colleagues and 'the system' have encouraged you to explore and take risks in your teaching and research?" The responses, as shown in Table 6.11, indicate that only 9 percent feel that risk taking is encouraged, while a large proportion of these

TABLE 6.10. Institutional Conditions Hindering Success

Response Categories	Humanities (N=10) N	%	Social Sciences (N=22) N	%	Biological Sciences (N=10) N	%	Physical Sciences and Math (N=21) N	%	Total Group (N=63) N	%
Nonsupportive university environment	–	–	3	20	3	60	4	27	10	23
Lack of funding	4	44	4	27	–	–	3	20	11	25
Heavy teaching/ administrative responsibilities	6	67	7	47	2	40	7	47	22	50
Lack of research time	1	11	2	13	–	–	–	–	3	7
Lack of good graduate students	–	–	–	–	1	20	2	13	3	7
Nature of the field	–	–	–	–	–	–	1	7	1	2
Poor facilities	1	11	3	20	–	–	3	20	7	16
Other	1	11	1	7	–	–	1	7	3	7
No data or non-scorable response*	(1)		(7)		(5)		(6)		(19)	

Note: Percentages are based on the number of individuals, by group, who gave at least 1 codable response. Up to 3 responses were coded. Therefore, the percentages in any column may add to more than 100.

*This category is inflated by inclusion of "nonresponses" (e.g., responses of faculty members who indicated that their success had not been hindered).

highly active, successful faculty members (42 percent) feel that risk taking is discouraged. To the extent that overconforming behavior may be dysfunctional to the organization, this finding suggests a basis for concern. Further content analysis of the interview transcripts should shed light on the meaning of these perceptions on faculty behavior.

IMPLICATIONS FOR INSTITUTIONAL POLICY ON FACULTY VITALITY

This study has been premised on the idea that the institution determines to a high degree a faculty member's vitality, that vitality is a result of individual and organizational interaction, and that consideration of faculty vitality cannot be separated from the missions of the institution. We have

TABLE 6.11.   Is Risk Taking Encouraged?

Response Categories	Humanities (N=10)		Social Sciences (N=22)		Biological Sciences (N=10)		Physical Sciences and Math (N=21)		Total Group (N=63)	
	N	%	N	%	N	%	N	%	N	%
Yes, encouraged	1	10	3	15	–	–	1	6	5	9
Under some conditions	–	–	3	15	3	30	6	35	13	23
Neither encouraged nor discouraged	–	–	9	45	–	–	5	29	14	25
Personally indifferent to restraints	2	20	1	5	2	20	2	12	7	12
Discouraged	6	60	4	20	7	70	7	41	24	42
Other	1	10	–	–	1	10	1	6	3	5
No data or non-scorable response	–		(2)		–		(4)		(6)	

Note: Percentages are based on the number of individuals, by group, who gave at least 1 codable response. Up to 3 responses were coded. Therefore, the percentages in any column may add to more than 100.

presented selected findings from the interviews with a sample of highly active faculty members at the University of Minnesota which suggest that faculty members like these, who may serve as models of vitality and productivity for others, make assessments of themselves, their colleagues, their students, and their institution relative to effects on their performance and their academic career development. From these assessments, some institutional policy implications may be framed. These policy suggestions will be grouped into three areas: provide environmental support for the scholarly development of the faculty, provide institutional support for faculty research activities, and provide differentiated support for individual faculty needs.

Provide an Environment Supportive of the Scholarly Interests of the Faculty

A recurring theme throughout the interview is the general quality of the institutional environment as it reflects concern for scholarly interests. More specifically, faculty speak of the importance of administrative attitudes and behavior as reflective of scholarly concerns. A biologist speaks of this as a sharpening of purposes: "I think there's a crying need for a definition of purpose in the University . . . it would be a tremendous morale booster for the whole faculty if we could define our purposes better, let people know where they are going, and give some direction to programs."

A mathematician laments that environmental pressures are affecting academic leadership adversely: "The main concern is that the universities are getting more and more administrative in nature and less educational. It's not just this university, it's happening all over the country . . . part of it is the accountability and part of it is the federal government."

And a psychologist argues that administrative responsibility extends to the interpretation of faculty interests and needs to the larger community: "We need to create an atmosphere of creativity. It's people who will sell us. I think we need sales persons at the very high administrative levels and that, I think, not only has direct benefits in terms of giving us the resources we need, but I think has relevance within. And I guess I consider that one of their major functions is to interpret us and sell us to the outside world."

Relative to this policy area of administrative attitudes and behavior as reflective of scholarly concerns, relevant action areas come to mind. These areas might include consideration of the specific selection criteria in academic appointments to assure genuine understanding of scholarship and its production and awareness of the impact for faculty of administrative statements and actions with implications on the value of faculty work.

Another theme is the need to recognize the full range of faculty accomplishments. A mathematician suggests that all faculty members need differential recognition and support, depending upon career stage: "For a young person, what's needed is time and a certain number of senior people around who encourage, discuss problems, that sort of thing . . . at the next stage . . . you don't need that much guidance anymore. But I think you still need some people with interest in what you're doing."

Good treatment of colleagues and administrators stimulates a positive reciprocal effect, in the view of an English professor: "I think that what has made a difference to me is that . . . I was treated very well within the department and by the college and the university and that feeling . . . translates itself into a desire to do well and justify the good treatment . . . the support of colleagues . . . who have made a real difference to me has been instrumental."

Relevant policy areas include the assurance that faculty accomplishments are considered fully in formal reward systems such as tenure and promotion and salary adjustment reviews and in informal collegial interactions as well. Appreciation of faculty contributions including those that are not as readily counted as publications and granting agency dollars may be of fundamental importance to the quality of an institution with multiple missions.

A third theme is the need to encourage development of an intellectually stimulating community of colleagues. Faculty vitality may be infectious and it spreads by contact. A psychologist comments: "Having good people in a program or department fosters having . . . intellectual resources. I think we can look back and see that great institutions have in fact been created by bringing in a core of great people . . . they infect each other."

A historian finds career satisfaction in personal relationships which are based on common intellectual interests: "Well, I think the most satisfying thing for me, these days anyway, is the personal relationships with people whose company and intellectual companionship I enjoy . . . this ranges all the way from undergraduates to very senior scholars."

Policy action areas associated with this theme involve the careful attention to recruiting and hiring of intellectually vital faculty members, the recruitment of intellectually curious students, and support of opportunities for interdisciplinary activities and scholarly exchanges.

Support Faculty Research Activities

Even at large, land grant universities, where professional and service functions have always had an honored place, research-oriented faculties have embodied dominant norms in the institution and are chiefly responsible for its image. Thus, it is not surprising that our faculty samples expressed strong support for freedom of inquiry, and valued it highly. To a historian, this import and freedom pervades his professional activities: "I basically make decisions about the classes and what I teach. I have a good deal of freedom in my intellectual pursuits. And I have a good deal of freedom to organize my work week the way that I want to organize it."

Freedom of intellectual inquiry relates very directly to the job satisfaction of a geologist: "The freedom to pursue these very interesting problems that I'm working on and decide what problems I want to work on. That's one of the very, very satisfying aspects of the job."

Freedom and career success are associated, says a biologist, but there are costs as well: "I think unquestionably the freedom, the freedom that I've had has contributed to my success. The size of the university is a double-edged sword. It lets you have an awful lot of freedom and presents you with enormous opportunities . . . the other side . . . is that you're always weighed down by paper work."

Policy action areas related to support for freedom of inquiry and freedom to organize one's work to suit individual considerations include maintaining and protecting this important condition against bureaucratic encroachments. To many, freedom is regarded as one of the most essential and attractive aspects of a faculty position. Another action area is to advocate and exercise caution in developing policies and practices that press faculty toward research directions guided primarily by funders' interests that are not compatible with those of the researcher.

A second theme revolves around the provision of adequate time for research. As stated by a mathematician, time must be factored into the process that produces research: "There has to be some sort of atmosphere of expectation; and the other thing is there has to be free time — that's part of the university's job. That's the part that is disappearing."

Institutional leave programs, such as sabbaticals and single quarter leaves, should be maintained and enhanced to extend the precious resource of concentrated time. Policy action areas also include recognition that research is not produced when teaching and administrative loads are burdensome, especially for young faculty.

A third theme focuses on the continuous need for provision of "seed" money to initiate research activities and to carry people through funding discontinuities. A psychologist speaks of the special value of seed money: "The research that we're involved in now which is a major project, would not have been possible without funds from the graduate school . . . there's no question I think . . . the university having its own money to start new people, to help people through rough times, to initiate a brand new novel project that requires funding is absolutely necessary."

Fourth, since highly active faculty consider that research and graduate training form an integrated core of activities, the concerns about quality of students and support for graduate students are very much in the policy domain at present. Concerns for the quality of graduate students come from various disciplines. For example, an art historian speculates: "I'm not sure that we are getting the best minds into our graduate programs anywhere in the traditional liberal arts disciplines. I think they may be going into professional schools, law, medicine, engineering and so on, but not into history, philosophy, and the languages."

Graduate students are important assets to the research stimulation of faculty, in the view of a biologist: "In general when I have a new idea, I'm more likely to talk with my students about it than with any colleagues . . . I consider the graduate students in the department as having been very important to many of the ideas I've had . . . I couldn't imagine instructing grad students, helping them along, without it being exciting to me and I hope to them."

Entrepreneurial activity is necessary, according to a psychologist, who works to ensure support of graduate students: "My main occupation is pimping for my graduate students, in the sense of getting money for their projects and supporting their research and my research too. Making sure that they get research assistantships so that they don't starve to death."

Policy action areas relative to the support of high quality graduate students include assurance of a reasonable level of institutional support to provide employment opportunities during graduate study and supporting national programs, which aim to sponsor scholar-scientists in limited numbers until the academic market improves as projected for the 1990s.

Finally, the adequacy of library and laboratory facilities is a policy theme affecting highly vital faculty in differential ways. A productive geologist claims he is adversely affected by substandard facilities: "The laboratory facilities in this building are lousy; they're crowded, they're dirty, they're not dirty from the standpoint of mud puddles on the floor, but from the standpoint of dust falling out of the ceiling and no temperature control in the laboratories, so on and so forth."

As faculties age, so also do the physical facilities and the resource collections of the campus. Their maintenance and "revitalization" must also be planned for.

Provide Differentiated Support for Individual Faculty Needs

The first two sets of policy themes and recommendations express the general concerns of the group of highly active, productive faculty members we have interviewed for institutional conditions that contribute to a dynamic, intellectually stimulating, productive university faculty environment. The last set lists some emergent concerns of a more individually specific nature. Given the characteristics of the Phase I sample, these concerns were not typically problems that they had faced in their careers, but were identified as problems that colleagues had experienced. At least four themes emerged, the first of which dealt with faculty members whose research interests had run dry. For them, collegial support and encouragement is very critical and astute administrative guidance and seed money are important if they are to take risks and move off in new directions.

The second theme focused on faculty members whose research is not attractive to the programmatic emphases of funding agencies. Policy action areas are similar to those of the first theme, with collegial support and seed money of particular importance to the continuation of the faculty member's creative efforts. Dollar amount of externally sponsored grants is perceived as carrying inordinate weight in the reward structure of some units under the press of current conditions.

The third theme arose from the discontinuities experienced by faculty who are hired for specific jobs under one set of understandings about performance and reward expectations and find that the reward system and opportunity structure do not accommodate to their situations. Aside from cases of clear inequity which must be adjusted, this theme suggests that some individuals will become seriously "stuck" in their careers. To get them "moving," collegial and administrative support, extension of alternative assignments, extended leaves to try out new jobs, or faculty outplacement may be considered.

The fourth theme concerns assistant professors confronting high demands for meeting promotion and tenure requirements at a time when future rewards are increasingly uncertain. We need to be aware that most of their colleagues, particularly those in our Phase II cross-sectional sample, established their careers under exceptionally favorable conditions for graduate training and for the "neophyte" stages of their faculty careers. The youngest cohort, which is relatively small and often scattered at present, faces a much more rigorous tenure and promotion review than was the case over a decade ago. Policy actions involving sponsorship/mentorship of their first years, offsetting some of the tension and competition inherent in their situation with sufficient support to encourage risk taking and productivity, and addressing work climate issues will be important for ensuring the vital faculty futures so essential to higher education in years ahead.

NOTES

1. "Ideal type" is used here in the Weberian sense of the term. Such a type is assumed to have both normative and explanatory significance, which derives from the assumption that values and norms formulated as part of it may influence the actions of participants in the social system under consideration (Parsons & Platt, 1973, p. 158).

2. In order to extend the exploratory inquiry of models of faculty vitality and as a basis for development of comparative data, a representative faculty sample was drawn from the same university colleges during 1981–82. Applying stratified random sampling procedures to specially drawn personnel data system listings, requisite proportions of tenured senior faculty were obtained and interviews were completed with 84 persons.

The parallel interview study with the representative group was accomplished to provide essential baseline data. For larger scale studies beyond the University of Minnesota such as models and problems of faculty vitality in our institutional reference group, the Committee on Institutional Cooperation institutions, or differential models of faculty vitality in other kinds of institutions (state college systems, or small private liberal arts colleges for example), or specialized studies such as career vitality issues of women and minorities, or generational cohort differences in career vitality, benchmark institutional case studies are the essential first step.

3. In the editor's introduction to a special issue of *Sociology of Education,* Donald Light observes that Fulton and Trow in their paper "Research Activity in Higher Education" (in the same issue) have located "one breed of faculty who does everything—publish, teach and administrate. As the authors say, this researcher is clearly not isolated in his laboratory or study. Instead he is a triple threat: you can't keep a good man down" (Light, 1974, p. 23).

4. Attributes of the qualitative paradigm include: concern with understanding behavior from the actor's own frame of reference; closeness to the data (having an "insider's" perspective); grounded, discovery oriented, exploratory, expansionist, descriptive, and inductive; process oriented; valid: "real," "rich," and "deep" data; ungeneralizable, single case studies; holistic; assumes a dynamic reality (Reichardt & Cook, 1979, p. 10).

Part III

POLICY OPTIONS IN FACULTY VITALITY

The chapters in Part III of the book focus on a number of major institutional policy options as possible responses for maintaining faculty vitality. Wherever possible, policy inferences based on data and analysis are presented. Chapter 7 introduces Part III by reviewing the various types and patterns of faculty development programs most commonly employed as responses to institutional concern for faculty vitality. Attributes of both successful and weak program characteristics are discussed. Alternatively, midcareer change practices and options are examined in Chapter 8 as possible responses to concerns for faculty vitality. Current institutional practices are reviewed along with recent survey results indicating faculty preferences for midcareer change. Special identification is made of various incentive practices and policies that might "induce" midcareer change for faculty. Chapter 9 examines the practice of outside professional consulting and aspects of its relationship with faculty vitality. The extent, pattern, and impact of faculty consulting are examined empirically and policy guidelines are suggested. Chapter 10 addresses likely relationships between issues of faculty vitality and the recent emergence of unionization in higher education. Consideration is given to questions of who has unionized and why; the effect of collective bargaining on institutional change, faculty governance, compensation, and productivity; and alternatives to the collective bargaining model. The final chapter in Part III deals with the practice and potential use of retirement benefit plans as policy options to affect the retirement timing and postretirement work plans of faculty. Although faculty members do not appear to be anxious to retire and institutional options for adapting retirement programs to changing demography and budgets are limited, some programs and policy alternatives such as phased retirement programs do exist for encouraging faculty to alter their retirement plans, thereby enhancing both faculty and institutional vitality.

Chapter 7

Maintaining Faculty Vitality Through Faculty Development

John A. Centra

"It is necessary to discuss not only the vitality of societies but the vitality of institutions and individuals. They are the same subjects. A society decays when its institutions and individuals lose their vitality." This quote from John Gardner's book, *Self-Renewal* (1965, p. 2) captures why faculty vitality is critical. Although colleges and universities are only one of the many types of institutions that make up society, they are crucial to society's growth and welfare. And a vital faculty, along with vital students, leadership, programs, and financial resources, are what help make up a vital institution.

Currently, a number of circumstances are adversely affecting the vitality of faculty members, individually and collectively. Inflation and poor economic conditions have resulted in program and staff reductions at many state and private institutions. Faculty, in some instances, have not only been distracted from teaching and research but also have been seriously demoralized. In addition, financial restraints can be expected to tax the practice of shared governance: institutions may increasingly centralize decision making to deal with financial crises. The declining rate of growth in higher education over the past decade or so has reduced job opportunities at competing institutions, thereby making it difficult for faculty members to renew themselves by changing jobs. Faced with less turnover and less new blood,

Portions of this chapter were adapted from an article by John A. Centra, "Faculty Development in Higher Education," in *Staff Development: New Demands, New Realities, New Perspectives,* ed. Ann Lieberman and Lynne Miller (New York: Teachers College Press, © 1978, 1979 by Teachers College, Columbia University), pp. 205–218.

institutions cannot depend on new staff to help keep them vital. To counter-act this prospect, many colleges expanded their faculty development pro-grams in the 1970s. Government and foundation grants aided some of these institutions in establishing a variety of practices to renew or assist faculty in their varied roles. This "movement," if it can be called that, seems to have tailed-off considerably in the last few years, falling prey to budget cuts and staff reductions.

What the effects of these programs have been and what the conse-quences of cutting back on faculty development activities will be are ques-tions that need to be considered. In this chapter, a historical view of faculty development is presented, concentrating especially on its heyday in the mid-dle to late 1970s. Discussion is also directed to what the consequences of deemphasizing faculty development could be to the vitality of higher educa-tion institutions. But first we present some further thoughts on the concept of vitality.

ON THE MEANING OF VITALITY

We are all familiar with the typical dictionary meanings of vitality: physical or mental vigor; the capacity to live and develop. The key phrase is, for our purpose, to develop. Mere survival or existence is not enough. Existence needs to be purposeful, to be constantly renewed. Continuous renewal, in fact, is John Gardner's key to vital institutions and individuals. As he states in *Self-Renewal* (1965):

> Every individual, organization or society must mature, but much depends on how this maturing takes place. A society whose maturing consists simply of ac-quiring more firmly established ways of doing things is headed for the grave-yard—even if it learns to do these things with greater and greater skill. In the ever renewing society, what matures is a system or framework within which continuous innovation, renewal and rebirth can occur. (p. 5)

According to Gardner, as individuals mature they often narrow the scope and variety of their lives: "Of all the interests we might pursue, we set-tle on a few. Of all the people with whom we might associate, we select a small number." Some individuals are fortunately able to renew or develop themselves. This self-renewal is what society and our educational system should, of course, encourage. Organizations too should foster the renewal and development of their staffs as a means of maintaining organizational vitality. Fifteen years ago, a group of us were involved in a project to define and assess vitality in institutions of higher education. To gain perspective on what an instrument should measure, we first conducted a questionnaire survey. The president, the dean of students, an associate professor of English, and the editor of the student newspaper at a cross section of 307 colleges and universities were sent an open-ended questionnaire, asking them to suggest characteristics that describe a vital college or university. Although there was no consensus in the responses we received, it is interesting to note what the most frequently volunteered kinds of ideas about institutional vitality were; they included the following:

1. Openness to innovation and experimentation.
2. Concern for sound undergraduate instruction.
3. Participatory campus governance.
4. Staff loyalty to institutional objectives.
5. Communication among students, faculty, and administrators.
6. Intellectual orientation and growth in students.
7. Close student-faculty relationships.
8. Faculty scholarship and research.
9. Nature and quality of faculty. (Peterson et al., 1970, p. 4)

A productive and committed faculty that is open to innovation is one of the primary themes that runs through this list. That same theme reappeared in a conference we held at that time to explore further the concept of institutional vitality. Conference participants concluded that a number of elements determined the vitality of institutions, including having appropriate leadership, enough money, and vital faculty members and students with "purposeful involvement with the institution" (Peterson & Loye, 1967).

If faculty development programs can be viewed as a conscious effort by institutions to renew and maintain the vitality of their staffs, then it is apparent that this effort has been anything but constant, as a historical look at faculty development demonstrates.

FACULTY DEVELOPMENT: A HISTORICAL VIEW

Colleges historically have expected faculty members to bear the responsibility for their own professional and personal development. During the early decades of American history when knowledge was thought of as a more or less fixed quantum of Christian truth, the primary function of education was to get undergraduates to absorb as much of this truth as possible (Hofstadter & Hardy, 1952). Faculty self-development was largely a matter of maintaining spiritual and moral resolve. The majority of faculty members prior to the Civil War were, in fact, clergymen (Rudolph, 1962). Over the years, the concept of knowledge broadened, and the role of a more secularized faculty was not only to help transmit this knowledge but also to create new knowledge through research. The responsible faculty member tried to keep abreast of the field and to acquire whatever new skills were needed to advance knowledge. To facilitate research and publication, the more affluent universities added paid leaves of absence and sabbaticals in the 1890s (Rudolph, 1962). It is interesting to note that the sabbatical was viewed largely as contributing to a faculty member's research productivity. Concern with teaching or discussions of different instructional methods were rare. In fact, in the voluminous correspondence between President Gilman of Johns Hopkins and President Eliot of Harvard, both giants in the history of higher education, issues even remotely related to teaching were never mentioned (Rudolph, 1962).

Prior to the 1960s, very few institutions had initiated faculty development programs, although many had established practices designed to orient new faculty or to help update faculty members. A 1960 survey of 214 southern colleges by Miller and Wilson (1963) found such practices as pre-college workshops, financial assistance for attendance at professional meetings, sabbaticals, and occasional department conferences on teaching or research available at many institutions. But the authors concluded that there was "a dearth of well-articulated, comprehensively designed *programs* for faculty development." A briefer survey, conducted in the late 1960s with a broader sample of institutions, reached a similar conclusion (Many, Ellis, & Abrams, 1969). Still further evidence for this finding emerged from the results of a questionnaire study done as part of the AAUP Project to Improve College Teaching: Eble (1971) reported that faculty members at some 150 schools stated almost unanimously that their institutions did not have *effective* faculty development programs. Eble further noted that few institutions set aside specific percentages of their budget for faculty development.

A handful of universities, however, did begin instructional improvement programs in the late 1960s. Alexander and Yelon (1972) collected information on about 14 so-called instructional development (or educational development) programs, including Syracuse University, Michigan State University, McGill University, and the University of Minnesota. Although the centers at these universities differed in their emphases, most tried to function as catalysts in affecting change by assisting faculty volunteers in analyzing and solving instructional problems. Curriculum and course changes were implemented by clarifying objectives and designing new instructional procedures and materials.

The instructional development model was only one of three components of faculty development that emerged in the 1970s. Bergquist and Phillips (1975) identified personal development and organizational development in addition to instructional development as related but different components of faculty development. Gaff's book, *Toward Faculty Renewal*

(1975), which was based on information received from 55 colleges and universities, also identified the same three general areas.

Personal development and organizational development programs might be viewed as efforts by some institutions to maintain staff and organizational vitality. Personal development focused on faculty members themselves rather than the courses they taught. Faculty growth and renewal was promoted through such activities as interpersonal skills training and life-planning workshops. In fact, the combination of activities related to the affective development of faculty members and those directed toward improved teaching behavior come closest to defining what many people meant by faculty development in the 1970s. Organizational development sought to improve the institutional environment for teaching and decision making and included activities for both faculty and administrators. Team building and managerial development were part of organizational development. Team building, according to Bergquist and Phillips (1975), attempts to improve the ability of a group, such as an academic department, to make decisions. Through weekend retreats or by employing a consultant, the group is expected to deliberate on its own structure, operations, or climate. Within a department, for example, faculty members might discuss the future directions the department should take.

The various approaches and activities that emerged for faculty development in the 1970s were a response to conditions that were appearing at that time, such as a decrease in faculty mobility and less new blood. A *Change* magazine monograph titled *Faculty Development in a Time of Retrenchment* (Group for Human Development in Higher Education, 1974) eloquently professed the need for faculty development and prescribed what to do and how to begin. This widely read monograph inspired many institutions to expand their efforts. Seed money was in some cases provided by government grants from the Fund for the Improvement of Postsecondary Education (FIPSE), National Institute of Education (NIE), and other federal agencies; foundation grants from Lilly, Danforth, Kellogg, and others; and in a few states, legislatures earmarked funds specifically for instructional improvement at public institutions. For institutions without the necessary funds, low-cost, self-development practices were suggested as a means of helping faculty members "change environments, risk new exposures, alter habitual patterns, or undertake new challenges" (Brown & Hanger, 1975).

In 1976, the Exxon Education Foundation gave this writer a grant to study faculty development practices. Specifically, the study was directed at the following questions: What were the practices most in use and how effective did they seem to be? Which groups of faculty members are most involved? How are development activities organized and financed?

A STUDY OF FACULTY DEVELOPMENT
IN COLLEGES AND UNIVERSITIES

The study began with a letter sent to the presidents of every college and university in the United States asking whether their institutions, or any part of their institutions, "had an organized program or set of practices for faculty development and improving instruction." Of the approximately 2,600 accredited, degree-granting institutions in the country (two-year colleges, four-year colleges, and universities), we heard from just under 1,800. About 60 percent (1,044) said that they had a program or set of practices and identified the person on campus who coordinated or was most knowledgeable about it. Another 3 to 4 percent said that they were planning such programs. Assuming that the nonrespondents would be less likely to have programs, it was estimated that perhaps half, or slightly over half, of the postsecondary institutions in the United States provided some sort of program or set of staff development activities. Of course, the estimate depends on how the institutions surveyed chose to interpret what constitutes an organized program or set of practices.

Each of the 1,044 college coordinators was sent a four-page questionnaire in the spring of 1976, and 756, or 72 percent of the group, responded. Generally, the respondent was a director of instructional development or faculty development, a dean or associate dean, or a faculty member spending part time as coordinator. Ninety-three doctoral-granting universities, 315 four-year colleges, and 326 two-year colleges were in the final sample.

To learn about specific development activities, we asked the respondents to estimate the proportion of faculty at their institutions that used each of 45 practices and how effective they thought the practices were. The list included activities directly related to instructional improvement as well as those dealing with personal development efforts such as improving self-awareness, interpersonal skills, and the like. The practices fell into four general categories: (1) workshops, seminars, or similar presentations; (2) analysis or assessment of instructors by students, by colleagues, by the use of videotape, or by other means; (3) activities that involved audiovisual aids, technology, or course development; and (4) institution-wide practices such as sabbaticals and annual teaching awards.

A major purpose of this study was to determine what patterns of development practices predominate among colleges and universities. That is, given the 45 practices listed in the questionnaire, is it possible to identify reasonable categories of activities based on the extent of faculty use among institutions? To explore this question, responses from each institution to the 45 practices were factor analyzed, enabling a grouping of the practices according to the extent to which they were used at the 756 institutions. The resulting factors or groups of practices were then related to the additional information collected about the institutions and their programs. The latter included the proportions of the various groups of faculty involved in development practices on each campus, how activities were funded and organized, and institutional characteristics such as size, type, and source of control.

Four factors or groups of development practices seemed to define patterns of estimated use of the practices among institutions. These factors were high faculty involvement, instructional assistance practices, traditional practices, and emphasis on assessment. The four factors and the practices that have significant loadings on each factor are listed in Table 7.1. A brief discussion of the four factors follows.

1. *High faculty involvement.* The development practices in this first group tend to involve a high proportion of the faculty at the colleges that use them. Many of the practices are run not only for the faculty but *by* the faculty as well: Experienced teachers work with inexperienced teachers, and those with special skills offer assistance to others. Good teachers, older teachers, and those needing improvement all tend to be involved.

   Several of the practices in this group were more likely to be used by the smaller colleges in the sample and seem appropriate for small college settings. Workshops on institutional purposes or on academic advisement are examples. In the wake of declining enrollments and higher costs, many smaller colleges have examined their goals more closely. These colleges would also see good academic guidance and attention to individual students as special strengths. Small institutions are less likely to afford full-time specialists in teaching or instructional development—thus the reliance on "master teachers" or faculty with expertise. Because of the emphasis on close personal relationships in most small colleges, these colleges could be expected to provide counseling and other personal development practices for faculty. Smallness, finally, also apparently encourages more informal assessments by colleagues, or more self-assessment, rather than formal systems of teaching evaluation.

2. *Instructional assistance practices.* Instructional development is an important aspect of this second group of practices, as evidenced by the high factor loading for "specialists to assist individual faculty in instructional or course development." The second practice, specialist assistance to the faculty in improving teaching skills or strategies, is part of both instructional development programs and broader teaching improvement or faculty development programs. Three of the additional practices also deal with providing assistance in the instructional process: (1) in teaching and evaluating student performance, (2) in applications of instructional technology to teaching, and (3) in the use of audiovisual aids. Work-

TABLE 7.1. Factor Analysis of the Estimated Use
of Faculty Development Practices

Group 1 (Factor 1): High Faculty Involvement	Factor Loading
Workshops, seminars, or programs to acquaint faculty with goals of the institution and types of students enrolled	.65
"Master teachers" or senior faculty work closely with new or apprentice teachers	.61
Faculty with expertise consult with other faculty on teaching or course improvement	.60
Workshops or programs to help faculty improve their academic advising and counseling skills	.57
Personal counseling provided individual faculty members on career goals and other personal development areas	.53
Workshops or presentations that explore general issues or trends in education	.51
Informal assessments by colleagues for teaching or course improvement	.48
System for faculty to assess their own strengths and areas needing improvement	.46

Group 2 (Factor 2): Instructional Assistance Practices	Factor Loading
Specialists to assist individual faculty in instructional or course development by consulting on course objectives and course design	.75
Specialists to help faculty develop teaching skills such as lecturing or leading discussions, or to encourage use of different teaching/ learning strategies such as individualized instruction	.70
Specialists to assist faculty in constructing tests or evaluating student performance	.69
Assistance to faculty in use of instructional technology as a teaching aid (e.g., programmed learning or computer-assisted instruction)	.65
Specialists on campus to assist faculty in use of audiovisual aids in instruction, including closed-circuit television	.56
Workshops or presentations that explore various methods or techniques of instruction	.42

Group 3 (Factor 3): Traditional Practices	Factor Loading
Visiting scholars programs that bring people to the campus for short or long periods	.58
Annual awards for excellence in teaching	.52
Sabbatical leaves with at least half salary	.43
Workshops or seminars to help faculty improve their research and scholarship skills	.43
Summer grants for projects to improve instruction or courses	.43

TABLE 7.1. (Continued)

Temporary teaching load reductions to work
  on a new course, major course revision,
  or research area   .39
Use of grants by faculty members for developing
  new or different approaches to courses
  or teaching   .37
Travel grants to refresh or update knowledge
  in a particular field   .33

Group 4 (Factor 4): Emphasis on Assessment	Factor Loading
Periodic review of the performance of all faculty members, whether tenured or not	.55
Travel funds available to attend professional conferences	.47
Systematic ratings of instruction by students used to help faculty improve	.41
Formal assessments by colleagues for teaching or course improvement (i.e., visitations or use of assessment form)	.40
A policy of unpaid leaves that covers educational or development purposes	.40
Systematic teaching or course evaluations by an administrator for improvement purposes	.40

---

shops or presentations exploring methods of instruction, the last practice with a significant loading, would logically fit in with other practices in this group. These instructional assistance practices were found in many of the two-year colleges and in a number of the universities in the sample. Few of the four-year colleges included them. Public rather than private institutions were also somewhat more likely to have these practices. Not surprisingly, most of the institutions had development units or offices on campus. Finally, in comparison with other practices, the practices that comprise this group were more likely to be evaluated in some way.

3. *Traditional practices.* As Table 7.1 indicates, the practices in this group included visiting scholars programs, annual awards in teaching, sabbatical leaves, grants for instructional improvement or travel, and temporary teaching-load reductions. The only workshop or seminar included was one designed to help faculty improve their research and scholarship skills. Thus, with the exception of the use of small faculty grants to improve instruction, these practices have been used by many institutions for a number of years and are, therefore, fairly traditional.

By themselves, the activities involve a relatively small number of faculty at any one time. The practices in this group, as further analysis indicated, were most likely to be used at universities and larger, four-year colleges.

4. *Emphasis on assessment.* Four of the six practices with significant loadings in this group emphasize various assessment techniques as means of improving instruction. Formal ratings by students, by colleagues, and by administrators are among those listed in Table 7.1. A periodic review of all faculty members is also a common practice. It is interesting to note that the less formal assessment or analyses practices, such as the use of in-class videotapes or informal assessments by colleagues, are not part of the group.

Travel funds to attend professional conferences and unpaid leaves for educational or development purposes also had significant loadings on this factor.

Among the types of institutions, two-year colleges (particularly public, two-year colleges) tended to emphasize the practices in this group.

These four descriptions provide a view of development programs somewhat different from the heuristic models discussed by Bergquist and Phillips (1975) and by Gaff (1975), though the instructional assistance category does overlap with their shared concept of instructional development.

Judging by the additional information provided by the institutions in the sample, programs in faculty development varied in other ways as well as those just described. Some colleges had a few uncoordinated practices with minimal budgets. Limited faculty development programs, if they can be referred to as programs, were most likely to be found in the sample among the small colleges with under 1,000 students enrolled. It should be added, however, that several larger institutions—including some of the most prestigious—reported (in response to the initial letter) that they did not have programs in faculty development.

Some development programs appeared to operate on the fringes of the schools they served: Coordinators reported that generally there was minimal faculty participation and, in some instances, that a significant part of the support for the programs came from foundations or the government.

Over 40 percent of the institutions (two-thirds of the universities) had some kind of development unit. Some had decentralized offices. A few units included several specialists in such areas as instructional development, evaluation, technology, and media. The majority, however, had more modest staffs—often only a director or coordinator—and were found frequently at medium-sized, two- and four-year colleges; most of these units had existed only two or three years and had not yet been evaluated adequately. In fact, less than a fifth of all institutions had completely evaluated their programs or activities.

Certainly an evaluation of an institution's program would include a close look at the characteristics of faculty members who participate. Ideally, we would hope that faculty who really need to improve would be among those most involved in development activities. Yet, this did not generally appear to be the case. The survey questionnaire included six general descriptions of faculty members and asked the respondents to estimate the extent to which each group was involved. The results are summarized in Table 7.2. Among the six types of faculty, the most actively involved in development activities were "good teachers who want to get better"; at about 70 percent of the institutions, half or more of this faculty group were involved. The least actively involved were "faculty who really need to improve," followed by older faculty—those with over 15 or 20 years of teaching experience—and younger faculty in their first years of teaching. Nontenured and tenured staff participated about equally.

Given the fact that participation in most development activities is usually voluntary, it should not be especially surprising that good teachers who want to get better were said to comprise the major clientele. It is surprising, however, that on many campuses teachers needing improvement were minimally involved. At 40 percent of the institutions, very few of the teachers who needed to improve participated (item 6 of Table 7.2). At another 38 percent, some (less than half) of these same teachers were involved. Combining these figures gives a total 78 percent of the colleges and universities where, according to the respondents' estimates, a minority of the faculty needing improvement were involved in development programs.

It is also noteworthy that faculty in their first year or two of teaching appeared to be moderately involved in development activities and those with over 15 or 20 years of experience only slightly involved. Both are criti-

TABLE 7.2. Estimates of Faculty Involvement in Development
            Activities

		Percentage of 756 Institutional Respondents Indicating			
	Very few	Some	About half	Most	No Response
1. Younger faculty in their first years of teaching	13	31	23	27	06
2. Faculty with over 15 or 20 years of teaching experience	22	45	17	09	07
3. Nontenured faculty	08	34	25	19	14
4. Tenured faculty	09	41	23	10	17
5. Good teachers who want to get better	03	21	28	43	05
6. Faculty who really need to improve	40	38	08	06	08

cal target groups among faculty, especially first-year teachers, as the data in Figure 7.1 (from another report) clearly demonstrate. Diagrammed are student ratings on a 5-point Likert scale of the teaching effectiveness of a sample of almost 9,000 teachers from approximately 100 colleges in the United States (see Centra & Creech, 1976, for further information on the study). Teachers in their first or second year of teaching received the lowest ratings. Teachers with 3–12 years of experience received the highest ratings, while those with more than 12 years dropped slightly in average student ratings of effectiveness.[1]

Assuming that the ratings are fairly valid measures of effectiveness, as much of the research indicates, these findings suggest that beginning teachers in particular and, to some extent, teachers in their middle or later years (i.e., over 12 years) are groups that could particularly profit from teaching improvement activities, and probably for different reasons. Beginning teachers have generally learned little in graduate school about teaching per

FIGURE 7.1.   Ratings of Teacher Effectiveness, by Years of Teaching (N=8,863 Teachers)

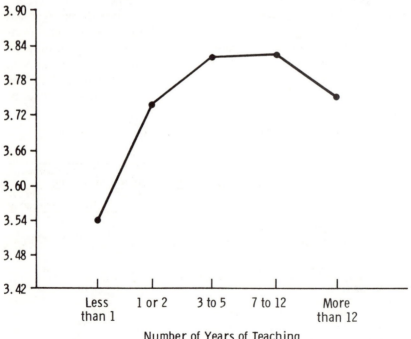

Number of Years of Teaching

se; therefore, their first years on the job are critical to learning about teaching as well as about their other professional roles. Teachers who have taught for some time are another story; some of them have possibly become stale in their methods, preparations, or outlook, which can become apparent to students.[2] We have even come up with a label for this condition: faculty *burnout,* of which we will say more shortly. Faculty development for some older teachers, then, may be largely a matter of breaking into their routine and getting them to try something different.

Involvement in development practices by the six types of faculty members was also investigated within each type of institution. Universities generally had poorer participation rates in development activities than either two- or four-year colleges. As illustrated in Figure 7.2, respondents from about 55 percent of the universities reported that very few of the faculty who really needed to improve were involved in development activities. This was the case at only 40 percent of the two- and four-year colleges. The dual emphasis on research and teaching in universities is one reason for these institutional differences. For many university faculty members, research and scholarly writing are an essential part of their jobs; indeed, they may be assessed largely on the basis of their publication records. Though they may also teach, such faculty members are less likely to participate in faculty development activities aimed at improving their performance as teachers.

EVALUATION OF PROGRAMS

Only a small number of faculty development and instructional improvement programs have been formally evaluated, and most evaluations have relied on reports by faculty participants. In general, faculty have viewed well-run programs as beneficial to both themselves and their institutions (Blackburn et al., 1980; Nelson & Siegel, 1980). Menges and Levinson-Rose (1981) reviewed studies that investigated teaching improvement programs in which evidence of improved teaching was used as criteria for effective programs. Studies based on five categories of interventions were reviewed: grants for faculty projects, workshops and seminars, feedback from student ratings, micro-teaching and minicourses (practice-based feedback), and concept-based feedback. In 62 percent of the better designed studies, the results indicated that the intervention had helped produce better teaching. Although even these studies were sometimes flawed, it would appear that in the majority of instances the teaching improvement programs were reasonably successful. Studies providing hard evidence for the positive effects of personal and professional development practices are more difficult to conduct and thus have rarely been reported. However, it is unlikely that the

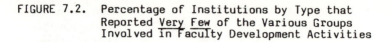

FIGURE 7.2.   Percentage of Institutions by Type that
              Reported <u>Very Few</u> of the Various Groups
              Involved in Faculty Development Activities

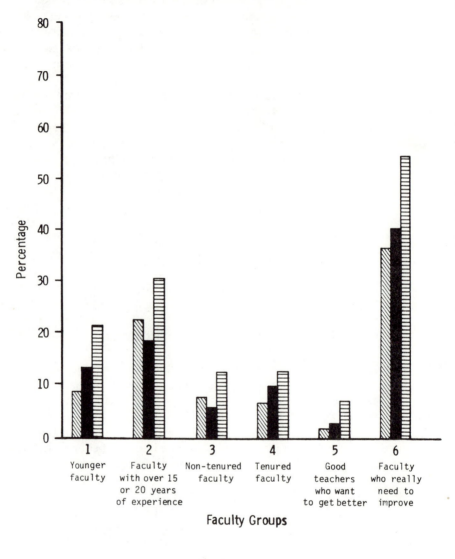

lack of a positive impact has led to the current status of faculty development programs on many campuses; rather, that status is the result of the shortage of financial resources coupled with the lack of a strong advocate group for such programs.

THE PRESENT

There seems little doubt that institutional programs and funds for faculty development have been greatly reduced since my 1976 study—not in all states but in most. Staffs have been cut back or, in some instances, eliminated; and funds for even the long-established practices are becoming tighter: an American Council on Education survey found that 3 percent fewer sabbaticals were granted in 1980 than two years earlier. Attendance at professional conferences is down because travel funds have been cut drastically at many institutions.

Reductions in faculty renewal activities along with other kinds of retrenchment help fuel the disease that has come to be called faculty *burnout.* Faculty burnout is characterized by physical and emotional exhaustion and feelings of being professionally stuck. At a recent national conference on faculty burnout (see *The Chronicle of Higher Education,* March 24, 1982, pp. 1 and 8), the following points were made: "Burnout comes from plugged-up mobility and a general sense of retraction—if not outright retrenchment—with declining economic and social status. It includes fatigue and absence of challenge" (Joseph Katz, Director of Research for Human Development and Educational Policy, SUNY, Stony Brook).

The main causes, according to Ayala Pines, a research associate at the University of California, Berkeley, are "lack of significance in your work" and "lack of control over your environment." One estimate was that 20 percent of the academic population suffers from burnout (Herbert J. Freudenberger, American Psychological Association). How might higher education institutions deal with burnout? Long-range career planning and "a commitment to develop their human resources with the same vigor with which they develop their physical resources" were among the suggestions offered by participants at the conference.

CONCLUSION

If maintaining faculty vitality is a critical goal for institutions, then faculty burnout is a clear symptom that we are falling short of achieving that goal. What then? In this paper I have argued that faculty development activities, in their broadest sense, can help keep a faculty vital. But given the current financial picture generally, can institutions be expected to spend money on these activities? Would not faculty members themselves rather see reductions in faculty development programs than in faculty positions? Would not many teachers prefer higher salaries to renewal programs if given the choice? Unfortunately, decisions increasingly being forced on institutions are of a "no-win" type. Not tending to the well-being of a university staff — and this includes adequate salaries as well as adequate opportunities for renewal — is shortsighted. Diminishing the vitality of a staff in this way critically affects the quality of an institution, maybe not today or tomorrow, but eventually.

NOTES

1. The difference between first-year teachers and those with 3–12 years of experience was about half a standard deviation ($p < .001$). The difference between teachers with more than 12 years and those with 3–12 years was statistically significant ($p < .05$), but not especially large. Because the data are cross-sectional rather than longitudinal, we cannot conclude that the pattern illustrated in Figure 7.1 would necessarily hold for individual teachers over time. Longitudinal studies of teachers in their first two years of teaching have, nevertheless, found similar levels of improvement as shown by the ratings in Figure 7.1.

2. It should be emphasized that there is nothing significant about the twelfth year of teaching; it simply happens to be the final category used. The drop in ratings suggests only a trend. If the last classification had, for example, been twenty years or more experience, the drop might be more dramatic.

Chapter 8

Maintaining Faculty Vitality Through Midcareer Change Options

Carl V. Patton and *David D. Palmer*

A legitimate question these days might well be whether the faculty body in higher education is truly interested in what it is doing. We will cite statistics later that suggest a substantial minority of today's academics may not be happy with their careers. True, a fraction of the members of any field are certain to be discontent, and today's academics, as a group, may be no more unhappy than those of a decade or two ago. However, recent trends in academe should cause us to consider whether today's indicators of discontent are a bellwether of things to come. It is not unreasonable to wonder whether the continued trend toward reduced job opportunities in academe, decreased student numbers, fewer chances for promotion, less opportunity for advancement, and the pressure and tension associated with academic life under static or shrinking budgets, will have a devastating impact on faculty vitality. Can faculty members do their best in an environment where job advancement is blocked, where financial rewards appear limited, where some faculty members are aging in place, and where job security is questionable? If faculty members do not remain vital, then individual institutions and academe will not remain vital. This chapter will review some of the means to enhance individual and institutional vitality, primarily midcareer redirection and retraining for faculty members. These programs are intended both

Portions of this chapter appeared in an article by David D. Palmer and Carl V. Patton, "Mid-Career Change Options in Academe: Experience and Possibilities," *Journal of Higher Education,* Vol. 52 (July/August 1981), pp. 378–398, and are used by permission. Copyright © 1981 by the Ohio State University Press.

to help faculty members shift directions at midcareer and to help institutions gain flexibility so that they can respond to changing demands.

Other contributors have discussed the concept of vitality, but let us state briefly some of the aspects of individual and institutional vitality that are closely associated with midcareer redirection. From an individual's standpoint, vitality can be defined in terms such as those of Gardner (1978, pp. 60–73), to refer to vigor, enthusiasm, and personal growth and development. Institutional vitality can be defined as the sum of the creativity of individual faculty and staff members, flexibility to respond to changing needs and demands, and the ability to adapt to larger-term trends and requirements. An organization will be vital only if its members are vital, and organizations can create opportunities to enhance faculty vitality. But toward which faculty members should organizations direct their efforts? While efforts may have to be directed primarily at individuals who are *now* members of the institution, the diverse needs of these groups of people will require a range of actions. We see as many as a half-dozen potential groups with specific needs. These groups include (a) those individuals who would prefer to retire before the mandatory age, (b) those persons who would prefer to teach in a different field, (c) those individuals who would prefer a nonfaculty position within the college or university, (d) those persons who would prefer to shift to a career outside of academe, and (e) those individuals who would like to try a new position or career if only to test their preference for their current position.

Colleges and universities can assist these persons with career assessment and development with the result that such persons may be more vital in their new work and life, if they shift to a new career or new work setting. Likewise, those who investigate the possibility of a career change, or experiment with a change but reject it in favor of their current position, may be more vital because doubts about their current situation have been removed. If wise hiring decisions are made as persons leave for careers elsewhere, the newly hired replacements may be more vital in the approach to their work than those who left.

If colleges and universities can meet the changing needs of students (by responding to enrollment shifts) and those of faculty (by facilitating career development and personal assessment), then the institutions themselves will remain vital and will be better able to meet society's needs. How to respond to these needs has been the focus of some of our work in recent years. We have investigated early retirement incentives and career change options as vehicles that colleges and universities can use to respond to budgetary stringencies, declining enrollments, shifting student interests, and the manpower problems already cited. We have also suggested that early retirement incentives might be used to cope with a possible short-term reduction in the retirement rate as some professors postpone retirement in response to the recent increase in the mandatory retirement age.

By enticing certain faculty members to retire earlier than originally planned, academe's ranks can be opened to new faculty members, especially women and minorities who have needed skills. Research has indicated that there are faculty members who, under certain circumstances, would retire early (COFHE, 1981; Montgomery, 1981; Palmer & Patton, 1978; and Toevs & Hanhardt, 1982). Furthermore, analyses of academics who retired early, both those who retired without inducements (Patton, 1977) and those who were financially induced to retire early (Kell & Patton, 1978), indicate that they are satisfied with their decisions. To some professors, early retirement may be a way to move out of an untenable situation; to others it may provide the financial support for a career change.

Early retirement incentives may also be of considerable use to certain institutions by enabling a number of important replacements during times when such replacements would otherwise not be possible. Early retirement schemes in most cases should be viewed as a means to permit this type of qualitative change, rather than as a mechanism for quantitative change, that is, substantial change in the size or composition of a faculty (Patton, 1979).

LIMITATIONS OF INCENTIVE EARLY RETIREMENT

The benefits of incentive early retirement notwithstanding, certain institutions may find such options will not serve their needs. A major consideration is the age distribution of a college or university faculty body. Some commentators have held that academe is populated heavily by persons of near-retirement age. However, Patton's analysis of the 1975 Carnegie Council national data (Patton & Foertsch, 1978), Palmer's analysis of the 1973 American Council on Education Data (1976), Palmer's analysis of the 1977 Ladd-Lipset data (1979), and Corwin and Knepper's 1978 survey (1978) show that on a national basis the population in academe has greater percentages of faculty members in the younger age categories. If an institution is among the majority, having few faculty near retirement age, it should examine the possibilities of incentive early retirement primarily for allowing modest changes in faculty composition. Even replacement of a few faculty positions in declining fields with positions in high demand fields could result in worthwhile *qualitative* changes. The institution with many professors nearing the mandatory retirement age is the exception. For the relatively few institutions with high proportions of older faculty members, induced early retirement may provide for *quantitative* changes by opening many faculty positions to new employees.

A second limitation involves the temporal nature of early retirement options. Inducing early retirements has a major, one-time effect (Patton, 1979, pp. 115–161). When the first group of early retirees is inducted to retire earlier than planned, an increase in the retirement rate is experienced. However, after this initial group has retired, and even if the inducements are continued and encourage the same proportion of persons to retire earlier than planned, the overall retirement rate will return to approximately the preincentive rates as those who would have retired are no longer employed because of induced early retirement.

A third limitation is cost. Incentive early retirement can be expensive, especially if inducements have to be set high and inflation protection is included. The benefits for each institution must, of course, be weighed against these costs. Many organizations find that, on balance, early retirement incentives are valuable (Lublin & King, 1980; *Time,* 1983; *Wall Street Journal,* 1982).

IS MIDCAREER CHANGE THE BETTER OPTION?

In those cases where early retirement would have a limited effect, inducement of job change at midcareer may be an alternative. The attractiveness of this alternative is heightened when the impact of exit rates at various faculty ages is modeled. At all ages, a small percentage of the faculty body leaves because of market inducements. At the younger ages, tenure denials cause exits, and at the older ages early retirement schemes increase the exit rate. Increasing terminations at both extremes of the population distribution will permit new hirings, but early retirement at best encourages termination approximately ten years earlier. Tenure denials, of course, exit faculty members thirty to forty years before normal retirement, but this alternative has limited usefulness since denying tenure to highly qualified and sometimes desperately needed individuals because of a lack of positions makes little sense. Furthermore, boosting the tenure denial rate has at best a "churning" effect since usually other young untenured appointees in turn will be terminated a few years later.

The thirty or more years between the time of tenure decision and retirement can harbor a number of people who have "burned out," people who would be happier in another field, or who, although performing well, are caught in fields for which there is little demand. Midcareer change programs have been suggested as ways to encourage these people to leave academe and in turn to open up job opportunities for people with needed skills.

Although the concept of midcareer change has appeal, relatively little has been done in business or academe to prepare employees for a career change. Businesses and industries regularly offer in-service training, but these programs are usually intended to upgrade good employees or to enhance the upward mobility of those already on the move. Private business has done little to prepare people for jobs with other firms (Pascal et al.,

1975; Patton, 1979; Ricklefs, 1981; Thompson, 1977b; *Time,* 1982; Zambrano, 1976).

Exceptions to the general lack of assistance in private business do exist. In recent years, a number of firms assisted employees through out-placement programs. Out-placement is a method of dealing with the firing of employees, especially executives, managers, and professional staff employees, in a manner that is designed to be beneficial to both the corporation and the terminated employee (Bailey, 1980; Gooding, 1979; Jackson, 1980; Scherba, 1978). Firing of executives is now more commonplace than in the past because of lowered profits, increased mergers, and frequent consolidations. These types of organizational changes often result in firms having an excess number of executives and managers. Those who are fired are usually *not* fired for incompetence, but because they are no longer necessary.

Out-placement programs assist the fired individuals in coping with the psychological and social consequences of being fired and in the development of a job search campaign, including skills assessment, resumé writing, job hunting, job interviewing, and how to select the best job. The self-assessment phase often results in career change or redirection. Companies have found that out-placement can be less costly than severance pay and more effective in maintaining the morale of those who stay. Gooding (1979) notes that hundreds of major companies use out-placement, although many keep that fact confidential.

Out-placement is usually performed by specialized, professional consulting firms, because the employer does not have the necessary expertise. Also, fired employees may be reluctant to discuss personal and professional issues with colleagues and friends. Finally, those involved in out-placement feel that fired employees will devote more attention to the job search if they are not trying to delay leaving as long as possible.

CAREER CHANGE EFFORTS IN ACADEME

Academics use a number of ways to move between university settings, government, and business. Programs such as the Economic Policy Fellowships of the Brookings Institution and the Congressional Science and Engineering Fellowships of the American Association for the Advancement of Science offer professors the opportunity to experiment with new kinds of work in new settings. Although these are not meant to be recruitment programs, participants often use the opportunity to move out of academe. In some programs as many as half of the participants remain in nonacademic positions. Since these programs are administered by outside agencies, colleges and universities have little say about who participates, except for a possible veto when a leave of absence is requested by a potential participant.

Early retraining programs include those offered at the State University

System of Florida, the Pennsylvania State College System, the State University of New York (SUNY), and the University of Wisconsin (Neff, 1978; Patton, 1979). Basically, these programs were intended for faculty members in departments with declining enrollments. Selected faculty members would receive their regular salary plus a grant to pay the cost of relocation for study, tuition, and other expenses associated with graduate study. The length of time for study ranged from one semester to one year.

Little new funding was involved in these programs since the major cost, the retainees' salaries, was paid out of existing budget lines, although two of the programs were financed in part by the Fund for the Improvement of Postsecondary Education. Retraining ranged from preparation in an allied specialty within the same discipline to training for a new, unrelated discipline. A few participants earned advanced degrees, but this was not typically a program purpose. The content of the retraining programs has been determined on an individual basis for each participant, and retraining has taken place, in most cases, within the participant's home institution. However, arrangements have been made for retraining at other institutions within the same state.

Candidates for retraining were generally selected only if a new placement had already been negotiated, and placements have been made primarily at the home institution or university system. Although these programs tended to begin with a centralized application and screening process, they later shifted to a decentralized, campus-based process of initial screening. The programs formally receive applications from interested faculty members, but these persons are often encouraged to apply by third parties or through the realization that their position may eventually be abolished. While these efforts have apparently benefited individual faculty members and caused existing talent to be better utilized, they tend not to produce career change.

A program at Loyola University in Chicago, also begun with partial support from the Fund for the Improvement of Postsecondary Education, places faculty members, administrators, and staff in positions outside the university for a one-year period. Participants, who are on leaves of absence from Loyola, are paid at approximately the same rate they would receive at the university. Before the end of the one-year period, participants must decide whether to return to Loyola (Barry & Naftzger, n.d.). Approximately half of the individuals placed have chosen to leave the university permanently. Loyola's career development program includes a workshop on personal and professional goals. After attending this workshop a person may decide to attempt a one-year placement. If so, the person would attend workshops on skills assessment, resumé writing, and interviewing. The participants then arrange to interview with corporations that have been contacted by the program director. Placement has taken from two to nine months. Loyola is expanding its workshops to serve the needs of spouses as well as potential career changes.

CAREER ASSISTANCE EFFORTS IN ACADEME

A number of programs less directly aimed at career change have been devised for faculty members. Typical programs encourage faculty members to develop career plans (Baldwin et al., 1981). In addition to sessions on goal setting, growth plans, and financial planning, some programs may include workshops for people who want to prepare for a shift to employment outside of academe. Another approach permits faculty members to undertake up to a year of study in a related discipline, with the intent that the new knowledge will be incorporated into the faculty member's teaching and research (Broudy, 1978).

1. The Career Renewal Project began as an outgrowth of a retrenchment scare at the Pennsylvania State College System. Career design workshops are used to facilitate the development of individual renewal plans. The workshops are intended to assist people who want to renew their careers as well as those who want to prepare for transition to nonacademic employment (*PROD,* 1980). Two of three workshops are aimed at life goals, career goals, and planning. The third workshop is intended to prepare participants in resumé writing, job searching, and interviewing.
2. The Southwest Field Training Project is directed at educators who needed to review their careers and career goals (*Debrief,* 1979). This project brings together academics in a wilderness setting to learn about themselves, their limits, and their goals. Participants serve as a resource network following the experience.
3. Campus to Corporate Careers Program is a Texas-based project intended to link business and industry to PhDs in the liberal arts who are seeking careers in business (Texas Bureau, 1980). The program consists of a six-week effort of career/life planning and assessment, with seminars, group discussions, and self-study intended to market the skills of participants. Any retraining necessary would take place at the new job.
4. The Career Opportunities Institute at the University of Virginia also stresses personal assessment, but does not require participants to have plans to leave academe. The program helps academics decide whether a career outside academe might be a way to fulfill their professional goals and it also helps them identify their marketable skills. The six-week summer program includes personal career counseling, meetings with successful career changers, and coursework in business. Half of the par-

ticipants in the program have moved to jobs outside academe (Jacobson, 1983).

Many other assistance programs are being launched. The efforts are coming from colleges and universities, private entrepreneurs, business and industry coalitions, and associations for higher education (AAHE, n.d.; Baldwin et al., 1981; *Chronicle of Higher Education,* 1983). Programs are also being run to inform graduate students in low employment fields about job opportunities outside academe (Furniss, 1981b, pp. 84–95).

RETRAINING FOR EMPLOYMENT ELSEWHERE

The question remains whether institutions have the incentive to pay for career-change programs, especially for efforts that would retrain workers for employment *elsewhere.* One proposal would have the federal government subsidize the retraining of workers through the unemployment compensation system (Thompson, 1977a). The most immediate solution might have to come from colleges and universities themselves if counseling and workshop programs fail to encourage career change. We can envision an option where a middle-aged professor would leave for retraining, and the funds spent on his or her retraining would be recovered through the higher productivity of the replacement. If the career changer is not replaced, the savings would equal the value of his or her budget line until retirement, minus the cost of the retraining package.

Consider an associate professor in a "declining" field who is earning $25,000 per year. If this person sees little chance for advancement, and expects salary increases perhaps at a rate only half that of a professor in a field in demand, he or she may very well be interested in an option that includes full pay for one year, tuition and fees, travel and relocation expenses, and a severance payment. The cost to an institution might include $25,000 in salary, $6,000 in tuition and fees, $4,000 in relocation funds, and perhaps a $10,000 payment to finance the period during which the career changer will be seeking a new job. Thus, for $45,000 it may be possible to free one position. If the career changer is not replaced, this cost can be recovered in less than two years. If replaced, but with an employee who earns, say, two-thirds of the career changer's salary, the cost can be recovered in approximately five years. In those instances where the changer is to be replaced, but where there is a cash flow problem, the changer's position could be left vacant until the retraining expenditure has been paid back through the vacant salary line (approximately one year after the training year concludes). This means an institution must be willing to do without one faculty position for two years or be willing to advance itself the funds to support both the career changer and a replacement under the realization that the costs eventually will be recovered.

Another possibility might be an arrangement to guarantee for a given number of years the salaries of faculty members who agree to leave the institution. The college or university might agree to pay the midcareer changer the difference (up to a fixed proportion) between his or her prior faculty salary and the salary from the new position for up to three years. The cost and recovery time for such a scheme would depend upon the difference in salaries. For example, assume a $25,000 per year associate professor took a $15,000 per year job; the subsidy would be recovered in a little more than a year, if the midcareer changer were not replaced. Were this person replaced with a faculty member paid two-thirds that of the midcareer changer, the subsidy would be recovered in less than four years. This scheme also requires an institution to take a longer-range view of its human resources and budgetary policies.

TO WHOM DOES A CAREER SHIFT APPEAL?

Before colleges and universities implement midcareer change schemes, we need to know the nature and the extent of the appeal of the programs. If these schemes were to appeal to the more active researchers, the better teachers, the more prolific writers, and the grant seekers, then it would seem reasonable to question their usefulness. On the other hand, if they were to appeal to the less active, it may benefit academe to encourage faculty members to take the options. With these issues in mind, the authors developed a series of questions that were incorporated within the 1977 Ladd-Lipset Survey of the American Professoriate.[1]

Conducted in the spring of 1977, the survey obtained an achieved sample of more than 4,200 faculty members at 160 universities and colleges. The questionnaire contained items about the respondent's views on changing or redirecting his or her career, plus items dealing with relative academic success and satisfaction with life outside academe (Ladd & Lipset, 1978).

We analyzed questions dealing with (1) those persons who would be equally or more satisfied with life outside academe, and (2) those persons who had seriously considered leaving academe permanently during the past two years.

Several measures of scholarly activity were used to determine whether faculty members who are attracted to the notion of midcareer change differ from those who are not. We analyzed respondent inclination toward midcareer change by publication records, involvement in research, and self-rating of comparative academic success. Because the type and extent of academic involvement varies by field and type of institution, the data were controlled both for four broad categories of fields and for two categories of institutions. The four fields were the social sciences, the humanities, the natural sciences, and business and applied fields. Institutions were categorized as research and doctoral institutions on the one hand and comprehensive and liberal arts institutions on the other. This distinction between types of institutions recognizes, among other things, the different emphasis placed upon research at doctoral institutions versus colleges.

Least Active Researchers and Writers

The more likely career changers would seem to be those persons who feel they would be at least equally happy with life outside academe. By examining this variable, we find that 32 percent of today's academics feel they would be equally or more satisfied outside. The percentage of individuals who feel they would be at least equally happy outside academe varies, by field and type of institution, from a low of 19 percent in the humanities to a high of 43 percent in the natural sciences, both at comprehensive and liberal arts institutions.

A greater portion of the less research-oriented academics believe they would be happier or at least as happy outside academe. Table 8.1 shows by field and type of institution that those now engaged in scholarly or scientific research are less likely to believe they would be happier outside. From 19 to 43 percent of the faculty members currently involved in research feel they would be equally or more happy outside academe, compared with a range from 26 to 68 percent of the faculty members who have never been engaged in scholarly or scientific research.[2]

The practice of using books and articles published as an indicator of academic involvement also suggests that those who would be equally or more happy outside academe are less active than their colleagues. The more articles a faculty member has written, the less likely he or she is to believe that life outside academe would be equally or more satisfying. A similar relationship exists for number of books published, with the exception that the more prolific book writers in business and applied fields at research and doctoral institutions say they would be happier outside. Of course, measuring scholarly productivity by counting the number of books and articles without respect to their quality can be misleading. This problem is discussed elsewhere, and it has been argued that books and articles should be used as measures, albeit with caution (Ladd, 1979; Patton & Marver, 1979).

Academics Who Rate Themselves as Less Successful Than Their Colleagues

More than one-quarter of the faculty members in American universities and colleges seriously considered "leaving academic life permanently" dur-

TABLE 8.1. Percentage of Faculty Who Would Be Equally or More Satisfied with Life Outside Academe (by Involvement in Scholarly or Scientific Research Within Field and Type of Institution)

Research and Doctoral Institutions

	Social Sciences (N=366)			Humanities (N=353)			Natural Sciences (N=844)			Business/Applied (N=257)		
	Never	Past	Now	Never	Past	Now	Never	Past	Now	Never	Past	Now
	66% (2)	25% (32)	24% (322)	41% (16)	40% (23)	25% (314)	51% (50)	57% (87)	31% (707)	45% (20)	33% (50)	43% (187)
		$p<.01$			n.s.			$p<.01$			n.s.	

Comprehensive and Liberal Arts Institutions

	Social Sciences (N=315)			Humanities (N=398)			Natural Sciences (N=682)			Business/Applied (N=165)		
	Never	Past	Now	Never	Past	Now	Never	Past	Now	Never	Past	Now
	55% (45)	8% (60)	40% (210)	32% (43)	10% (73)	19% (282)	68% (92)	49% (192)	34% (398)	26% (47)	47% (70)	37% (48)
		$p<.001$			$p<.02$			$p<.001$			n.s.	

Note: Numbers in parentheses are numbers of cases. Statistical significance was determined by the chi-square test.

ing the two years preceding the survey. Controlling for type of institution and field, the percentages range from a low of 22 percent for those in business and applied fields to a high of 38 percent for those in the natural sciences, both at comprehensive and liberal arts colleges. For all faculty members at research and doctoral institutions, the percentage is 27; for all faculty members at comprehensive and liberal arts colleges, it is 31.

Other studies have shown that publication rates tend to be positively associated with other measures of academic activity (Fulton & Trow, 1974; Marver & Patton, 1976; Patton & Marver, 1979) and negatively associated with an interest in early retirement (Hansen & Holden, 1981a; Palmer, 1979). In the current data, the number of books and articles published during one's career tends to be *negatively* associated with a serious consideration of leaving academe. The less involved in writing, the more likely it is that a faculty member has seriously considered leaving academe during the past two years.

The suggestion that it is the generally less active faculty members who have considered leaving academe is strengthened when we examine the respondent's *self-rating* of academic success compared with persons of the same age and qualifications and their consideration of leaving. The relationship is striking. Table 8.2 shows that a greater percentage of the faculty members *who regard themselves as unsuccessful* have seriously considered leaving.

Also, a greater percentage of younger faculty members have seriously considered leaving academe. This is important, of course, because it is the younger faculty members to whom midcareer options must appeal. It is also important because these options should not compete with the appeal of early retirement schemes to the older faculty members. However, we should not overlook the possibility that a career shift appeals to fewer older academics because those to whom it might have appealed left academe when they were younger. We might also be skeptical about the statements made by persons not yet granted tenure. They may be more receptive to a possible career shift because they recognize they may have to make one if they are not granted tenure.

Examining the relationship between happiness outside academe and considerations of leaving, we find that 55 percent of the respondents neither have seriously considered leaving nor believe they would be at least equally happy outside. On the other hand, 17 percent have both seriously considered leaving academe and believe they would be at least equally happy outside. The remaining 28 percent of today's academics have mixed feelings: 13 percent have seriously considered leaving academe even though they believe they would not be equally happy with life outside, and 15 percent feel they would be at least equally happy outside but they have not seriously considered leaving.

These percentages suggest there is indeed a substantial number of

TABLE 8.2. Percentage of Faculty Who Have Seriously Considered Leaving Academe During the Past Two Years (by Self-Rating of Comparative Academic Success Within Field and Type of Institution)

Research and Doctoral Institutions

	Social Sciences (N=373)			Humanities (N=379)			Natural Sciences (N=877)			Business/Applied (N=272)		
	Not	Fairly	Very	Not	Fairly	Very	Not	Fairly	Very	Not	Fairly	Very
	57% (39)	30% (250)	26% (84)	43% (51)	27% (256)	16% (72)	43% (56)	26% (636)	22% (185)	39% (11)	29% (176)	23% (85)
	p<.01			p<.01			p<.01			n.s.		

Comprehensive and Liberal Arts Institutions

	Social Sciences (N=300)			Humanities (N=469)			Natural Sciences (N=701)			Business/Applied (N=176)		
	Not	Fairly	Very	Not	Fairly	Very	Not	Fairly	Very	Not	Fairly	Very
	85% (35)	25% (199)	28% (66)	64% (26)	21% (390)	7% (53)	58% (68)	37% (476)	36% (157)	99% (12)	20% (113)	15% (51)
	p<.001			p<.001			p<.01			p<.001		

Note: Numbers in parentheses are numbers of cases. Statistical significance was determined by the chi-square test. "Not" = not successful in the academic setting; "fairly" = fairly successful; "very" = very successful.

academics who might be willing to participate in some type of career change program. Whether the relatively active or the inactive are the persons who would be happier outside academe is an important question. Should they be the more active, then institutions will need to search for other ways to deal with their dissatisfaction and to retain their services.

Studies of early retirees in academe show that those who know others who retired early are more likely to retire early themselves (Patton, 1977). With this in mind, we tried to discover if the number of colleagues a faculty member knew who left academe for other careers is associated with considerations of leaving. The results, shown in Table 8.3, reveal a strong relationship. The more midcareer changers the respondent knew, the more likely he or she was to have seriously considered leaving academe.

These data suffer the usual disadvantages of self-reported information. The respondents may not do tomorrow what they say today. Since the less active apparently know how they stand in relation to their colleagues, they may have used the survey as a catharsis and may no longer be midcareer change candidates. Furthermore, these findings are derived from data collected before the recent increase in the mandatory retirement age and before the dramatic increase in the cost of living during the past several years. However, more recent studies are finding similar results. Early retirement incentives appeal to the disaffected, and they do not appeal disproportionately to faculty members who consider themselves to be the better teachers (Toevs & Hanhardt, 1982). Informal reports from colleges and universities now implementing early retirement and career change options suggest that the general thrust of these findings still applies. However, individual institutions must use these national data and findings from other institutions with caution. For example, when the national data are examined by field or are otherwise disaggregated, some relationships tend to weaken. Although we should recognize these possibilities, personal interviews with midcareer changers and persons who have taken incentive early retirement lead us to believe that there are indeed many academics who would be happier outside of university and college life. Institutions that devise career options would be well-advised to collect data about their own situations (Kreinin, 1982).

CONCLUSIONS AND IMPLICATIONS

Many academics, especially those who have been less active in the research and publishing areas, have contemplated leaving the halls of academe. But what are the prospects for these potential career changers? Several researchers have collected data that show that a career in academe is no longer the only route to success and happiness for the PhD holder (Gottschalk, 1982; Jacobson, 1983; Lovett, 1980; Solmon et al., 1981). Others, however, have

TABLE 8.3. Percentage of Faculty Who Have Seriously Considered Leaving Academe During the Past Two Years (by Number of Colleagues Known to Have Left Academe During the Last Five Years Within Field and Type of Institution)

Research and Doctoral Institutions

	Social Sciences (N=361)			Humanities (N=499)			Natural Sciences (N=732)			Business/Applied (N=270)		
	0	1-2	≥3	0	1-2	≥3	0	1-2	≥3	0	1-2	≥3
	21%	28%	46%	10%	33%	35%	19%	25%	34%	17%	26%	38%
	(79)	(158)	(124)	(99)	(135)	(143)	(221)	(356)	(300)	(76)	(103)	(91)
	$p<.001$			$p<.001$			$p<.001$			$p<.01$		

Comprehensive and Liberal Arts Institutions

	Social Sciences (N=302)			Humanities (N=467)			Natural Sciences (N=700)			Business/Applied (N=178)		
	0	1-2	≥3	0	1-2	≥3	0	1-2	≥3	0	1-2	≥3
	21%	27%	53%	19%	18%	28%	42%	27%	59%	12%	8%	46%
	(99)	(108)	(95)	(144)	(157)	(166)	(145)	(356)	(199)	(45)	(66)	(67)
	$p<.001$			$p<.05$			$p<.001$			$p<.001$		

Note: Numbers in parentheses are numbers of cases. Statistical Significance was determined by the chi-square test.

raised the quite legitimate question of whether jobs will be available for career changers, have noted that very little voluntary career change has taken place, and have pointed out that as people grow older they are less likely to make such change (Arbeiter, 1979). We share these concerns. Although faculty members now changing careers are finding jobs outside academe (Feinberg, 1982; Gottschalk, 1982; Jacobson, 1983; Solmon, 1979), an increase in the number of career changes may strain the availability of jobs. Institutions interested in options that might increase vitality will have to keep these factors in mind; the problems should not be used as reasons to avoid action. Our review of initial midcareer change programs in academe, career development, and out-placement activities in business, as well as our findings from the Survey of the American Professoriate, reveal important implications for institutional leaders and other policymakers considering midcareer change efforts in higher education.

Improved Information

More information must be obtained regarding employment patterns of PhDs outside academe. In many fields, high proportions of PhD degree recipients have been traditionally employed in business and government. In others, nonacademic employment is relatively new. The efforts of federal agencies and professional associations for several disciplines in gathering information must continue, and their findings should be disseminated broadly. In addition, universities and colleges could help by obtaining valuable information from alumni who have followed nontraditional careers. Our findings also suggest that more faculty feel that nontraditional careers are acceptable once they are made aware of the options. Hence, nonacademic career information should be disseminated to faculty members, department chairpersons, and academic administrators. This information should also find its way to graduate students. Those in midcareer as well as those just entering should be aware of the rich diversity of opportunities.

Personal Assessment

Faculty members and administrators should be provided with opportunities for self-assessment of their personal and career goals in order to help them determine whether their current position provides the best opportunity for personal and professional satisfaction. Some faculty members will develop career change strategies through self-administered, self-assessment techniques or through their participation in seminars. Others will require more assistance through formal programs offered by universities and colleges. In either case, books on self-assessment are available (Furniss, 1981b; Robbins, 1978, pp. 149–156; Souerwine, 1979) and seminars and short courses are being offered. Undoubtedly, more assistance will become available.

Colleges and universities considering formal career change programs need to plan these efforts carefully. Such plans must be attractive to faculty, acceptable to departments, and financially viable for the institution. Our review of recent experience with midcareer change and incentive early retirement programs revealed the following factors that should be considered by institutional leaders.

Program Focus

Institutional leaders must determine their needs and then the type of program best suited for them. Most career change efforts thus far have not been designed for, and consequently have not resulted in, a movement of faculty members to nonacademic institutions. Institutions experiencing minor shifts in student enrollment among fields and among specialties within fields may only require programs that provide for upgrading and transfer of faculty from one specialty to another or from one campus to another. Those institutions experiencing dramatic downturns in enrollments within some fields or across the whole institution, however, can benefit from programs that facilitate faculty members leaving higher education to pursue new careers.

Engendering Faculty Support

Many faculty members are receptive to the idea of midcareer change. They have seriously considered leaving higher education, and they would expect to be equally or more satisfied with life outside academe. Providing information about alternative careers and providing opportunities for self-assessment may be sufficient to induce career change for some faculty. For most, however, personal counseling on preparing resumés, on job searching and on job interviewing may be necessary because recruiting and selecting processes in business and government differ from those in higher education. Also, we should recognize that faculty members interested in career change may take a long time to reach a decision to change. In Robbins' study of successful career changers, she found it took people more than a year to decide to leave their previous jobs—most said the hardest part of their career change was deciding to do it (Robbins, 1978).

Academics may be more disposed to career change if they are actively involved in developing the program and if the risks associated with change are reduced. Change programs should involve the active participation of faculty and their representatives. Faculty senates and collective bargaining representatives could be helpful in the design and implementation stages when the programs are intended to help faculty members and when faculty leaders believe the programs will help their constituents.

Individual faculty members may be more willing to attempt career change if the risks are minimized. Tenured faculty who take positions outside of higher education should be on leave of absence for no less than a one-year period. Exiting faculty may have to be provided with a salary supplement for one or two years in those instances where the initial salary of the new position is below their previous faculty salary. However, it is not likely to be necessary in most cases for two reasons. First, faculty salaries have fallen farther below salaries for most professionals. Second, 60 percent of the out-placements in the private sector received higher salaries in their new positions (Gooding, 1979).

Out-placement activities in business do not usually involve retraining. In higher education, however, retraining is often a critical component of the career change program. Retraining can range from short courses to improve the quantitative skills of those in the humanities, since PhDs in the humanities who are employed in nonacademic jobs tend to need stronger quantitative skills (Solmon, 1979, p. 61), to regular graduate degree-granting programs (Robbins, 1978, pp. 139–143). Institutions that include retraining as a part of their program should provide adequate financial support for educational expenses, plus salary and benefits during this period.

Acceptability to Departments

Department chairpersons and deans must be assured some return from these programs. If participation in midcareer change programs means that a department will lose a faculty position, then most units will be reluctant to encourage their members to explore these programs. Partial, and perhaps temporary, funding to offset such a loss may be needed to encourage participation. Also, department chairs may fear that the least valuable will stay and the most valuable will leave. Their fears might be alleviated if some flexibility is built into the program. In addition to any general publicity regarding the program, department chairs could discourage some faculty members from leaving and encourage others to think about participation. Institutions should be prepared either to offer special incentives to retain the most active and valued faculty members or to hire replacements. Experiences with incentive early retirement programs have revealed that the less active were most attracted to the programs, although some departments lost valued faculty. However, in those situations, department chairpersons reported that equally competent replacements were hired (Patton, 1979).

Financial Viability for Institutions

Several factors must be considered before deciding to offer midcareer change programs for faculty. Each institution should forecast changes that are likely to occur if no midcareer change programs are instituted. If projections of faculty age composition by department over a five- to ten-year period reveal that high proportions of faculty members will reach normal retirement age, a midcareer change program may not be necessary. On the other hand, projections of age compositions at most institutions will show that relatively few retirements will occur during the next five to ten years (Corwin & Knepper, 1978; Palmer, 1979; Patton, 1979).

The proportion of faculty with academic tenure in each department or unit should be calculated and projected for the next five to ten years. Institutions with higher proportions of tenured faculty should consider midcareer change programs.

Faculty receptivity to midcareer change should be examined by asking such questions as: To what extent are faculty disposed to career change? Do those who are most receptive to the concept tend to be the least active? Are they the more productive scholars? The better teachers? The overall national pattern in which those who are least active in research are more interested in career change may not apply within a particular institution.

The midcareer change efforts can vary from the ad hoc, informal, information dissemination approach to a formal program. The costs of formal programs depend upon the availability of internal expertise versus outside consultants and program components. Many institutions may have sufficient expertise within their placement offices and schools of business administration to provide guidance on job opportunities, resumé writing, job search techniques, and interviewing skills. Others will require external consultants. Members of boards of trustees may be able to have their corporations offer programs to improve career change skills for faculty and may hire some of those who leave academe.

The eligibility criteria will influence the cost. Baldwin (1979b) found that, among tenured faculty, full professors more than five years from retirement were most likely to have considered alternative career paths. Universities might limit eligibility for career change programs based on academic rank or years of employment. An important cost consideration is the inclusion of a retraining component and, if included, the extent of retraining supported by the institution. While it appears that retraining will often be necessary, it is not certain how much retraining will be required before career changers enter their new positions. As noted earlier, in at least one program all retraining is the responsibility of the new employer (Barry & Naftzger, n.d.). Modest retraining efforts at the originating institution, however, will be inexpensive if prospective career changers can take courses on a space-available basis.

Initial experience with midcareer change programs demonstrates that they have the potential to increase institutional flexibility during periods of declining student enrollments and shrinking budgets. The prospects for wider use of midcareer change programs are bright if they are carefully planned to satisfy the needs of faculty, department chairpersons, and employing universities and colleges.

NOTES

1. David D. Palmer was an associate of the 1977 survey and had primary responsibility for the retirement and midcareer change component of the 1977 Survey of the American Professoriate.

2. The analyses are based on data corrected for sampling ratios and response rates.

Chapter 9

Maintaining Faculty Vitality Through Outside Professional Consulting

Carol M. Boyer and *Darrell R. Lewis*

Faculty consulting has been viewed traditionally as an important form of public service and faculty vitality in higher education. Nonetheless, concern about the appropriateness of outside professional consulting activities of full-time faculty members has increased in recent years as consulting activity reportedly has increased, as public sentiment toward post-secondary education has changed, and as greater accountability has been sought. The central concern, however, appears to be the same today as it was forty years ago, namely, whether outside professional consulting results in "shirking . . . university responsibilities" (Patton, 1980) or "diffusion of energy" (Wilson, 1942).

On the one side are those who argue that faculty consulting may result in neglect of students and other university responsibilities, abuses of academic freedom, conflicts of interest, and illegitimate use of institutional resources. On the other side are those who argue that faculty consulting enhances both research and teaching, that conflicts of interest and other abuses are very uncommon, and that faculty consulting benefits both the institution and society as well as the individual.

Unfortunately, much of the argument both for and against outside professional consulting is based on anecdotal information and misperceptions of its nature and intent. Empirical evidence even on the incidence of

The authors contributed equally to the research and writing of this chapter. Portions of this chapter appeared in an article by Carol M. Boyer and Darrell R. Lewis, "Faculty Consulting: Responsibility or Promiscuity?" *Journal of Higher Education,* September/October 1984, *55,* pp. 637–659, and are used by permission. Copyright © 1984 by the Ohio State University Press.

faculty consulting, not to mention its nature or effects, is sorely lacking. Moreover, the evidence that does exist appears to be inconsistent. One study shows, for example, that the proportion of faculty at four-year colleges and universities who received consulting fees increased from 13 percent in 1962 to 48 percent in 1975 (Dillon, 1979). Another set of studies shows that the percentage of faculty members who consult for pay was considerably smaller and did not change between 1969 and 1975; that is, 37 percent of American academics consult for pay, 19 percent consult more than one-half day per week, and only 6 percent consult more than one day per week (Patton, 1980; Patton & Marver, 1979; Marver & Patton, 1976). A third study purports that over 54 percent of faculty members at major universities devote some portion of their normal workweek to paid consulting and that 16 percent of them spend more than 10 percent of their workweek consulting (Lanning, 1977).

In view of current economic and demographic conditions as well as forecasts for higher education, both the debate about outside professional consulting and concern for faculty vitality are likely to intensify. This chapter sheds some light on both of these important faculty issues. It does so by (1) exploring aspects of the relationship between outside professional consulting and faculty vitality, (2) providing a taxonomy for examining the *potential benefits* — to the individual, the institution, and society — and the *potential conflicts* or costs that could result from outside professional consulting, (3) presenting a review and synthesis of existing literature and data on faculty consulting, and (4) introducing new and previously unreported data from the National Research Council. Consideration also is given to pertinent theoretical, social-philosophical, and policy implementation issues.

CONSULTING AS A TRADITIONAL FACULTY ROLE AND RESPONSIBILITY

A consultant, defined generally, is "one who gives professional advice or services regarding matters in the field of his special knowledge or training" (*Webster's New International Dictionary,* 1959, p. 573). Applying that definition to higher education, faculty consulting is the extension and application of an individual's professional or scholarly expertise outside the academic institution. Consulting, as defined here, is not limited to remuneration and other economic self-interest considerations. Rather, consulting is viewed as a traditional faculty role and responsibility that has long been recognized as an important form of public service on the part of both individual faculty members and the academic institution. As such, faculty consulting relates directly to the tripartite university mission of teaching, research, and service.

By providing a broad range of opportunities for constant renewal and purposeful development, faculty consulting also relates directly to faculty and institutional vitality. According to Gardner (1978, 1963), such renewal and development depend upon conditions that encourage individual growth and fulfillment. In his words, "A society concerned for its continued vitality will be interested in the growth and fulfillment of individual human beings" (1978, p. 73). Outside professional consulting, then, is clearly one of several means of maintaining faculty and institutional vitality that, in turn, is linked inextricably both to the intellectual, social, psychological, and economic well-being of individuals within an academic institution and to the mission of that institution.[1]

In spite of these traditional linkages among outside professional consulting, institutional mission, and faculty vitality, concern about the ethical and economic issues surrounding faculty consulting has persisted in higher education. In fact, concern about the "diffusion of energy" that allegedly results when full-time faculty members engage in outside professional consulting first surfaced in the literature over forty years ago (Wilson, 1942). Increased concern in recent years has been attributed both to reported increases in consulting activity and to changes in public sentiment toward postsecondary education, along with declining resources and calls for greater accountability on the part of colleges and universities (see, for example, Aggarwal, 1981; Dillon, 1979; Lanning, 1977; Patton, 1980). Nonetheless, the central concern appears to be the same today as it was in 1942, namely, whether outside professional consulting by individual faculty members results in the shirking of their university responsibilities.

SOME COMMON COMPLAINTS AND MISPERCEPTIONS

In discussions about faculty consulting, several complaints and misperceptions frequently surface. Among them: "faculty consulting is increasing and getting out of hand," "less outside consulting will result in increased faculty productivity" (or conversely, "increased consulting results in reduced faculty productivity"), and "faculty consulting is really 'moonlighting' and 'double-dipping' at the public's and students' expense." These complaints and misperceptions result basically both from a lack of current knowledge about the nature and extent of outside professional consulting activities, and from a muddled understanding of the "true" costs and benefits that result from faculty consulting.

What is the empirical evidence? Is faculty consulting increasing? Are faculty who consult teaching less or with less effectiveness, or conducting less research than nonconsulting faculty? Will less consulting result in increased faculty and institutional productivity? What are the *true* costs and benefits that result from faculty consulting activities? In the following sections, in an attempt to answer some of these questions, the existing research literature will be reviewed and some new data from the National Research Council will be introduced. Even before these data are considered, however, and before addressing the more fundamental question of whether more or less faculty consulting activities should take place, it is essential to have a clear conceptual understanding both of the true costs and benefits that result from outside professional consulting, and of the necessary trade-offs between costs and benefits in such activities.

Trade-offs Between Costs and Benefits in Faculty Consulting

Informed decisions about alternative faculty roles and responsibilities — as with most decisions dealing with alternative allocations of institutional resources — must be based on *cost-effectiveness*. The latter can be determined only by systematic comparison of the costs (or resources to be used, or alternative services not provided) with the benefits (or outcomes to be achieved).

In an accounting sense, costs are defined as the total outlays necessary to achieve a given set of outcomes. More generally, costs can be defined as the value of alternatives or other opportunities forgone in order to pursue a particular course of action, hence the term *opportunity costs*. For example, each time an academic institution decides to approve or encourage the investment of faculty time in consulting, total outlays include both the direct costs of any institutional resource employed (e.g., equipment, facilities, materials, and faculty time) and the indirect costs of any institutional output (i.e., teaching, research, or service) forgone by taking faculty members away from their typical everyday activities.[2] Benefits, as defined here, are the opposite of costs in that they represent opportunities gained or outcomes achieved by engaging in some activity. For example, one of the principal benefits said to accrue to an academic institution when it "invests in" (i.e., permits or promotes) some faculty development activity is an increase in the marginal product of its faculty that, in turn, contributes to an increase in subsequent total faculty output. Thus, in the case of outside professional consulting, we could hypothesize that such consulting enhances faculty and institutional vitality by improving faculty effectiveness in subsequent teaching and research activities.[3]

More About Cost-Effectiveness

Cost-effectiveness, then, is a rational technique for selecting from alternative activities *the* activity that will achieve either a given set of outcomes at the lowest cost or the greatest number of benefits at given costs.

The underlying concept is that the benefits (or outcomes to be achieved) must be weighed against the costs (or resources to be used); the lower the costs with given benefits, or the greater the benefits with given costs, the greater the cost-effectiveness. It is important to recognize, however, that activities that are low in cost are not necessarily cost-effective or low in quality. Similarly, activities that are cost-effective are not necessarily low in cost or low in quality. Cost-effectiveness is complicated further because usually there are any number of ways to achieve a given set of outcomes, some of which are more cost-effective than others.

Comparisons of cost-effectiveness are used at least implicitly in most rational decisions both within and outside higher education. Such comparisons usually are expressed as judgments or ratios that may or may not have required the use of other, more formal techniques such as monetary benefit–cost analysis. Determining how best to conceptualize (or define) and measure the various costs and benefits is a difficult but important task, since different conceptualizations undoubtedly will lead to different comparisons of cost-effectiveness. The use of several such comparisons can be particularly useful in situations where benefits cannot easily be specified or measured in monetary terms, as is surely the case in higher education and in most assessments of faculty consulting.[4]

POTENTIAL BENEFITS OF
OUTSIDE PROFESSIONAL CONSULTING

The benefits of outside professional consulting have been recounted several times in recent years (see, for example, Aggarwal, 1981; Dillon, 1979; Dillon & Bane, 1980; Eddy, 1982; Golomb, 1979; Patton, 1980; Weston, 1980–81; Wildavsky, 1978). In this section, such benefits will be examined from the perspective of who benefits—the individual, the institution, or society.

Benefits to the Individual

Benefits of outside professional consulting doubtless accrue to the individual faculty member who does the consulting and, as such, demonstrate clearly the link that exists between outside professional consulting and faculty vitality. For example, in addition to supplementing the university salary and presumably contributing to the economic well-being and morale of the faculty member, consulting enables the faculty member to gain "valuable learning opportunities for professionally and academically enriching work . . . and to test academic teaching and research against real-world experience" (Aggarwal, 1981, p. 17). Consulting enhances the faculty member's teaching capabilities by providing a valuable source of real-world examples for the concepts and theories taught in the classroom. Moreover, consulting enables the faculty member to stay current and abreast of practical needs and developments in his or her field. It also provides ideas and inspiration for further research, helps to build the faculty member's professional competence and reputation, and provides external confirmation of both the quality and the relevance of the faculty member's expertise and specialized talents.

Benefits to the Institution

For most benefits of outside professional consulting to the individual faculty member, there are corresponding benefits to the employing academic institution. Each such benefit demonstrates clearly the links that exist both between faculty and institutional vitality and between consulting activities and institutional vitality. For example, by supplementing the individual's university salary, consulting enables the academic institution to attract and retain outstanding faculty in various professional and applied areas. It has been claimed (Golomb, 1979) that it is fairly easy for faculty members in some departments (e.g., electrical engineering) to double their university salaries by consulting on average only one day per week. In the words of one such faculty member: "Eliminate faculty consulting, and either the salaries of such people become prohibitively expensive to the university, or they will be lost to alternative forms of employment which are available to them" (Golomb, 1979, pp. 34–35).

Permissive consulting in such cases can be perceived as indirect salary supplement by the institution for "market retention" purposes. This is a very common practice in most American schools of medicine and business. (In fact, major medical schools currently permit up to 100 percent of the institutional base salary to be supplemented by clinical and consulting practices.) If the market rate of pay per unit of time for the external practice is greater than the institutional rate, then such permissive institutional consulting policies are clearly cost-effective—even if there are *no other* faculty vitality benefits. Consulting also complements the effectiveness of research and teaching; helps build the professional reputation of the department and university (as well as the individual faculty member); strengthens the university's presence in, and service commitment to, the broader community; and builds public good will toward the university. Moreover, consulting sometimes results in summer work or internship experiences and post-degree career opportunities for students trained by faculty who are respected professionally and known outside the university community. And finally, by providing access to private sector and government contracts as well as foundation grant monies, consulting aids in the advancement of institutional resources.

Benefits to Society

Most of the benefits of professional consulting to outside agencies are fairly self-evident and complementary to the missions of most academic institutions. Most importantly, university-based consulting provides public and private agencies with access to a great pool of specialized talent and expertise that can be applied to a wide range of problems that affect society. As Bowen so aptly states: "Just as a hospital or an auto repair shop is of value on a standby basis, even if never used, so a college or university is valuable because of the talent it has in readiness to advise on technical questions or policy issues that may arise in government at any level, in the household, on the farm, in the business firm, in the labor union, or in the school" (1978, p. 320). And, as Golomb points out, "this is *talent which it is more economical to rent than to buy*" (1979, p. 36). In a clearly cost-effective manner, then, agencies in society can draw on the talent and expertise of faculty members on an as-needed basis without the full costs attendant with long-term, full-time commitments. Consulting also aids in the transfer of research findings to the broader university community. As Golomb asserts, "Faculty consulting is probably the most efficient mechanism imaginable through which the latest research can be incorporated into the technology" (1979, p. 35). And finally, in some fields, consulting provides public and private agencies with opportunities to assess the professional competence of the university's faculty and to determine the extent of correspondence between specific training needs and the university's educational resources.

POTENTIAL CONFLICTS OF OUTSIDE PROFESSIONAL CONSULTING

Just as the benefits of faculty consulting have been recounted several times in recent years, so too the potential conflicts and costs of faculty consulting have received considerable attention (see, for example, Aggarwal, 1981; Dillon, 1979; Eddy, 1982; Golomb, 1979; Marver & Patton, 1976; Patton, 1980; Patton & Marver, 1979; Weston, 1980–81; Wildavsky, 1978). Among the conflicts most frequently mentioned is possible neglect of students and other university responsibilities. Indeed, as stated earlier, the central concern today appears to be whether outside professional consulting by faculty members results in the shirking of their university responsibilities. Patton and Marver explain the basis for such concern in this way: "Today's observers are upset about what they perceive as 'double dipping' by well-paid faculty members. Their concern is not with the earnings of extra income per se; rather, these critics level their arguments at faculty members who earn outside income *on university time*" (1979, p. 176, emphasis added). Discretionary use of time has long been an accepted part of the traditional

definition of faculty role and, as such, is linked directly to the maintenance
of faculty vitality. Nonetheless, as Dillon points out, "to many observers it
appears that the availability of income-producing commitments . . . may
result in faculty who choose to spend time on what pays and not necessarily
on that which is of highest academic priority" (1979, p. 39).

Other closely related conflicts of faculty consulting are possible abuses
of academic freedom and conflicts of interest that result in "unconscious
compromise of academic objectivity and impartiality" (Dillon, 1979, p. 39).
Here the basic concern appears to be that faculty members serving as consultants may skew their research toward studies most likely to be profitable
to the private corporation. Such concern certainly is visible today at major
research centers in higher education. For example, debate has been especially strong recently at Stanford, Harvard, Yale, and the University of
California, where many faculty members are involved in the competitive
and profitable fields of bioengineering and computer electronics (*New York
Times,* 1983). Another potential conflict of faculty consulting is the possible
illegitimate use of institutional resources, for example, the case of an individual professor who uses without permission libraries and other university facilities, supplies, computers, or staff to support consulting activities. Still another possible conflict of faculty consulting, the question of
property rights, arises when such consulting results in the creation of intellectual property for which the patent or copyright may rightfully belong
to the university.

INSTITUTIONAL POLICIES ON FACULTY CONSULTING

In a number of recent studies, attempts have been made to identify those
elements that are most commonly included in university policy statements
on outside professional consulting. In one study, for example, Dillon and
Bane (1980) examined 98 different institutional policy statements or sum-
maries and found that about 70 percent contained provisions regarding
faculty time limitations, prior approval of outside consulting activities, and
noninterference of such activities with regular university responsibilities.

In another, much smaller study, Weston (1980–81) obtained from 14
public and private institutions information on institutional policies and procedures related to the outside professional activities of faculty members. He
found three elements common to most institutional policies, namely, definitions of the activity to be regulated, descriptions of the limitations on that
activity, and specification of formal approval that is required prior to pursuing that activity.

In still another, more recent study, Teague (1982) reviewed some 230
written institutional statements on outside faculty consulting. He identified

four areas that were consistently addressed in about half the documents: prior approval, conflict of interest, allocation of faculty time, and reporting of consulting activities. He concluded, however, that many of the current institutional policies on outside faculty consulting fail to address formally many important considerations of the outside consulting arrangement. It is important to note that Teague did find that nearly every written institutional policy statement on faculty consulting started with an acknowledgment of the benefits of outside professional consulting both to the individual faculty member and to the institution, but included the stipulation that such activity: "(1) . . . not interfere with the faculty member's institutional obligation; (2) enhances the faculty member's professional development; and, (3) is consistent with institutional goals and objectives" (1982, p. 182). The second provision can be interpreted clearly as a formal acknowledgment of the direct link between outside professional consulting and faculty vitality. Indeed, the second provision could easily be modified to read either "enhances the vitality of the individual faculty member" or "enhances the faculty member's professional development and vitality."

EXISTING RESEARCH AND SOME NEW RESULTS

Reported Incidence of Faculty Consulting to Date

Although prior to 1960, much of the literature on the academic profession was based on anecdotal information, the past two decades have witnessed a number of relatively large-scale empirical studies of college and university faculty (see, for example, Parsons & Platt, 1968; Trow, 1972; Bayer, 1973; Kemerer & Baldridge, 1975; Ladd & Lipset, 1975a; Wilson et al., 1975; Roizen et al., 1978). However, only the 1969 and 1975 Carnegie surveys (Trow, 1972; Roizen et al., 1978) and the 1975 Ladd and Lipset survey (Ladd & Lipset, 1975a) dealt specifically with questions of faculty consulting and included supplementary income data. Therefore, empirical studies on the incidence of faculty consulting have been based almost entirely on one or the other of these data bases.

Dillon (1979) juxtaposes data collected in the Ladd and Lipset (1975a) survey with that reported in an earlier study of Dunham and others (1966) and indicates that the proportion of faculty at four-year colleges and universities who received consulting fees from any source over a 12- to 24-month period more than tripled in 13 years, increasing from 13 percent in 1962 to 48 percent in 1975.

In another analysis of the 1975 Ladd and Lipset survey data, Marsh and Dillon (1980) again show that nearly half of all college and university faculty reported some paid consulting activity for the preceding two-year period. Most importantly, Marsh and Dillon found that supplemental income activities did not interfere with other activities traditionally expected of faculty. In brief, they found that faculty who earned more supplemental income were more active in research, but no less active in other regular on-campus activities such as teaching.

Still another set of studies is based solely on the 1969 and 1975 Carnegie survey data. Patton (1980) summarizes the findings from two earlier analyses of these data (Patton & Marver, 1979; Marver & Patton, 1976) and indicates that the proportion of faculty members who reported consulting for pay over a 24-month period did not change between 1969 and 1975: 37 percent of American academics consult for pay, 19 percent consult more than one-half day per week, and 6 percent consult more than one day per week. As for the effects of consulting, Patton and Marver report that when they controlled for rank as well as type and quality of academic institution, they found that: "On a number of measures, academics who engage in paid consulting tend to be more active in the academy than their colleagues who do not consult for fees. The paid consultants spend more time teaching and advising, more of them are engaged in research, and they have written more books and articles" (1979, p. 175). Patton interprets these data to suggest that "paid consultants are *at least* as active in their college and university roles as their peers who do not consult for pay" (1980, p. 184).

Using the same data as that used by Marver and Patton in the first of their two studies, Lanning (1977) indicates that 54 percent of a subsample of faculty members at major universities devote some portion of their normal workweek to paid consulting, and that 16 percent of them spend more than 10 percent of their workweek consulting. Moreover, he found that paid faculty consultants not only teach nearly as much as faculty noncon-sultants, but also publish more, subscribe to more professional journals, communicate more with their colleagues at other institutions, and appear to be more satisfied with their careers and their universities than faculty non-consultants.

In summary, it is important to note that even though the studies reported here were based almost entirely on the Carnegie or Ladd and Lipset data, some of the results appear to be inconsistent, especially those regarding increases in outside consulting activities over time. Such inconsistency could be the result of either among-study differences in sampling techniques, questionnaires, and research methods or, in the case of Dillon (1979), comparison of results from two possibly noncomparable samples and studies. It is especially important to note that the studies reported here all collected data with questionnaires that sampled consulting activity for different periods of time. More importantly, none is recent enough to reflect any change in paid consulting activity that could be attributed to recent demographic or economic changes in higher education.

Some New Empirical Results

The National Research Council (1982) made available from its 1981 Survey of Doctorate Recipients recent data regarding faculty consulting that previously had not been examined. Data for the Survey of Doctorate Recipients (SDR) are collected biennially by the National Research Council (NRC) from a stratified random sample of all science, engineering, and humanities doctorates in the United States who earned their degrees between 1938 and the present. (The NRC also maintains a longitudinal data base that consists of data from its five surveys conducted since 1973.) These data were analyzed by the authors for purposes of this study. Additional NRC data on all PhD respondents whose primary employment was in a university or four-year college then were drawn from the 1975 and 1981 SDR samples.[5] Our NRC subsample sizes were 16,447 PhDs in 1975 and 15,574 in 1981. For descriptive data from these samples, see Tables 9.1, 9.2, and 9.3.

Most importantly, our 1981 NRC data (Table 9.3) indicate that only 20.8 percent of the PhD faculty in fields allied with science and engineering and only 12.4 percent of the PhD faculty in the humanities devote any portion of their professional work time *during the academic year* to outside consulting activities. Overall, only 18.7 percent of these faculty devote any professional time to outside consulting activities during the academic year. These results are surprisingly low, especially when compared directly with results as high as 37 to 54 percent from the previous studies by Patton (1980), Dillon (1979), and Lanning (1977). ·

Why the apparent discrepancy in results? Two fundamental differences in the samples may provide some explanation. First, the NRC survey sampled only for the academic year and did not allow for the reporting of any extraordinary consulting activity that took place during the summer. All previous studies sampled over 12- and even 24-month periods that obviously included summers. Therefore, given that most institutional consulting policies are concerned with faculty activity during the academic year, our NRC data may be more appropriate for examining the relevant incidence of faculty consulting. Second, our NRC data did not include doctorate recipients from some professional fields such as business and education. Rather, our NRC data only included doctorates in fields allied with science and engineering (including mathematics, computer science, physics/astronomy, chemistry, earth/environment, engineering, agriculture, medicine, biology, psychology, and social sciences) and in the humanities (including history, art history, music, speech/theater, philosophy, other humanities, English/American language and literature, classical language and literature, and modern language and literature). Inasmuch as the excluded professional fields may induce and afford even greater consulting activity, our NRC

(*continued on page 191*)

TABLE 9.1. Median Annual Salaries of Doctoral Scientists and Engineers Employed Full Time, 1981 (by Years Since PhD and Type of Employer--in thousands of dollars)

	All Fields	Math.	Comp. Sci.	Phys./ Astrn.	Chem.	Earth/ Envir.	Engr.	Agric.	Med.	Biol.	Psych.	Social Sci.
TOTALS	$34.8	$31.8	$34.8	$36.9	$36.9	$34.9	$40.2	$33.1	$36.5	$32.5	$30.9	$30.9
Years Since PhD												
5 or Fewer	26.6	23.9	32.3	29.6	29.6	28.0	33.0	25.4	28.4	23.9	24.0	24.3
6-10	31.3	29.1	36.8	34.6	33.5	32.6	37.9	30.4	35.1	28.1	28.4	29.2
11-15	36.5	32.9	-	37.1	37.0	38.6	42.5	35.1	38.8	33.8	33.9	35.0
16-20	39.6	37.2	-	-	40.7	39.7	45.3	37.3	47.9	37.3	36.6	37.1
21-25	41.9	41.9	-	43.7	40.9	-	48.4	38.2	46.0	39.8	40.7	39.5
26-30	45.5	-	-	48.4	45.9	-	50.2	40.9	-	44.0	42.9	44.0
Over 30	46.6	47.2	-	-	47.5	50.3	50.3	42.0	50.1	46.0	-	44.9
TOTALS	$34.8	$31.8	$34.8	$36.9	$36.9	$34.9	$40.2	$33.1	$36.5	$32.5	$30.9	$30.9
Type of Employer												
Educational Institution	31.1	30.5	29.5	34.0	31.3	30.5	36.2	31.3	33.5	30.5	29.0	29.8
4-Yr. Col./Univ./Med.Sch.	31.3	30.6	29.4	34.2	31.4	30.6	36.2	31.3	33.6	30.6	28.9	29.8
2-Yr. College	28.2	-	-	-	30.0	-	-	-	-	25.8	28.0	27.1
Elem./Sec. School	29.2	-	-	-	-	-	-	-	-	-	30.7	-
Business/Industry+	40.3	36.4	40.1	39.5	40.3	40.5	41.6	35.4	44.6	38.2	40.3	38.9
U.S. Gov't, Civilian	40.4	39.3	-	-	39.8	40.7	44.2	38.9	39.6	37.6	-	44.2
State/Local Gov't	28.9	-	-	-	-	27.5	-	30.4	-	-	27.9	29.2
Hospital/Clinic	31.1	-	-	-	32.6	-	-	-	-	35.4	30.1	-
Other Nonprofit Organ.	35.5	35.7	-	37.0	37.2	34.7	40.5	-	-	33.1	30.5	30.4

Notes: Median salaries were computed only for PhDs employed full time, excluding those in the U.S. military. Academic salaries were multiplied by 11/9 to adjust for a full-year scale. Medians were not reported for cells with fewer than 20 cases reporting salary or with a sampling error of more than ± $2,000.

Adapted from Tables 1.7 and 1.8 in National Research Council, Science, Engineering, and Humanities Doctorates in the United States: 1981 Profile (Washington, DC: National Academy Press, 1982).

+ Includes self-employed.

TABLE 9.2. Median Annual Salaries of PhDs in the Humanities Employed Full Time, 1981 (by Years Since PhD and Type of Employer--in thousands of dollars)

					Field of Doctorate					
	All Fields	Hist.	Art Hist.	Music	Speech/ Theater	Phil.	Others	Eng./ Amer. Lang. & Lit.	Class. Lang. & Lit.	Modern Lang. & Lit.
TOTALS	$26.3	$27.0	$25.2	$26.0	$28.3	$26.0	$27.1	$26.2	$24.9	$25.4
Years Since PhD										
5 or fewer	20.4	20.2	19.8	21.6	21.2	20.2	21.0	20.9	18.1	19.1
6-10	24.4	24.7	25.2	25.4	26.2	24.2	26.9	24.0	23.0	24.2
11-15	28.9	28.5	–	30.7	29.2	29.5	–	29.7	–	28.0
16-20	32.7	34.4	34.6	32.0	–	34.3	38.3	30.9	–	32.2
21-25	35.1	36.5	–	–	–	33.2	–	35.2	–	34.6
26-30	39.2	40.1	–	–	–	–	–	–	–	–
Over 30	40.2	–	–	–	–	–	–	–	–	–
TOTALS	$26.3	$27.0	$25.2	$26.0	$28.3	$26.0	$27.1	$26.2	$24.9	$25.4
Type of Employer										
Educational Institution	26.5	27.5	25.4	26.4	28.4	26.5	27.9	26.4	25.4	25.6
4-Yr. Col./Univ./Med.Sch.	26.5	27.3	25.3	26.4	28.3	26.6	27.9	26.5	25.3	25.5
2-Yr. College	26.6	29.6	–	–	–	–	–	24.1	–	–
Elem./Sec. School	25.6	–	–	–	–	–	–	–	–	24.4
Business/Industry+	21.8	18.5	–	–	–	18.5	–	–	–	–
U.S. Gov't	25.4	25.5	–	–	–	–	–	–	–	–
Other/No Report	22.3	–	–	–	–	–	–	19.0	–	–

Notes: Median salaries were computed only for PhDs employed full time, excluding those in the U.S. military. Academic salaries were multiplied by 11/9 to adjust for a full-year scale. Medians were not reported for cells with fewer than 20 cases reporting salary or a sampling error of ± $2,000.

Adapted from Tables 2.7 and 2.8 in National Research Council, Science, Engineering, and Humanities Doctorates in the United States: 1981 Profile (Washington, DC: National Academy Press, 1982).

+ Includes self-employed.

TABLE 9.3. Science, Engineering, and Humanities Doctorates Employed Full Time as Faculty in Colleges and Universities in the United States, 1981

	Faculty in Science & Engineering	Faculty in Humanities	Totals	Faculty in Science & Engr.		Faculty in Humanities	
				Consult.	Non-consult.	Consult.	Non-consult.
Sample size	10,742	4,832	15,574				
Percentage of sample	69.0%	31.0%	100.0%	20.8%	79.2%	12.4%	87.6%
University employment	79.4%	66.5%	75.4%	84.1%	78.4%	75.0%	65.5%
Professor rank	42.6%	31.8%	39.2%	43.2%	40.6%	37.7%	29.7%
Tenured	64.6%	76.0%	68.1%				
Professional research	74.8%	48.0%	67.0%	74.3%	74.9%	52.2%	47.4%
Applied research	31.0%	11.9%	25.0%	43.6%	27.7%	17.6%	11.1%
Basic research	53.5%	38.0%	49.0%	44.7%	55.7%	38.0%	38.0%
Attention to problem of national interest	60.3%	55.0%	58.0%	71.2%	56.4%	67.4%	53.3%
Professional, academic-year consulting	20.8%	12.4%	18.7%	100.0%		100.0%	
Consulting more than one day a week	5.6%	2.2%	4.6%	26.9%		17.7%	
Base academic salary (average in thousands)	$26.9	$23.1	$25.7	$28.3	$25.5	$26.5	$22.7
Supplemental income (average in thousands)	$3.8	$2.2	$3.3	$7.5	$2.8	$5.1	$1.7
No supplemental income	35.6%	41.3%	37.4%				
Supplemental income exceeding $9,000	9.8%	3.9%	8.0%				

Source: Primary data from National Research Council, Science, Engineering, and Humanities Doctorates in the United States: 1981 Profile (Washington, DC: National Academy Press, 1982).

sample may be biased downward and the results, in turn, underestimated. Nonetheless, the significant differences in reported faculty consulting activity among the samples studied cannot be explained solely by such exclusions and differences in sampling techniques. At the very least, the 37-percent incidence reported by Patton (1980) is more likely to reflect actual consulting activity than the percentages reported by Dillon (1979) and by Lanning (1977); the aggregated 19 percent incidence found in our NRC data, in turn, is more likely to reflect actual academic-year consulting activity for the reasons already stated.

Of all PhD faculty in our 1981 NRC sample (Table 9.3), we also found that only approximately 5 percent consult for more than one day a week; this is comparable with Patton's (1980) earlier 6 percent finding.[6] Of all PhD faculty in our 1981 NRC sample, 68 percent were professors or associate professors, with 65 percent of the science and engineering faculty and 76 percent of the humanities faculty tenured, indicating a mature and experienced group of career faculty. Important from the perspective of society, over 58 percent of all surveyed PhD faculty in colleges and universities devote a "significant proportion" of their professional time and attention to issues of national interest (e.g., energy, health, defense, environmental protection, space, crime prevention, housing, food), with 60 percent of the science and engineering faculty and 55 percent of the humanities faculty so involved. In addition, 75 percent of all the science and engineering faculty and 48 percent of the humanities faculty devote some proportion of their professional work time to research activities, with 25 percent of the total group involved in applied research and 40 percent in basic research.

If we employ multivariate analysis and control for field, rank, type of institution, income, and research activities, our NRC data indicate that *faculty who consult* (1) are more likely to be full professors and at a university; (2) have higher faculty salaries *and* professional gross incomes; (3) are more likely to be in the science and engineering fields, with some subfields such as engineering and computer science more active than others; (4) pay more attention to issues of national interest (e.g., 71 percent of the consulting faculty versus 56 percent for nonconsulting science and engineering faculty); and (5) devote *at least* the same amount of time to research as their nonconsulting colleagues. In short, our NRC data and results are highly consistent with those of Marsh and Dillon (1980), Lanning (1977), and Patton (1980) who found that consultants are *at least* as active in their faculty roles as their peers who do not consult. In addition, our NRC data indicate that consulting faculty appear to be *more attentive* to society's concerns and priorities than their nonconsulting colleagues.

It is important to note here that although consultants have higher average academic salaries than their nonconsulting peers, the percentage of professional work time devoted to consulting by consultants is not related to their base salaries. This is especially important because it indicates that faculty who consult are not motivated to do so primarily for economic reasons. Rather, the highest paid faculty are paid high salaries because they likely are both the highest quality and most experienced faculty, and in fields most in demand by society (in terms of both competitive labor-market salaries and demand for consultants). In short, it appears that the highest paid faculty who are most in demand are not exploiting their consulting options.

Is faculty consulting activity increasing? Contrary to conventional wisdom, our NRC data indicate that from 1975 to 1981 faculty increased their consulting activities, but only in minor ways. Because the 1975 survey included only faculty from the science and engineering fields, we compared those data only with data from the same cohort in 1981. We found that the proportion of science and engineering faculty who consult increased but only from 19.3 percent in 1975 to 20.8 percent in 1981. Moreover, we found an even smaller percentage increase in rate of faculty consulting; only 5.2 percent consulted for more than one day a week in 1975 as compared to 5.6 percent in 1981. These results substantiate and extend the earlier findings of Patton (1980), namely, that the proportion of faculty who consult did not change between 1969 and 1975. Only in the one other, earlier comparison by Dillon (1979) of *two different* surveys conducted in 1962 and 1975 has there been any data-based reference to substantial increases in faculty consulting activity.

Estimated Earnings Beyond University Salaries

A reason frequently cited for the alleged increases in paid consulting activity is the declining economic position of the academic profession over the past decade or so. From 1970–71 to 1980–81, for example, in the United States real faculty salaries declined by almost 21 percent to 79.3 percent of their 1970–71 level, with most of that decline occurring between 1975–76 and 1980–81 (American Association of University Professors, August 1981). During 1981–82, however, most faculty members received salary increases that enabled them, for the first time in almost a decade, to maintain their economic position over the previous year (American Association of University Professors, July–August 1982).

Nonetheless, in light of the results presented in the previous section and in spite of the significant decline in real faculty salaries that occurred during the latter 1970s, it does not appear that more faculty were induced to seek outside professional consulting activities to supplement their university base salaries. Rather, the relatively steady number of faculty members who consult is consistent with our earlier finding that the percentage of professional time devoted to consulting is not related to base salary. Again we can state, and even more affirmatively, that faculty are not motivated to consult primarily for economic reasons.

Just how large a proportion of university base salary is accounted for by supplemental earnings? According to a 1980–81 *Chronicle* survey conducted by John Minter Associates (*Chronicle of Higher Education,* 1981), reported outside income averaged $3,873 or 16.2 percent of base salary. Sources of outside income included research or teaching at other institutions as well as external consulting and other services. Two other studies yielded similar results. Marsh and Dillon (1980) analyzed data from the 1975 Ladd and Lipset survey and found that reported supplemental earnings averaged $2,700 or about 15 percent of base salary. Consulting, as might be expected, was one of two main sources of reported supplemental earnings. Based on comparable survey data collected two years later, Ladd (1978) found that reported outside earnings still averaged about 15 percent of base salary.

Our NRC data also permitted us to examine supplemental income and its relationship to faculty consulting and vitality. As shown in Table 9.3, over 64 percent of science and engineering faculty and 59 percent of humanities faculty supplement their university base salaries with consulting, summer and/or overload teaching, royalties, and the like. (Alternatively and as shown in Table 9.3, it also is important to note that approximately 36 percent and 41 percent of these two faculty groups, respectively, do not receive any supplemental professional income.) In 1981, the average supplemental annual income derived from such professional activities was only $3,800 for science and engineering faculty and $2,200 for humanities faculty. This represents only 12.5 percent of total professional income for science and engineering faculty and 8.8 percent for humanities faculty. When compared directly to base salary, reported supplemental income averaged about 14 percent for the two groups combined. The latter is highly consistent with the results from the earlier surveys reported above (Marsh & Dillon, 1980; Ladd, 1978), namely, that extra professional income averaged about 15 percent of base salary. Again, the consistent pattern of supplemental earnings averaging between 14 and 15 percent of base salary reinforces further our earlier observations concerning the limited relationship between salary level and induced consulting activities.[7]

In addition, less than 10 percent of the science and engineering faculty and 4 percent of the humanities faculty earned more than $9,000 in supplemental earnings that, in turn, represents on average only about one-third of their base salaries. Clearly, the vast majority of faculty is not getting rich from supplemental earnings.

It is important to note that reported salaries and supplemental earnings are not distributed evenly across disciplines or fields. In our NRC data, for example, supplemental earnings account for a much larger proportion of faculty base salary for science and engineering faculty than for humanities faculty.[8] Consistent with these results is the observation that for science and engineering faculty the 1981 median annual salary ($31,300) was significantly lower than for their counterparts in business/industry or the federal government ($40,000). On the other hand, the 1981 median annual salary was significantly higher for humanities faculty ($26,500) than for their colleagues in the private sector ($21,800). (See, for example, Tables 9.1 and 9.2.)

In short, these results and observations indicate a clear economic argument for permissive consulting policies in higher education. When consulting does take place, it is reasonable to assume that it results in a satisfactory economic and professional arrangement for individual faculty members because of its voluntary and consensual nature. In addition, with a 1981 unemployment rate of only 0.8 percent for all PhD scientists and engineers seeking full-time employment in the United States and only another 0.6 percent seeking changes from part-time to full-time employment status (National Research Council, 1982, p. 32), we can safely assume a very tight labor market in which individuals in these fields have employment options. Thus, from the perspective of science and engineering faculty, employment in higher education—with its voluntary consulting options—is a professionally satisfactory trade-off in terms both of opportunities for professional activities and of economic rewards.

From the self-interest perspective of the institution, it is clearly cost-effective to hire science and engineering faculty on an average of at least $9,000 below the market and then "rent" them out (even on an overload basis) for $3,800 or less. This is an especially good bargain when we know from the research literature that such faculty are at *least* as productive as their nonconsulting colleagues (and, in many cases, exhibit even more faculty vitality) and are not shirking their university responsibilities.

From the perspective of agencies in society outside the institution, we know that consulting arrangements result from voluntary agreements. We also can assume that consultants generally are worthy of their marginal revenue product. At least in the United States private sector, financial self-interest would not allow otherwise. By "renting" science and engineering faculty from higher education, outside agencies in society are getting a bargain. They are paying only the marginal cost for such expertise, whereas if they had to hire such individuals full time, they would be required to pay the full average cost of employment for each individual.

Similar arguments can also be put forward for permissive faculty consulting policies for humanities faculty. Again, as in the case of science and engineering faculty, we can assume that consulting results from voluntary agreements and that consultants generally are worthy of their marginal revenue product. It is important to note that in 1981, PhDs in the humanities had a surprisingly low unemployment rate of only 1.5 percent (National Research Council, 1982, p. 58). Even adding those PhDs in the humanities who were seeking changes from part-time to full-time employment status (2.2 percent), their total underemployment plus unemployment rate was only 3.7 percent in 1981. Apparently, employment options existed for PhDs in the humanities, at least until as recently as 1981, although because of salary levels it is very unlikely that most humanities faculty would elect such options. Significant for the economic welfare of PhD humanities faculty is the salary differential reported above, namely, $26,500 for humanities faculty versus $21,800 for their colleagues in the private sector. In short, university and college employment pays a premium of almost $5,000 a year in median salaries.

From a purely economic self-interest perspective, colleges and universities would not have to permit consulting for humanities faculty in order to retain them. In addition, because of the salary differential, with higher education paying the premium, there is some basis for the academic institution truly "renting out" (and "inloading") some of the consulting activities of its humanities faculty. However, the limited participation rate of humanities faculty (only 12 percent), extent of involvement (less than 2.2 percent consult more than one day a week), and size of supplemental income (only $2,200, or less than 8.8 percent of total professional income) probably renders the issue moot. Nevertheless, as in the case of science and engineering faculty, both the research literature and our NRC data indicate that humanities PhD faculty who consult are *at least* as productive as their nonconsulting peers. Given the other noneconomic benefits for faculty vitality that accrue to individual faculty members and their respective institutions as a result of consulting, the trade-off in opportunity costs even for PhD humanities faculty is on average indeed small.

CONCLUSIONS

The question of how academic institutions ought to measure the costs and benefits of faculty consulting has *not* been the focus of this paper. Rather, what we did was to provide new empirical evidence and a taxonomy that should prove useful to academic institutions as they develop guidelines governing outside professional consulting.

Our review of the literature and analysis of recent NRC data suggest that faculty consulting has been overestimated and underappreciated. Observers of faculty consulting too often focus on only the visible costs to the institution. Even then, many such costs appear to be based on misperceptions, tending as they do *not* to recognize the substantial benefits of faculty consulting that also accrue to the individual and the institution — both in terms of pure economics and in terms of faculty vitality.

Our analysis of the NRC data suggests that concern about the increasing nature of faculty consulting is unfounded. First, our analysis indicates that only 20.8 percent of PhD science and engineering faculty and only 12.4 percent of PhD humanities faculty in four-year colleges and universities devote *any* portion of their professional work time to outside consulting during the academic year. These results are surprisingly low, especially when compared with results as high as 37 to 54 percent from previous studies. Second, and contrary to conventional wisdom, our analysis of the NRC data indicates that from 1975 to 1981 science and engineering faculty in four-year colleges and universities increased their consulting activities only in minor ways. Third, from our NRC data reported supplemental income averaged only about 14 percent of base salary for the two faculty groups combined; the latter being highly consistent with the results of other studies. Fourth, faculty do not appear to be highly motivated by economic considerations in their selection and frequency of consulting activities. And finally, our analysis supports and extends previous studies which showed that consulting faculty are more attentive to society's concerns and priorities and are at least as active in their faculty roles on campus as their nonconsulting colleagues.

This paper has only touched some important policy issues. We have suggested, for example, that rational decisions about guidelines for faculty consulting should come to grips not only with the trade-offs between the costs and benefits of faculty consulting but also with recognition of the *full* dimension of the costs and benefits of such consulting. More explicitly defined guidelines governing faculty consulting clearly may be in order, provided such definition does not mean more restrictive policies and procedures. To the contrary, the evidence we have suggests that guidelines for faculty consulting ought to be permissive — but not promiscuous.

NOTES

1. Doubtless this view is consistent with that presented by John Centra (1982), who also draws heavily on Gardner's concepts of renewal and development in discussing the meaning of vitality and its relationship to faculty development.

2. The presumption usually has been that consulting activities take place at the expense of forgone benefits to the institution, with nonconsulting faculty providing the standard against which the regular, on-campus activities of faculty who consult are compared. If, however, faculty who consult are doing so at the expense of forgone leisure time, then the opportunity costs would be borne by the individual and not by the academic institution. The latter has not yet been investigated in the literature, but needs to be.

3. Since the marginal product of labor can be increased by a change in the quality of labor employed, outside consulting by faculty will yield institutional benefits *if* the faculty members enhance their stock of knowledge and experience, and *if* the institution can appropriate some or all of this increase in the marginal product of its faculty to subsequent teaching and research.

4. Thompson (1980), Kirschling (1979), and Lewis and Kellogg (1979) have addressed these issues of specification, measurement, and analysis especially as they relate to comparisons of cost-effectiveness in higher education.

5. The 1975 SDR sample was 62,470 PhDs and the 1981 SDR sample was 63,022 PhDs with an overall sampling rate of 13.5 percent. See National Research Council (1982) for details concerning the methodology and sampling techniques employed in these surveys.

6. As noted by Teague (1982) in his recent survey of written institutional policies dealing with faculty consulting, "one day per week" is the most common maximum amount of institutional time permitted for outside employment by faculty.

7. It is important to note again that all professional supplemental income does not come solely from external consulting, but results from all forms of professional activity including summer teaching and research. Such activities should and can be perceived as natural on-campus extensions of regular faculty work load, but should not be confused with "outside professional consulting" activities. In this regard, our 1981 NRC data (Table 9.3) indicates that faculty who reported no academic-year consulting activity did report professional supplemental income that averaged annually between $1,700 and $2,800. Presumably, this supplemental income came from academic-year overload teaching or summer teaching, research, and consulting activities. These averages account for over 7 percent of base salary for humanities faculty and over 10 percent for faculty in the science and engineering fields as compared to the 15 percent for all faculty as reported in this and other studies (Marsh & Dillon, 1980; Ladd, 1978). Consequently, it is fair to assume that on average, *at the most,* less than half of all supplemental income can be attributed to outside professional consulting during the academic year.

8. Moreover, earnings comparisons are not always based on comparable data. For example, all salary data collected by the American Association of University Professors (AAUP) in conjunction with the National Center for Education Statistics (NCES) reflect average base salaries by rank reported on a 9-month basis, with 12-month earnings converted to their proportional 9-month equivalents. Thus, when faculty earnings are compared to those of other occupations, the former will appear artificially low because they exclude supplemental earnings (e.g., from summer or overload teaching, research, or administrative assignments, and consulting or other services). A similar problem arises when faculty earnings are compared across institutions, depending on whether the data reflect average salaries for *all* faculty members or average salaries for *continuing* faculty members. Since the latter excludes new hires who most likely would be relatively low paid, its results would tend to overstate both average salaries and percentage increases from one year to the next. This problem arises at least annually when AAUP/NCES data are compared with those collected in a survey conducted for *The Chronicle of Higher Education* by John Minter Associates of Boulder, Colorado (see discussion in American Association of University Professors, 1982a).

Chapter 10 | **Maintaining Faculty Vitality Through Collective Bargaining**

William E. Becker, Jr.

Collective bargaining on the part of faculty at four-year institutions of higher education started in 1966 with the organization of the faculty at the United States Merchant Marine Academy. It was not until 1969, however, when faculty at the City University of New York (CUNY) organized, that faculty around the country began to look to the unions as a way to increase their pay and power in institutional governance and personnel decisions. By the mid-1970s, the American Federation of Teachers (AFT), American Association of University Professors (AAUP), and the National Education Association (NEA) were advocating collective bargaining as a viable mechanism for guaranteeing faculty due process in all forms of personnel and governance issues. According to Margaret Schmid (1979, p. 108), "Collective bargaining is simply a logical extension of the ongoing attempts of faculty to assert a reasonable measure of control over their professional careers."

While increases in the economic status and political clout of faculty have been the pots of gold promised by the AFT, AAUP and NEA, not all academics view collective bargaining as a way to fulfill this promise. For example, William B. Boyd, president of Central Michigan University, likened collective bargaining to the Midas touch—"Not that everything it touches turns to gold, but that everything it touches turns rigid."[1] The observation by Joseph Garbarino (1975a) that collective bargaining replaces custom

An earlier version of this paper was presented at the University of Minnesota Symposium on Faculty Vitality, 27 May 1982. Participants in that symposium provided helpful comments. Editorial and research assistance was provided by S. Becker and V. Ollis.

with contract, collegial consensus with majority rule, consultative committees with bargaining teams, and continuous discussion of discrete issues with periodic open-ended constitutional conventions has caused many academics to question whether the vitality of a faculty will be enhanced or impaired by collective bargaining.

This paper provides a review of some of the key issues related to collective bargaining and faculty vitality in higher education. Consideration is given to the following: who has unionized and why; the effect of collective bargaining on institutional change; faculty governance, compensation, and productivity; and alternatives to the collective bargaining model.[2]

WHO HAS UNIONIZED?

Based on the trend of precollege teachers to unionize, early estimates of union growth in higher education gave rise to the belief that by 1980 at least 70 percent of the faculty in higher education would be unionized (Begin, 1979, p. 246). By the start of the 1981–82 school year, only 737 of some 3,000 college and university campuses had recognized union agents; 458 of the unionized ones were public, two-year colleges (see Table 10.1). Except for multicampus institutions such as those of the State University of New York (SUNY), where state law mandated full-system participation, and possibly Rutgers, the University of Hawaii and the University of Florida, no leading research university (such as any of the 50 institutions classified as

TABLE 10.1. Summary of Faculty Bargaining Decisions to Organize, 1981

	Four-Year Institutions			Two-Year Colleges			Grand Totals
	Public	Private	Total	Public	Private	Total	
AAUP	31	31	62	22	1	23	85
AFT	63	27	90	149	7	156	246
NEA	56	17	73	248	3	251	324
AAUP–AFT	26	0	26	1	0	1	27
AAUP–NEA	3	0	3	7	0	7	10
Independent and other	5	8	13	31	1	32	45
TOTALS	184	83	267	458	12	470	737
Bargaining rejected	32	42	74	17	3	20	94

Source: The Chronicle of Higher Education, September 23, 1981, p. 6.

"Research University I" by the Carnegie Commission that are members of the Association of American Universities) had unionized. As of January 1, 1982, only about 25 percent of all faculty members (141,000 faculty members) were working under formal labor agreements with institutions of higher education.[3] Clearly Garbarino's (1974, p. 309) use of the term "creeping unionism" to describe the slow expansion of faculty collective bargaining is most appropriate.

To sort out the factors that have contributed to the growth of unionization of faculty in higher education, it is worthwhile to distinguish the legal, institutional, and socioeconomic variables that seem to affect the acceptance of collective bargaining.

State Laws

The locations (such as Massachusetts, Michigan, New York, New Jersey) of the original or pioneering institutions that accepted collective bargaining suggest the importance of legislation enabling collective bargaining. In particular, Garbarino (1980a, pp. 75–77) shows that in the 22 states and District of Columbia that give faculty the legal right to elect an exclusive bargaining agent, 85 percent of the public institutions of higher education are unionized. In 11 of the 23 jurisdictions, all the public institutions are unionized (see Table 10.2). In states without legislation, no major research institutions have authorized a faculty election of an exclusive bargaining agent. For example, the University of Wisconsin, Indiana University, the University of Illinois, and Ohio State have formally refused union organizers' requests for a faculty vote. Before the statutory requirements became effective in California (on July 1, 1979), the administrations at the 27 unorganized campuses would not authorize union elections. The only states without enabling legislation and where a significant amount of organization has occurred are Ohio, Illinois, and Maryland.

Since 1975, no state except California has passed a public employee, exclusive bargaining law covering faculty in four-year institutions. Given the relationship between the passage of such laws and the level of organization to be found among faculty in the state, it is unlikely that there will be any great expansion of faculty unions in the foreseeable future. Furthermore, even if additional laws are passed, it does not appear that the higher quality, public institutions and the prestigious private institutions of higher education are going to quickly adopt collective bargaining.[4] The mere existence of state laws that mandate faculty-requested elections does not appear to influence faculty desire for collective bargaining. Faculty elections at the University of Minnesota (Twin Cities campus), Michigan State, University of Pittsburgh, University of California (Berkeley), Pennsylvania State, Oregon State, and University of Colorado ended in "no union" votes.

TABLE 10.2. Bargaining Status of Public Institutions, 1979

	Number of Institutions	
	Organized	Unorganized
States with bargaining laws and 100% organization:		
Connecticut (5), Delaware (2), Florida (9), Hawaii (2), Maine (7), Massachusetts (15), New Jersey (13), New York (37), Rhode Island (2), South Dakota (7), District of Columbia (3)	102	0
States with bargaining laws, less than 100% organization:		
Alaska (0-2), California (0-29), Iowa (1-2), Kansas (1-5), Michigan (9-3), Minnesota (7-1), Montana (4-1), Nebraska (4-3) New Hampshire (1-2), Oregon (3-5), Pennsylvania (16-2), Vermont (3-1) Excluding California	49 (49)	56 (27)
States without bargaining laws, with organization:		
Ohio (3-9), Illinois (5-7), Maryland (1-9)	9	25

Source: Joseph W. Garbarino, "Faculty Unionism: The First Ten Years," The Annals of the American Academy, March 1980, p. 76.

Table 10.1 shows that at private, four-year institutions 42 of 125 elections (34 percent) ended in "no union" votes, while on public, four-year college and university campuses the number of rejections was only 32 out of 216 elections (15 percent). Clearly, forces other than the mere existence of a statutory requirement affect union voting behavior.

Private Versus Public Institutions

The number of faculty union elections in the United States has fallen steadily since 1975. But until 1980, the percentage of faculty acceptances had been rising at private colleges and universities while decreasing at public institutions. Thus, prior to the United States Supreme Court decision in the Yeshiva case—which found Yeshiva University to be a "mature" private university where faculty share in the governance of the institution — private colleges and universities were viewed as strong candidates for collective bargaining. Subsequent to this February 1980 Supreme Court decision, some 40 similar cases have been brought before the National Labor Relations Board (NLRB), but only a few have been resolved. From the cases which have been resolved by NLRB, it is clear that faculty at private universities are not automatically considered to be managers.

For example, in the case of Bradford College, the NLRB found that full authority and responsibility for administration was delegated to the president by the trustees, who have overall control of the private college. Since faculty did not participate in collegial governance, the board ruled that they were not managerial employees and thus were entitled to vote on collective bargaining representation. It issued a similar ruling in a case involving physicians at Montefiore Hospital and Medical Center who are also faculty members at the Albert Einstein College of Medicine of Yeshiva University. In the Montefiore case the NLRB noted that the physicians were primarily concerned with patient care and not academic matters; each is primarily associated with a hospital and only secondarily with an educational institution. In the cases of Ithaca College, Thiel College, and the Duquesne University law school, the NLRB found that faculty were managerial employees and thus were not entitled to collective bargaining under the National Labor Relations Act.[5]

In the case-by-case decisions that the NLRB is making, it is not yet clear which characteristic of a faculty will make it nonmanagerial under the National Labor Relations Act and, therefore, entitle its members to form a union and negotiate with their institution. Thus, while the Supreme Court decision in the case of Yeshiva University will clearly limit the future unionization of faculty at private colleges, the extent of that limitation is not yet predictable.

Reorganization

The greatest catalyst to unionization is often given as conflict between a president and the faculty over reorganization of the institution. In the case of large state institutions, it was the reorganization of these institutions into a single, multicampus system that supposedly gave rise to unionization because of the impersonal and bureaucratic way that faculty felt they would be or were being treated in the new structure. For example, Begin (1979, pp. 248–250) reports that it was the 1966 reorganization of higher education in New Jersey that caused faculty to lobby for legislation and establish a union at Rutgers.

Changes in the structure and function of higher education institutions may have been an important factor at the early stages in the collective bargaining movement, but the importance of such changes appears to have vanished with the passage of time. For example, all the well-established public universities were organized as part of state multi-campus systems prior to 1976. Furthermore, the only instances where older and well-established institutions developed as single campuses are the universities of Connecticut, Rhode Island, Delaware and Rutgers. If concern over centralization and system-wide bureaucratic decision making were of such concern to faculty, then surely more traditional and well-established campuses would have organized as single units. Garbarino (1975a, 1980) has stated that single units of major universities are the least likely to organize. The impetus for organization usually comes from the newer and less prestigious campuses of a university system. At these newer campuses there is no history or tradition of faculty-administrator interaction and cooperation.

Union Opposition

The oldest and most prestigious institutions of higher education in the United States have been characterized historically by an administrative structure built on academic units (departments). Faculty members move through the ranks, and over the years they may become involved in departmental and college governance. Administrators are selected from departmental lines as opposed to peripheral service or support areas. Administrators view themselves as part of an academic department and may plan on returning to the department after their days of administrating are over. Informal lines of communication are thus maintained between administrators and faculty. Administrative decisions tend to be made by consensus, for to ignore the wishes of even a minority of faculty could create difficulties in a current administrator's later academic career. At institutions with traditional governance structures, faculty as individuals are not afraid to make their feelings known to administrators because they are colleagues.

Calls for unionization at the more prestigious or oldest institutions can be traced to a change in the structure of governance that has been imposed on or accepted by the faculty. For example, of the 100 oldest colleges in the United States, only 8 appear to have a single legal bargaining agent. Of these, 3 are junior colleges where administrators now have minimal academic credentials. The remaining 5 are now part of large systems where college and departmental control were captured by an outside administration that wanted or at least did not oppose collective bargaining. The State University of New York's Potsdam and New Paltz colleges were established in 1816 and 1828, but today are part of a 30-campus system that is centrally controlled. In the case of Rutgers (founded in 1766), Nelson (1982, p. 10) claims that faculty were encouraged by the university president to vote for the AAUP as an exclusive bargaining agent. Ohio does not have enabling legislation, yet the administration at the University of Cincinnati (founded in 1819) authorized a faculty election possibly to increase the centralization of the decision-making process or to cover its own inadequacies. At few if any of the 737 campuses that are unionized was there a strong incentive for a faculty group to oppose the organizational movement, since the faculty had already lost its historical power and its link with the administrators.[6]

Where administrators view themselves as academics and faculty view themselves as individual research or teaching entrepreneurs, there is a strong incentive for administrators and faculty groups to oppose collective bargaining, inasmuch as by definition collective bargaining makes administrators management and faculty employees. On the other hand, where administrators do not consider themselves academics, there is a strong incentive for faculty to form unions and for administrators to encourage or at least not object to such a move. A weak administration is always further ahead with a faculty that is unionized, because such an administration can always blame the union for any deterioration in productivity or working relationships that might develop. Where state law enabled the unions to call for a faculty vote (e.g., Minnesota, Michigan, California, Pennsylvania, Oregon), the unions were defeated on the most prestigious public campuses. A reason for these defeats can be traced to faculty members who joined together and formed "antiunion groups" to counter the union organizers. Where such groups were not encouraged by administrators or not formed by the leading academics on a campus, the union organizers have had a monopoly on the dissemination of information.

Economic Status

The 1969 unionization of CUNY faculty brought collective bargaining in higher education to national attention. The first CUNY contract provided for a salary schedule with a maximum salary of slightly more than $31,000. In 1970 dollars, the CUNY salary schedule was relatively high. The national publicity given to the CUNY salary scale suggested that collective bargaining was responsible. Early studies of the effect of unions on salaries (Birnbaum, 1974, 1976) added to the belief that unionization would raise salaries by 8 to 9 percent over what they would be in the absence of collective bargaining.

While some academic writers assert that faculty desire for higher compensation is of secondary importance in voting for unions, surely the early salary gains allegedly caused by the unions did not slow the unionization movement. Furthermore, the formalization of the salary determination process and the union organizers' promise to remove differentials between disciplines and ranks must have been appealing to those faculty at the lower end of the faculty schedule. The union's promises for the establishment of "equitable" and "fair" salary schedules with merit money allocated on the basis of standards must have also appealed to some faculty at the higher end of the schedule.

In summary, the low level of faculty unionization in states without enabling legislation suggests that additional growth in collective bargaining at public institutions of higher learning will not move forward at a rapid pace unless additional laws are passed. Given that the legislature's support for public employee bargaining has declined in most states, the passage of additional enabling laws seems unlikely at this time. (For example, in Washington, Wisconsin, and Indiana, the extension of collective bargaining laws to cover all postsecondary faculty has been an issue for years, yet such legislation has never been passed.) At private colleges and universities the Supreme Court decision in the Yeshiva case will probably slow the growth rate of unionization. Furthermore, unless the unions are successful in organizing more of the established and prestigious large schools in states with existing legislation, it is difficult to see how rapid growth in unionization can be obtained. As long as faculty at the prestigious and established institutions enjoy relatively high salaries and better working conditions (in terms of lower teaching loads with superior students, better office facilities and clerical support, and ample funds for leaves and travel) and as long as the administration at these institutions is supportive of faculty activities, there is little reason to expect that faculty unionization will occur at these quality institutions.

THE EFFECT OF FACULTY BARGAINING

The general institutional effects of collective bargaining in higher education are agreed upon by many reviewers of the existing literature. However, the consequences of these changes are disputed by these scholars. Whether faculty power, productivity, and pay are enhanced or retarded by unionization is a hotly debated issue. In this section, the recent literature related to the consequences of faculty collective bargaining will be reviewed; emphasis will be given to an assessment of the effects of unionization on institutional change and on faculty influence in governance; issues of faculty compensation and productivity will also be considered.

Institutional Change

Four general trends in higher education, which began with its rapid expansion in the 1960s, have been identified by numerous scholars. These trends are: (1) the growing centralization of decision making with decision-making power going to nonacademics, (2) the decay in faculty participation and influence through university senates, (3) the increasing formalization or bureaucratization of administrative processes, and (4) a greater concern with due process in the equal treatment of all individuals. Because these trends preceded the advent of unions on the higher education scene and because all of these issues relate to goals of unions, it is difficult to estimate or factor out the effect of unionization in these areas. As Garbarino (1980a, p. 82) states, faculty unions have tended to reinforce existing trends in higher education. The unionization of faculty neither caused nor reversed these trends.

Centralization of decision making. As public institutions of higher education expanded in the 1960s, coordination and duplication became major issues facing state legislatures. Following the industrial mode of management in this country, large systems were created; decision making moved from the campus to the headquarters of the system. The speed of movement of decision-making power toward the administration was increased by the financial problems many state systems had in the 1970s. Hiring, promotion, and curriculum decisions that were once made by departments moved to the dean's or campus vice-president's office. Budget and planning decisions that were once made by the deans' offices moved to the campus vice-president's office. Final budget and program authority once in the hands of the chief campus administrator moved to the system's presidential office or to a system coordinating board. Management specialists and bureaucrats, with no special experience in research or higher education operations, replaced many academics in the decision-making process. As Minter and Bowen (1982a and b) demonstrate, the fastest-growing budget area in higher education has been in noninstructional areas. The faculty's feeling of loss in power is real, and it is not surprising that faculty unions developed as a way of signaling and regaining "the power of the teaching cadres over the massive, universal system of higher education" (Light, 1974, p. 21).

Unfortunately, instead of returning power to the faculty and reducing the level of centralization, collective bargaining tends to speed up the process of bureaucratization and centralization. As noted earlier, the only instances where traditional, state university campuses voted to form unions as single campuses are the universities in Connecticut, Rhode Island, Delaware, and New Jersey. Where there is a system-wide union, power is not vested in the hands of the majority on one campus; the wishes of the voting faculty majority for the entire system are what the union leaders heed. Supporting the earlier research, Lienemann and Bullis's (1980) survey results from twelve unionized campuses in four states (Florida, New York, Minnesota, and Illinois) suggest:

Collective bargaining changed influence relationships in systemwide public university settings. A measurable shift in influence or power was observed from on-campus decision making levels to those off-campus. Three sets of on-campus decision makers (department faculty, faculty governance, and chairpersons/deans) lost influence over decisions as a result of bargaining; one (central administration) gained slightly. The greatest decline in influence occurred at the levels of department faculty and faculty governance. Central administration gained influence over five decision making areas, but lost influence over faculty workload/assignment of duties and, more pointedly, over salary decisions. (p. 22)

Unionization implies an increase of nonacademics in key decision-making positions. For example, the 1975 Purdue University Presidential Committee on Collective Bargaining concluded that the process of collective bargaining would require the following labor relations staff:

1. Vice-president for personnel affairs.
2. Attorney (negotiation/contract specialist).
3. Professional negotiators.
4. Clerical/secretarial assistants.
5. Computer scientist.
6. Research and model-building personnel.

The additional annual cost, in 1974 dollars, to Purdue for this nonacademic staff, and related incidental resource commitments, was estimated to be between $115,000 and $250,000 for negotiation and contract administration. This amount for collective bargaining cost would be added to almost any large institution's administrative budget. Because of the specialties needed, it is safe to assume that the personnel for these positions would not come from academic lines; the dollars, however, might. Thus, collective bargaining can be expected to result in an added impetus to centralize decision making and push the decision making further from the faculty and into the hands of nonacademics. This conclusion was best summarized by Baldridge (1982a):

Many factors challenge and undermine single-campus bargaining. While bargaining seems more collegial and adoptable on single campuses, pressures abound to force single campuses into large university systems and to amalgamate the union into massive bargaining units. Ironically, the advent of bargaining may itself be an incentive to the 'recentralization' of administrative power and authority. Collective bargaining also encourages an 'invasion of the technocrats' in which the traditional model of academics participating in governance gives way to the development of specialized personnel to interpret and administer contracts. (p. 9A)

University senates and faculty governance.   At the early stages of the union movement in higher education, many scholars warned that traditional forms of faculty self-governance, through faculty-dominated university senates, would be destroyed by the exclusivity clause in most union contracts. In fact, many universities warned faculty that if the faculty voted for a union then the university could not recognize the traditional faculty senate as a participant in the decision-making process. Just recently the University of Minnesota attempted to remove faculty on the Duluth campus from the university senate because that campus is now represented by an exclusive union agent. As Kemerer and Baldridge (1981), Begin (1979), and others have pointed out, however, in most cases faculty senates have not died or been negatively affected when faculty voted for a union representative.

At some institutions, such as CUNY and Rutgers, some faculty claim the union has strengthened the senate by forcing the administration to deal with it on academic matters. The union has restricted its domain to working conditions, due process issues and compensation matters. At Rutgers, according to Nelson (1982, p. 11), the union has supported and enhanced the powers of the senate. For example, in 1977 when the president of Rutgers attempted to narrow the scope of senate issues by declaring that "anything in collective bargaining or litigation or not specifically identified as senate business was not a subject for senate consideration," the AAUP local union supposedly carried out a difficult negotiation to resolve this bargaining conflict. Similarly, according to Polishook (1982, pp. 16–17), in a bitter 1972 and 1973 contract battle, when the CUNY president supposedly tried to restrict faculty participation in governance, the union argued on behalf of the senate to get the contract to specify that "the rights, and privileges, and responsibilities of the University Faculty Senate shall not be diminished during the terms of this agreement." Thus, what the union achieved was not assignment of governance rights to itself, but the preservation of existing faculty rights to participate in governance through the university senate.

While both Nelson's and Polishook's accounts testify to how faculty unions and senates can coexist, they point out one of the ironies of unionization. After a faculty unionizes, the union may have to spend a lot of time, money and faculty energy to regain what the faculty had prior to unionizing. Furthermore, in the case of most faculty senates, the only thing the union is fighting to maintain is the faculty's ability to advise the administration, since faculty senates have never had final decision-making authority. It is also worth pointing out, as participants at the 1981 Wingspread conference on collective bargaining learned, for every Rutgers or CUNY situation of relatively peaceful existence between a faculty union and senate there is a Massachusetts or SUNY-Buffalo story of union agents trying to enjoin the faculty senate from meeting and open warfare between the senate and union. Kemerer and Baldridge's (1981) work also suggests that if unions cannot win large economic gains for their members, they will move into governance issues as a way of justifying their existence.[7]

Formalization of administrative processes.   If there is one area where most writers agree on the effects of unionization, it is in regard to the formalization of procedures for making decisions. See, for example, Garbarino (1980a, pp. 82–83) and Baldridge (1982a, p. 9A). This point should not be surprising, inasmuch as the reason for drawing up a written contract is to ensure standardization of personnel policies. In the absence of a written contract, deviations from an implicit or explicit personnel policy are possible. Such flexibility may give the appearance of arbitrariness or may, in fact, reflect a sloppy situation. The collective bargaining contract will bring an immediate appearance of order in personnel practices. "Fairness," "equality," and "justice" in personnel practices are defined in the negotiation process and rigid procedures are prescribed and followed religiously in all personnel practices.

The legal necessity of equal application of these procedures to all cases (and the possibility of outside review of decisions made) forces the institution to demand extensive documentation on every decision made. Lienemann and Bullis (1980, p. 12) found in their survey of faculty on twelve unionized campuses: "Forty-six percent of the persons interviewed felt that bargaining had increased their paperwork, while only slightly more than one percent felt it had decreased" (p. 12). In addition, Lienemann and Bullis report that respondents frequently noted that the arrival of unionization resulted in an increase in time spent in meetings, both those required by the institution and those added by the union.

While there are benefits in the standardization that collective bargaining brings to an institution (the semblance of order, the availability of information on how and why decisions were made), there are also costs to the institution and to individual faculty members as well. An institution that signs a contract is locked into the conditions of that contract for the life of the contract. Such rigidity implies that the institution cannot respond to changing market conditions rapidly. The implication of additional resources directed to monitor and comply with the contract is that some administrative and faculty time once spent in academic pursuits is now lost. Possibly the most significant cost, however, is that adherence to procedures, as opposed to concern about performance, may lead to the protection of incompetence.

Due process and the protection of the individual.   While most writers on collective bargaining in higher education emphasize the job protection and due process protection that unions bring to their members, few acknowledge the way that collective bargaining reduces the freedom of those individuals who do not accept the primacy of the union. Unions do protect the individual who is treated in the manner that is contrary to the written letter of a contract. They ensure that due process provisions are negotiated to protect faculty rights, but only to the extent that those rights do not threaten the security of the bargaining agent. For example, even at the early stages of the union movement, a 1974 contract study by Baruch National Center for the Study of Collective Bargaining in Higher Education showed that slightly more than 16 percent of all four-year contracts contained some form of union security provision in the form of a closed agency shop. All contracts attempt to provide for at least an exclusive bargaining right.

Because of union influence, few faculty members have attempted to fight the unions on their desire to have security provisions. There are exceptions, however. At the University of Massachusetts, where the NEA lobbied through the legislature a state law requiring nonunion members to pay an agency fee, the NEA contract with the university specifies this fee to be equal to union dues. In 1981, the NEA sought to have five tenured faculty members fired for refusing to pay this fee unless the NEA disclosed how these fees would be spent. At Ferris State College in Michigan, four faculty members were threatened with firing for failure to pay an agency fee. Three eventually paid and one resigned (Kemerer and Baldridge, 1975). Other examples of such infringement of unions on tenured individuals' rights can be observed at Minnesota and Michigan institutions (Begin, 1979, p. 287).

The protection of some individuals' rights through the due process agreements that are negotiated by unions have come at the expense of other faculty members' previously obtained tenure rights and academic freedoms. The assessment of the net effect on faculty vitality is a question of the values attached to the two sides of the issue. Is a community of scholars made better off when previously held and specific individual rights are sacrificed to secure the future of the exclusive agent representing the faculty, or when the individual's rights are acknowledged at the possible cost of the agent and the faculty represented?

Compensation and Productivity

One of the major reasons for unionizing has always been to raise the economic status of those represented by the union agent. This goal has been accomplished in the industrial world by raising the average level of compensation while making the terms of individual wage assignment more "equitable" and "fair." The question to be raised here is whether or not faculty unions in higher education can raise the average level of unionized faculty compensation and at the same time make the salary distribution within an institution more "equitable." Consideration will also be given in this section to the effect on faculty academic performance that can be expected to result from any change in the method by which faculty are remunerated.

Levels of compensation.   Until recently, the literature on the effect of faculty unions on relative wages was interpreted by reviewers to "produce mixed results as to union impact, but most estimates fall within a range of 0 to 10 percent" (Begin 1979, p. 263). In particular, Begin's review of the pre-1978 literature states:

> Some of the articles (Birnbaum, 1974, 1976; Morgan & Kearney, 1977) identify a union wage impact. Birnbaum (1976) in a study of fifty matched pairs of union and nonunion four year institutions found a positive union differential of $1,500 (8.1 percent). Morgan & Kearney (1977) in a study of forty-six pairs of matched four year institutions found an average union effect of $625. In a regression analysis using salary changes from 1969–1970 to 1974–1975 as the dependent variable, the union-nonunion variable was the largest predictor (Morgan & Kearney, 1977). Some of the recent studies report a lessening (Birnbaum, 1977) or insignificant effect. (Brown & Stone 1977, p. 163)

Since Begin's review, several additional studies of the union impact of relative salaries have become available. Those newer studies, together with the studies cited by Begin, clearly suggest that while the faculty who organized early may have benefited from unionization such gains may no longer exist. For example, Leslie and Hu (1977a), using the Morgan and Kearney matched pairs data and regression analysis and incorporating many of the new questions raised by Brown and Stone, extended the 1974–75 salary data to include 1975–76. They found that while faculty at the unionized institutions continued to enjoy slightly larger salaries, their early advantage declined considerably.

After learning that the original Morgan and Kearney matched pairs data had mistakes in the way some institutions were classified, Leslie and Hu (1977b) repeated their study and found that the direction of the original findings was correct, but the direction of union advantage varied considerably when the duration of bargaining was considered. For the 1974–75 data, the size of the union compensation advantage was positively related to length of time unionized. Most recently, Guthrie-Morse, Leslie, and Hu (1981) report that for the 1970–78 period

> the nonunionized faculty achieved larger (unadjusted) salary gains than did the unionized faculties: $7,854 versus $7,704. . . . When the data are adjusted to reflect local cost of living differences between the union and nonunion samples, the performance of the union is further questioned. In each of the eight years, the average nonunion compensation was higher than the union average [$455 more for the nonunion]. (p. 242)

In addition, their regression analysis of salary determination showed that "although the union variable is significant in 1974–75, the year Morgan and Kearney studied, in all other years this is not the case" (p. 246).

They also observed that the organizational longevity effect, which Leslie and Hu (1977b) observed, was probably limited: "Relative compensation gains from bargaining in higher education tend to increase for several years and then probably begin to decline thereafter" (p. 248).

Another matched pairs study by Marshall (1979) examined campuses that entered into collective bargaining agreements in the 1971–73 period. Her comparison of the matched thirty union and thirty nonunion campuses terminated with 1976–77 data. She concluded, "There is little, if any difference between salary increases at union and nonunion institutions." She also noted that "as reported salary data becomes more recent, the relationship between salary increases and unionization declines" (p. 318).

Although somewhat dated, given the Guthrie-Morse, Leslie, and Hu (1981) study, the most comprehensive study of the effect of unionization on faculty salaries is that of Freeman (1978). Freeman used all reported AAUP data on compensation by rank for the period 1970–71 to 1976–77. After controlling for initial differences in compensation levels of unionized and nonunionized institutions and other school characteristics, Freeman showed in regression analysis that the direct impact of unionization on faculty compensation was not highly significant. There was, however, a slight, positive effect associated with the number of years organized. Freeman stated, "While it would be wrong to extrapolate the log-linear form beyond the period under study, as the effect of years organized is likely to level off as the variable increases, the results suggest much larger effects for schools that have been organized longer, with little or no union impact for those organized in recent years" (p. 19). On this point, Freeman's findings were consistent with Marshall's and Leslie and Hu's. If Freeman's sample had included salary data through 1977–78, we can only speculate as to whether or not he would have found the 1974–75 "peaking" of unionized salary increases, as found by Guthrie-Morse, Leslie, and Hu (1981).

The question of why faculties at institutions that unionized early in the 1970s may have received some general compensation benefit from unionizing, at least up to 1975, while faculties at institutions that organized more recently generated little if any, has not been resolved. If this observation reflects the fact that unions are able to win gains as time passes, then in the "long run" there may be some financial benefit to organizing. Given that the early studies as cited by Begin (1979) showed a union effect, while the later studies that covered the same time period and institutions as the earlier studies plus additional observations show little or no effect, the premise of long-run benefit seems doubtful.[8] On the other hand, if this observation is the result of greater potential for gains to those who organized first, or if it reflects a weakened academic market place, or if it is caused by nonunionized institutions increasing their faculty salaries to ward off the union organizer, there may be no general financial benefit to future organizing.[9]

Finally, it is interesting that while unions have had little if any effect generally in raising unionized faculty salaries relative to nonunionized faculty salaries, they do appear to have had differential effects at various types of institutions. For example, Guthrie-Morse, Leslie, and Hu (1981) reported that in their matched school study, using compensation data for each year from 1970–71 through 1977–78, unionization seems to have had a big effect on salaries at private and nonuniversity type, four-year institutions; they conclude:

> Unionism seems to yield relatively more, in terms of faculty compensation, in private than in public institutions. This supports the findings of nearly all previous work. It is also confirmed that it is the least complex colleges, those offering only the baccalaureate or the equivalent, that show the greatest union yield. Furthermore, it would appear that lesser complexity and private control interact to yield major, union compensation gains. (p. 252)

The idea that major public research/teaching universities do not benefit from unionization is further supported by Shively and Swan (1981). Their salary study of all AAUP "Type I" universities from 1970–71 to 1979–80, shows that faculty at "Type I" unionized campuses "received increases in compensation which were about equal to the national average for 'Type I' university faculty." They conclude, based on their study and the more general literature, that "unionization does not bring gains in compensation for university faculty" (p. 6).

It seems fair to infer that while the early unionization of faculty may have benefited some faculty, the later unionization of faculty has not. Faculty that may still benefit from unionization are those in private, small college settings. At this time, it does not appear that faculty at the major public research/teaching universities would reap immediate or even long-run financial benefits by organizing.

Distribution of compensation. While it does not appear that unionization greatly affects the level of average faculty salaries, relative to nonunion average faculty salaries, there is evidence that unionization does affect the distribution of salaries. This outcome should not be surprising since both "cognitive dissonance theory" and "equity theory" suggest that when individuals feel they are being treated unfairly, relative to the way others are being treated, or when they are receiving compensation that does not reflect their average contribution, they will unionize to correct the situation. In particular, if an institution has a merit-based pay system and individuals feel that the system is unfair, they may unionize to impose better screening of the performance on which merit money is allocated. If individuals feel that performance can never be measured precisely, they may unionize to get everyone an equal share of the wage pool.

The problem in establishing a priori why faculty might want to unionize can be seen in the two types of compensation redistribution that faculty might hope to achieve through unionization. Relatively high producers and "stars" might expect the union to improve and standardize the criteria on which merit money or cost of living money is allocated. As Becker (1979) has shown, they may want this because a system based on perfect screening of performance would increase the remuneration of all those above the modal performance level. Under perfect screening, high producers would no longer have to share their product with the low producers. On the other hand, those below the mean salary may argue that since a perfect screening method cannot be found, the union should negotiate an equitable method of establishing salaries in which all individuals with the same job classification are paid the same.

Clearly, "fairness" and "equity" mean different things to different people. In the process of voting for a union agent, it is to the organizers' advantage to use such words but never define them quantitatively. After a union agent has been established, however, it is impossible for both a meritocracy and an egalitarian pay system to exist simultaneously. Because unions supposedly make decisions on the basis of majority rule, one or the other type of salary determination process will come to dominate or the union contracts will reflect the unstable equilibrium caused by the membership search for the pay system by which the majority benefit. In the industrial world, the egalitarian pay schedule has come to dominate union contracts. In the entertainment and sports world, a two-tier system has emerged where the stars take care of themselves and the second class actors and players share relatively equally in the residuals. It is too early to tell what type of pay schedule will emerge in the unionized institutions of higher education but there is some indication that it may be the egalitarian type pay scale that emerges.

Begin (1979, p. 268) stated: "Merit does live in faculty contracts to reward the 'stars' despite expectations to the contrary." To support this conclusion, he cited work by the National Center for the Study of Collective Bargaining in Higher Education (1975) that showed that 18 of the 41 (46 percent) four-year institution contracts it reviewed did reference and provide for merit pay and only 1 prohibited such payments. Similarly, Bognanno, Estenson, and Suntrup (1977) found that of the 61 four-year institution agreements they considered, just less than half contained merit provisions.

Guthrie-Morse, Leslie and Hu's (1981) matched pairs study also indicates that less than half of the 30 unionized institutions they surveyed "considered merit in the awarding of salary increases, whereas nearly three-fourths of the nonunion institutions did" (p. 250). More interesting, however, is the observation that "the unionized institutions experienced many more changes in their salary procedures between 1968 and 1978 than did the nonunion institutions." Possibly these changes reflect the conflict between those looking for a more precise and universally acceptable way to measure academic performance and those wishing an equal distribution in the absence of such perfection. The idea that the egalitarians are winning is suggested by Guthrie-Morse, Leslie, and Hu's observation concerning the relative number of unionized institutions that have given up the idea of merit pay: "Fewer union institutions utilized the merit principle in awarding salary increases in 1978 than had done so in 1968. The figures were nearly constant in the nonunion sector" (p. 250). Furthermore, the union's efforts to preserve jobs, possibly at the expense of promotions based on merit, is somewhat supported by the Guthrie-Morse, Leslie, and Hu observation regarding the change in tenured faculty at the unionized versus the nonunionized institutions. "In 1974–75, tenure had been achieved by 53 percent of unionized faculty members and 57 percent of nonunionized faculty members. By 1977–78 the pattern had been reversed and the union tenure rate exceeded the nonunion rate by 3 percent, for a net gain of 7 percent" (pp. 249–250). While merit may live in faculty union contracts, it appears that it may be moribund.

Screening for productivity. The importance of merit based promotion and pay structures to faculty academic performance was demonstrated by Becker (1979). By assuming a faculty member receives satisfaction from academic accomplishments and that those accomplishments are of value to and rewarded by the employing university but that they are not measured precisely, Becker demonstrates within a specific model of professorial behavior that:

a. If the faculty member is above the modal academic accomplishment level in the distribution of such outputs, then a decrease (increase) in the employer's intensity of screening of this output will result in a decrease (increase) in this scholar's desire to produce the given output. (If he/she is below the mode, then behavioral changes are indeterminate.)
b. If screening is relatively precise, then changes in the merit, or income determination, weight given an academic accomplishment or output will produce like changes in the faculty member's desire to produce that output. (If the screening process is highly inaccurate, then the effect of changing merit weights is indeterminate.) (p. 1010)

While it is always dangerous to make real-world predictions on purely theoretical constructs, the implications of these theoretical results seem quite clear when applied to the faculty productivity effects resulting from a union-negotiated elimination of merit pay increases. The introduction of an egalitarian faculty union that negotiates the reduction of screening and merit pay in an institution will cause faculty members at the high end of the academic output distribution to reduce their productivity as the recognition of their contribution to the university is diminished.

Whether or not a given faculty would desire a merit-based pay system or an egalitarian pay system can be decided by considering the distribution of faculty output. For simplicity, assume that there is a unique, continuous, and unimodal distribution of faculty output. The position of any given faculty member in this distribution is not known to the university. In the absence of any screening, the university would have to label all faculty members as being equally productive. With the exception of the truly average member, all faculty members are incorrectly labeled. To exhaust the university product, all faculty would receive the mean faculty product value regardless of actual contributions to total output. The high producers in the university subsidize the low producers.

If, after a review of faculty performance, the university determined there are three identifiable ranges of faculty contribution, it would label faculty members as low, medium, or high. The university can pay each professor according to the mean product value for the group to which he or she is assigned. However, all professors receiving one of these individual labels need not be equally productive. As before, some may be at the high end of the now shortened productivity range of the three separate groupings and some may be at the low end. For example, let Distribution A in Figure 10.1 be the unknown but true faculty productivity distribution. Those getting a low label L^* could actually be of quality as high as $(L + E)$ or as low as quality $(L - E)$, where E is the error in measurement. Those at the high and low ends of each group range are still mislabeled and incorrectly paid, although not as badly as when there was no screening. Iteratively, through yet more intensive screening, the university could continue to reduce the measurement error. As long as there was some measurement error, however, those below the modal output (as at point L in Figure 10.1) can expect to be grouped with more who are better than worse. (For example, in Figure 10.1 the frequency of $L + E$ is greater than the frequency of $L - E$.) For those above the mode, just the reverse is true. Thus, with less than perfect screening, those with output below the mode can expect to get more than their true product value; those above the mode can expect to get less.

To put the argument in perspective, whether or not an individual professor desires no screening, as would be possible under an egalitarian union contract, or some screening, where the possibility of mislabeling is real, can depend on the individual's sense of his or her position in the output distri-

FIGURE 10.1. Academic Output Distributions

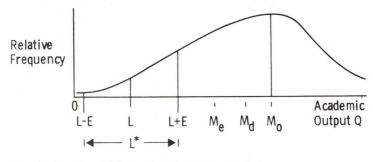

Distribution A – Distribution skewed to the left

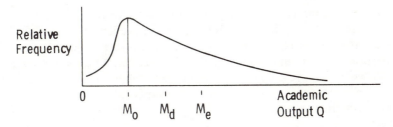

Distribution B – Distribution skewed to the right

bution. For simplicity, it is perhaps best to explain this by considering the actions of the median professor in the cohort (whose behavior is character-istic of those in the fiftieth percentile of the distribution). Where there is no screening, the professor actually producing at the median output level (M_d) could expect to receive, and would receive, the total faculty average or mean salary (M_e). If the actual output distribution is skewed left of the modal salary (M_o, see Figure 10.1, Distribution A), then there is no financial rea-son for the median professor to vote for a union advancing the egalitarian idea of no screening, for this would lower his or her relative salary to the average. If the actual output distribution is skewed right of the modal salary (M_o, see Figure 10.1, Distribution B), then the greatest financial gain that the median producer could enjoy would be obtained by voting for an egalitarian union; its no-screening policies would tend to raise his or her salary to the mean. In fact, as is evident from Figure 10.2, the highest salary achievable by the median professor in a right-skewed distribution is where no screening is employed.

FIGURE 10.2.   Income and Screening Levels
                for Median Faculty Member
                in Right Skewed Output Distribution

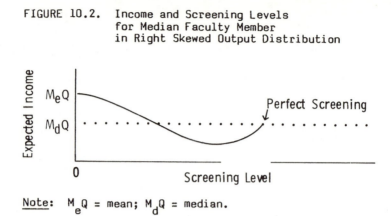

Note: M_eQ = mean; M_dQ = median.

Figure 10.2 indicates how the expected salary of the median professor in a right-skewed distribution would change as the level of screening is increased. At a zero screening level, the expected income would be the total distribution average and would exceed the median. But, as the screening process becomes more accurate through successive divisions of the cohort to obtain precise output-reward linkages, the expected salary falls below the median and then moves back up to it again as perfect screening is approached.

If the university was unionized, but was successful in excluding any discussion of the removal of a merit system, then for a right-skewed output distribution the union would argue for better and more precise methods of screening. As long as the union cannot negotiate away the merit system, the majority of faculty members (those above the mode in a right-skewed output distribution) are better off with a more precise screening method than with a slightly less precise screening method. However, in a right-skewed output distribution there are also a majority of faculty below the mean who could get maximum salaries if the merit system were completely removed and no screening took place. This majority can be expected to continue to pressure the union leaders to try to negotiate the removal of the merit system. Thus, under unionization, where faculty can negotiate how salaries are determined, there may be no stable equilibrium in terms of the process by which salaries are determined.

As already noted, Guthrie-Morse, Leslie, and Hu (1981, p. 250) found that unionized institutions experienced more changes during a decade of negotiation than did nonunion institutions. This finding is consistent with our theoretical predictions. Furthermore, since the majority of faculty in a right-skewed distribution will get the maximum compensation under an egalitarian pay system, it is not surprising that the unionized institutions are beginning to move slowly toward the complete removal of merit pay. Unfortunately, Becker's model of professorial behavior suggests that if screening of faculty is reduced, the high producers will either cut back on their academic productivity or leave the unionized institution. If the institution's wage pool is in fact determined, at least in part, on faculty productivity, then the loss of the high producer's output will imply a reduction in the size of the wage pool. In time, the average level of compensation to the unionized institutions should fall relative to the nonunionized schools, where salaries are determined on the basis of a faculty member's contribution to the institution. This prediction appears to be consistent with what empirical researchers are already beginning to find.

SUMMARY, IMPLICATIONS, AND RECOMMENDATIONS

Joseph Garbarino coined the phrase "creeping unionism" to describe the pace at which faculty collective bargaining was expanding in the late 1960s and early 1970s. If anything, that pace has slowed to the point of stalling in the 1980s.

Faculty rationale for considering unions in the 1970s was well founded. Enrollments in higher education rose while instructional budgets as a percentage of total institutional budgets fell. Relative to administrators' salaries and general-service staff salaries, faculty salaries were being devastated by price inflation. Faculties lost control of the governance process as single campuses became part of centrally managed systems. Lawyers, accountants, and system planners replaced faculty members as decision makers. Unionization held the promise to change all of this; unfortunately, it does not now appear that it did or that it can.

In the early 1970s, it appeared that collective bargaining could raise unionized faculty salaries above what would have been achieved in the absence of the union. By the mid-1970s, the unions' ability to extract additional dollars may have come to an end as administrators became more apt in dealing at the bargaining table, as the market in higher education became tighter, and as nonunionized institutions began to increase their faculty salaries — possibly to ward off the union organizers. At unionized institutions, collective bargaining was successful in standardizing the salary determination processes. But it appears that the idea of merit pay may have fallen victim to this formalization process.

Collective bargaining has strengthened faculty due process in salary determination, but it is not clear how unionization has strengthened faculty governance in more traditional senate settings or within the bureaucracy of a large, state system. In fact, the mere creation of a system-wide union appears to remove the governance process further from individual faculty members: Collective bargaining implies that it is the union agent who deals with the central administration's lawyers and personnel specialists. In addition, as unions find it tougher to win financial gains for their members, we may see them taking a more active role in governance issues that have historically been the domain of faculty senates; but to date (with few exceptions) unions appear to have avoided issues in the academic areas.

The question to be asked at this time is obvious: If faculty unions have not delivered on their promises, what can be done to reverse the tides that may be eroding faculty vitality and diminishing the role of higher education as a major force in the socioeconomic advances of our country? There are no easy answers, but perhaps much can be learned from the fall of our industrial sector from the position of innovator to that of follower. After all, it is the industrial model that many planners and administrators in higher education claim to be emulating.

From Arch Patton, retired director of the international management consulting firm, McKinsey & Co., we gain a particular insight as to what weakened United States firms in the world market. Unlike others who identify these weaknesses as being related to poor labor-management relations, uneconomical wage demands, inadequate plant investment, and marginal product quality standards, Arch Patton (1982, pp. 12–15) identifies our industrial weakness as the change that has taken place in line-staff relations since World War II. He states that "staff positions have far outstripped line jobs in number and influence, with serious consequences for the ability of U.S. industry to compete in world markets" (p. 12).

According to Patton, positions in areas such as engineering, manufacturing, and marketing have been downgraded in terms of pay, authority, and promotion expectations; areas which are less directly connected with production such as accounting, law, and public relations have been upgraded. While it was once common to have engineers as high company officials, it is now unusual even in the motor vehicle industries. Emphasis on staff positions in this country has resulted in a reduction in industrial productivity as the more able individuals seek training and promotion in staff positions. Those remaining in line positions adjust their productivity to the relatively lower levels of remuneration and influence. The poor quality standards, lack of concern, and generally bad labor-management relations that result are symptomatic of this situation and not the cause.

If Patton's assessment of industrial debility is correct, then prestigious and highly productive colleges and universities with their "up or out" promotion system, strong departmental control, faculty administrators, and a fairly pure form of merit pay may be the last bastion of the American entrepreneurial work ethic. This reward and governance system, which has provided great technological advances in the sciences and arts and is one of the few sectors in our economy that continues to attract foreign dollars, is being threatened by the same expansion of staff authority and influence that has impaired the productivity of industry here. The call for unionization in higher education is at least in part the result of higher education planners' attempts to implement our faulty industry model. Unfortunately, unionization of faculty in higher education can be expected to expedite and not retard the takeover of our colleges and universities by bureaucratic staff personnel.

To advance faculty vitality and enhance investment in higher education, anything that expands the number and influence of staff personnel in university decision making must be questioned and opposed where the staff personnel could undermine faculty productivity. It is essential that college and university boards of directors and chief executive officers get the message that the faculty and its vitality are, in Arch Patton's words, "the guts of the business."

To ensure that boards and presidents know what is going on in the bureaucracy, it is necessary that individual faculty members, departments, and colleges voice their needs and complaints.[11] Traditional academic departments have been, and probably will continue to be, the source of power within the institution if faculty in such units act as a group, documenting their needs, and demanding what is good for the program and the institution. Central administration cannot take power away from an academic unit that produces a unique, visible, and essential quality service — unless that unit allows it.

If administrators and boards of directors are smarter than their counterparts in the industrial world, they will have already spotted the early warning signs of mismanagement that the calls for unionization have signaled. They will have attempted to open *direct* lines of communication with faculty in departmental subgroups. They will insist that *all* key administrators and consultants, including those whose training is in law, accounting, or planning, have academic credentials. They will be trying to allocate resources on the basis of contribution to an academic product. In this environment, an active academic department is in a position to regain any power it may have lost and possibly increase the influence and economic status of its members. In the process it will enhance the vitality of higher education.

NOTES

1. Quoted from program description of "Information Seminar on Collective Bargaining," 5 December 1980.
2. These issues were selected for special consideration because many scholars have singled them out as the key issues related to faculty vitality and unionization.

For example, Garbarino (1975a, p. 255) wrote: "We conclude that the policies of the faculty unions reflect concern in three major areas: governance, tenure and job security, and salaries."

3. *Chronicle of Higher Education,* 28 April 1982, p. 2.

4. Whether state law encourages unionization or the existence of unions encourages the passage of state laws is not clear.

5. See Watkins (1982b) for a discussion of issues related to these decisions.

6. After a union was established, stony faculty opposition developed on a few campuses. But as the faculty at the University of Florida, Gainesville, learned in 1980, once a union is in place it is difficult to decertify it. The bargaining agent will fight to keep its power and state laws usually favor the bargaining agent.

7. Kemerer and Baldridge (1981, pp. 262–263) speculate that since a union is a political organization, its leadership must continually justify its existence. "As a result unions are always striving for greater benefits for their membership. When economic concessions are not forthcoming, unions will naturally look elsewhere for gains. One of those areas will be governance." This prediction appears to be supported by their 1979 survey results, where over half the presidents and faculty union chairpersons agreed with the statement, "Our union is gradually moving into educational issues, trying to influence curriculum and program decisions."

8. One might ask how it can be that unionization in higher education has not brought greater compensation when steel workers, plumbers, airline pilots, and precollege teachers have apparently profited so much from unionization. For example, Baugh and Stone (1982) report that the union/nonunion wage differential among precollege teachers reached 12 to 22 percent by the late 1970s and that real wages of precollege teachers rose during the 1974–78 period, while the real wage of nonunionized precollege teachers declined.

Unions have had the greatest strength in bargaining in sectors where there is a "profit" pool from which they can extract benefits (at the expense of the corporate shareholders), or where labor costs can be passed on to the consumer, or where their service is essential to the production of a product that is critical to the smooth operation of society.

By definition, universities are typically nonprofit institutions. While enrollments in higher education have risen, the average financial return to a degree recipient has been falling. Thus, institutions in higher education have not been able to pass on all of the increasing costs to students and taxpayers. Finally, while the product of higher education may be more sophisticated than that of others in the public sector, it may be much less needed in the short run. Society cannot function very long without policemen, firemen, and elementary school teachers. It can function in the short run without colleges and universities.

9. It is possible that at the early stages, college and university administrators and state legislators didn't know how to deal with the unions at the bargaining table. Kemerer and Baldridge (1981, p. 259) report: "There is also mounting evidence that administrators are less fearful of faculty bargaining now than in 1974 and are taking a tougher stance at the bargaining table."

10. Minter and Bowen (1982b, p. 7) report that by 1979, 54 percent of faculty at private institutions had tenure, while at public institutions 63 percent had tenure. Thus, Guthrie-Morse, Leslie, and Hu's sample data appears representative of the

population, but the net change in tenured faculty between union and nonunion institutions could be a chance occurrence because the new change does not appear to be highly significant.

11. An interesting model for faculty and administration interaction in governance processes can be seen in the Ashland College agreement. Following a unanimous vote by the faculty to rescind the authority of the AAUP to represent it in collective bargaining, a "faculty forum" was established. This forum comprises department chairmen and deans as well as faculty members. The agreement between the faculty and the administration also specifies that all committees established by the trustees will include one faculty member with voting rights.

Chapter 11 | **Maintaining Faculty Vitality Through Early Retirement Options**

Karen C. Holden

Both the early development of pension plans in higher education and the current interest in early and phased retirement programs are based on a common concern about the costs of an aging faculty and a common belief in the power of pension benefits to affect the retirement timing of faculty members. In 1905 Dr. William Osler, physician in chief of the Johns Hopkins University faculty, remarked in his retirement address: "It is a very serious matter . . . to have all our professors growing old at the same time. In some places only an epidemic, a time limit, or an age limit can save the situation" (Graebner, 1980, p. 4). Never one to trust to natural phenomena to improve an organization's efficiency, Andrew Carnegie was inspired in part by this address to establish in 1906 the Carnegie Foundation for the Advancement of Teaching (CFAT). A pension fund, administered by the CFAT, would encourage and enable the retirement of "many old professors whose places should be occupied by younger men" (Carnegie as quoted by Graebner, 1980, p. 109). Now in the 1980s we are faced once again with an aging faculty group, and once again personnel policy makers look to pensions and other fringe benefits as means of achieving retirement and age distribution goals.[1]

PUTTING RETIREMENT AND PENSIONS IN PERSPECTIVE

The separate effect of pensions, mandatory retirement provisions, and of other economic and personal factors on the retirement timing of faculty members was not studied during the first half of the twentieth century and, consequently, was not well understood. Most likely, pensions and associated mandatory retirement rules did play a key role in accelerating retirements during the crucial development period of pension plans.

Unencumbered by federal and state regulations or by long-term pension promises to faculty members, pensions could be easily manipulated during this early period to meet institutional hiring and age distribution goals. The rapid development of pensions in both the public and private sectors meant a significant and, to some extent, unexpected improvement in the financial lot of most college and university faculty members, providing to many for the first time an opportunity to retire. At the same time, in guaranteeing some income in retirement to faculty members, college and university administrators could in good conscience require retirement at a fixed age. By 1948, 85 percent of college and university faculty members were covered by some sort of retirement plan (Greenough, 1948), and almost 90 percent of all institutions reported some age of mandatory retirement (AAUP, 1950).[2]

The coupling of pension receipt to mandatory retirement age rules was approved by the American Association of University Professors (AAUP) and the Association of American Colleges (AAC), which beginning in 1950 issued joint statements establishing standards for pension levels and the age and strictness of mandatory retirement age (MRA) rules.[3] It is important to note that both an MRA and an adequate pension were assumed necessary to induce faculty members to retire. The 1950 statement asserted that "the retirement plan of the college should be such that . . . no large proportion of faculty members be retired considerably before their effectiveness is markedly diminished and no large proportion of faculty members remain in service after that time (AAUP, 1950)." Members of the joint AAUP-AAC committee felt that this goal was best met with a fixed retirement age between 64 and 70, and they recommended that no exceptions be made to this rule — that no extensions of service be granted; they deplored the number of colleges that permitted services beyond age 70, noting that such an extension, most often granted to administrators, "rarely provides vigorous administrative leadership" (AAUP, 1950, p. 150).

The regulatory climate covering academic retirement rules, and the attitudes within the academic sector have changed since 1950. Most obvious have been the stiffening of federal regulation with the passage of the Employee Retirement Income Security Act of 1974 (ERISA) and the 1978 Amendments to the Age Discrimination in Employment Act of 1967 (AADEA). ERISA restricts the ability of institutions to make short-term changes in pension plans in order to alter retirement income and thereby the timing of separation. The AADEA eliminated mandatory retirement prior to age 70 (as of July 1, 1982, for tenured college faculty members). The 1967

Act may be further amended to eliminate mandatory retirement entirely. Sentiment within the academic community, expressed through the joint statements of the AAUP and AAC, have also changed. In the 1958 joint statement, this shift was already apparent. While that committee continued to press for a mandatory retirement age, it was argued that recalls of retired faculty members made at the discretion of the institution could be beneficial for both the college and faculty member without undermining the basic goals of a mandatory retirement age (AAUP, 1958). The joint statement in 1980 maintained both organizations' favorable view of mandatory retirement, but supported extensions of service beyond mandatory retirement and recommended that institutions permit individuals to adopt a phased retirement schedule prior to mandatory retirement (AAUP, 1980).

Current Developments

Mounting fiscal problems caused by cutbacks in federal and state support for higher education and declining student enrollments have forced institutions to look for nontraditional ways of altering retirement rates and providing for new job openings. Yet, the emphasis continues to be placed on retirement pension programs for providing the flexibility required by personnel and budget planners. Now, however, the pension issues faced are substantially different from those of the first half of the century. The major question is no longer the relatively simple one of what replacement rate to provide at a traditional mandatory retirement age, but rather how to structure pension plans and retirement policies that will encourage retirement or part-time work at particular ages in order to alleviate budget problems facing the institution or to achieve education goals that may require the restructuring of departments or the development of new disciplines. Without a mandatory retirement age, can pension plans be structured to encourage retirement at an earlier than normal age? Research on the total labor force claims they can (Burkhauser and Quinn, 1980). Whether this is true for particular occupations, especially in higher education, is not clear. Can part-time work programs be structured that allow retirees to maintain their full-time work — but at lower costs to the institution? The numbers show such programs are possible. It is not clear whether faculty members would be responsive to such a phased retirement program. Does pension income play the key role in the retirement timing of faculty members that pension policy planners have always assumed? Little is known about the nonfinancial determinants of retirement for any labor group; evidence presented next provides some evidence that these are of perhaps unexpected importance in the decision of faculty members to retire.

The passage of the 1978 Amendments to the Age Discrimination in Employment Act (AADEA) of 1967 was a mixed blessing to higher education. The immediate impact was to compel all institutions with a mandatory retirement age below 70 (67 percent of all institutions in 1977) to increase this age to be at least 70 on or before July 1, 1982. The long-term impact will only be felt if and when faculty members alter their retirement behavior in light of this unexpected extension in their contracts.[4] At the same time, a mandate to the United States Secretary of Labor included in the 1978 Act and institutional concern about the effects of later retirements on institutional costs and productivity precipitated several studies of the effect of mandatory retirement age on the retirement behavior of faculty members (COFHE, 1979, 1980; Corwin & Knepper, 1978; Hansen & Holden, 1981b; Jenny, Heim, & Hughes, 1979; Mulanaphy, 1981; Patton & Foertsch, 1978). We now know more about college pension plans and retirement behavior than we ever have before. This information will be extremely valuable in setting retirement policy in a world without mandatory retirement. At the same time, it has illuminated the limits of using pensions to orchestrate the retirement timing of tenured faculty members. These studies show that retirement behavior is a far more complicated decision than was envisioned by the early developers of pension plans and retirement standards in higher education.

Focus on the 1980 Study

This chapter reports on the major findings of one of these studies, a 1980 survey and analysis of retirement policies in higher education and of the expected retirement timing of a representative sample of older faculty members in higher education. This study was undertaken in response to the mandate to the United States Secretary of Labor by the AADEA to examine the effect of a change in mandatory retirement age policies in higher education on the timing of retirement by tenured faculty members and on institutional costs and new hires. The data is described in the next section, followed by an overview of the types of retirement benefit plans in higher education and a summary of the estimated efforts of retirement benefit plans on retirement timing (the analysis is detailed in Hansen & Holden, 1981b). We then discuss the postretirement work plans of this sample of faculty members, focusing on the influence of expected retirement income. In the final section, we tie these two decisions together — retirement and postretirement work plans — by discussing changes in retirement programs that could be most successful in altering retirement timing and hours of work by older faculty members. Included in this discussion are some examples of recently developed early and phased retirement programs in higher education. Though few institutions have had sufficient time to measure the responses to these options in any systematic way, we can speculate on the probable success of particular types of programs from our own research results. The future will tell whether the expectations of college administrators and our predictions are correct.

DATA

The study from which these findings are drawn was undertaken to examine the effect of raising the minimum age of mandatory retirement from 65 to 70 on the retirement behavior of tenured college faculty members and on institutional costs and new hires. To do this, we generated the data we needed from two special surveys. First, we fielded in the spring of 1980 a questionnaire to institutions of higher education to obtain information on pension plans and other fringe benefits. We then drew samples of faculty members at responding institutions and sent questionnaires to individual faculty members to obtain information on expected retirement age, current work activities, postretirement work plans, publication records and other personal characteristics. Only those faculty members aged 50 or older were asked to complete the questionnaire. This survey design was adopted in order to allow us to match faculty and institutional pension data and thereby develop accurate and detailed information for individual faculty members on the pension benefits they would be eligible for at alternative ages of retirement. This represents a major advantage over other data sets that depend on faculty members themselves for information on future pension benefits; we know that amounts given are often inaccurate (if given at all) and represent benefit amounts that are themselves determined by expected retirement behavior and postretirement work plans.[5]

This data set has several shortcomings that need some mention. Our responses came primarily from faculty members at universities and four-year colleges. Two-year colleges and their faculty members were least likely to respond. It is possible that the few two-year colleges responding are not representative of the population of two-year institutions or of their faculties. With this exception, the distribution of respondents — both institutions and faculty members — by type of institution and between the private and public sector are fairly representative of the respective populations.

Inasmuch as our questionnaire was directed at faculty members 50 years of age or older, we have no information on younger faculty members. The decision to limit the range was mandated by our granting agency, but also is consistent with our own knowledge that the younger the faculty member, the lower the correlation between expected age of retirement and the actual age (Reimers, 1977). Of course, by surveying all age groups, we would have obtained valuable information from younger faculty members about their savings behavior for retirement; however, because the purpose of the survey was to study retirement behavior, savings behavior was not given a high priority in survey design. In the analysis of faculty retirement behavior, we look at the expectations of full-time faculty between ages 56–64, prior to the age of eligibility for unreduced social security benefits.

Although we have excellent information on retirement benefit programs provided by the employing institution, our data on social security are not very good. This shortcoming is not a major concern for two reasons. First, most of the faculty sample currently earn a salary well above the taxable maximum. Given probable earnings histories estimated from AAUP data on salary by rank, these faculty members typically would have always had earnings at or above the taxable maximum. This salary level means they will have the maximum Primary Insurance Amount (PIA) for their cohort and family status, which we can easily estimate. Second, although we asked each person about current and past coverage by social security, only a small percentage were able to respond. We suspect that because few know even this most basic information about past coverage, few can estimate future social security insurance benefits accurately.[6] As a result, small differences between workers in social security benefits payable at a future retirement age will have little impact on actual behavior. This is not to argue that faculty were assumed to be indifferent about social security coverage, just that how the system works and the effect of additional years of work on final benefits is largely unknown by currently employed faculty members. We do take into account whether faculty are covered by social security on their current jobs, for clearly it will matter whether a person expects to receive any benefits at all from social security or whether he or she can expect these benefits to change by some (unknown) amount with additional years of work.

RETIREMENT TIMING AND PENSION PLANS IN HIGHER EDUCATION

Age of Retirement

Compared to the retirement timing of workers in the general work force, retirement occurs late for faculty members. For one group of faculty members in our sample — those 56–64 years of age — expected age of retirement was 66.4 years of age (66.7 for those 62–64). This is much later than the actual median age of retirement of about 65 for a sample of males 62–64 in 1973 (Wertheimer, 1982) and the mean expected age of retirement of 62.5 recorded in a national survey of male workers conducted in 1980 (the same year of our survey) by Mathematica Policy Research (DOL 1982). Elsewhere we compare the marked shift towards early retirement for the total work force with available data on retirement age in higher education

(Hansen & Holden, 1981b). We find little evidence that a similar shift toward early retirement has occurred among faculty members in higher education.

Looking more closely at expected retirement age in our sample of faculty members 56–64 years of age (Table 11.1), we find that almost 18 percent of males and 29 percent of females expect to retire at 62 or earlier. The next bulge in expected retirement age is at age 65 when 35 percent of both sexes want to retire. Another large percentage expect to wait until 70 to retire (24.1 percent of males and 16.4 percent of females), with a smaller percentage (11.8 and 10.7 percent of males and females respectively) retiring in the interim. Only a small fraction expect to postpone retirement beyond 70. Compare these expectations to 1980 data, which show that 54 percent of eligible males in the United States between 62 and 65 were collecting social security benefits. Also consider the fact that studies comparing expected and actual retirement ages find the anticipated age of retirement is most often below the age at which workers actually retire (Reimers, 1977). Even among those faculty members in our sample aged 56–61 (i.e. those not yet eligible for early social security benefits), only 21 percent expect to retire prior to reaching age 65. Clearly, tenured faculty members expect to, and probably do, retire later than does the general worker.

Pension Plans Covering Faculty Members in Higher Education

The effect of pension variables in determining the timing of retirement has aways been a major focus of retirement-related research (see reviews of

TABLE 11.1. Expected Age of Retirement for Faculty Members, 56 to 64 Years of Age, 1980

Expected Age of Retirement	Males	Females	Totals
57–61	7.7%	9.3%	7.9%
62	10.2	19.5	11.9
63–64	4.1	3.8[a]	4.1
65	34.8	34.6	34.8
66–69	11.8	10.7	11.7
70	24.1	16.4	22.7
71+	7.4	5.6	7.1
All ages	100.0	100.0	100.0
N[b]	727	159	886

a. Fewer than ten cases.
b. This group of faculty were "sure" of their expected retirement age (see Hansen and Holden, 1981b, for a description of how retirement ages were asked for).

this research and comparison of results in Clark, Kreps, and Spengler, 1978; Danziger, Haveman, and Plotnick, 1981). Not unexpectedly, financial variables are shown to have an important effect although there is no consensus on the size of this effect and the manner in which pensions affect retirement timing. Recent research has argued that not only does the level of annual benefits matter but also (and perhaps more important) the change in lifetime pension income that would be realized with an additional year of work (Burkhauser, 1979; Burkhauser & Quinn, 1980). The argument is that if workers can expect a gain in lifetime income with an additional year of work, retirement is likely to be delayed. Burkhauser (1980) argues that only a pension in which a worker is equally well-off in terms of lifetime income at any retirement age is "neutral" with respect to retirement timing; all other pensions can be identified as encouraging or discouraging early retirement.[7] To calculate the extent to which pensions in higher education may encourage faculty to accelerate or delay retirement, it is necessary to have detailed information on pension plan benefit calculation methods and inflation adjustment pensions; then earnings are projected to the specified retirement age and inflation during retirement. When this is done for the Teachers Insurance Annuity Association (TIAA) and state pension plans covering faculty members in higher education,[8] assuming a typical earnings profile explained below and a 10 percent inflation rate, we find that on the average faculty members will lose lifetime pension income if they delay retirement past age 62 (Table 11.2). Although annual benefits will rise if retirement is delayed from 62 to 65, lifetime pension income will be lower on the average.

To understand why this happens, it is necessary to look at how TIAA and state pension plans calculate benefits and how we made these estimates. In calculating the annual annuity for which a person would be eligible at age 62 and 65 under each of the public and private institutional plans in our sample, we constructed a wage profile for an "average" full-time faculty member who started teaching at age 32 with a beginning salary of $3,200 and at age 64 earned $33,150 as a full professor. Annual salaries (taking account of changes in rank) were estimated from historical AAUP salary data and are available in Hansen and Holden (1981b). In the present value calculations, both the probability that a person will live to receive a benefit and an appropriate discount rate are taken into account. We assumed a real discount rate of 5 percent and an annual rate of inflation of 10 percent throughout a person's remaining lifetime.[9] The present values calculated for state plans reflect the inflation adjustments built into each plan, with the benefits from plans offering no adjustments discounted at 15 percent and those adjusting benefits by the full rise in the Consumer Price Index (CPI) being discounted at 5 percent.

The average benefits faculty members can expect to receive under each plan vary considerably across institutions because of wide variation in total

TABLE 11.2.   Annuity and Present Value of Benefits at Age 62
              When Retirement Occurs at 62 and 65

	State Plan[a]	TIAA[ab]	OASI[c]
Projected annual benefits			
at 62	$14,098	$8,903	$5,433
at 65	18,388	12,201	7,848
Percentage Change	+30.4	+37.0	+44.4
Present value at 62 if			
begun at 62	$97,002	$50,553	$62,139
begun at 65	83,458	42,139	68,962
Percentage change	-14.0	-6.3	+11.0

a.   Based on assumed salary profile.
b.   Teachers Insurance Annuity Association.
c.   Old Age and Survivors Insurance (Social Security).

contributions among institutions with TIAA plans and in benefit formulas among state plans. State plans differ in the number of years over which average salary is calculated, where this average is taken over three to five years. Usually, this average is first multiplied by years of service and the product is then multiplied by some factor,[10] which in our sample of state institutions ranges between 0.012 and 0.02. When a person covered by a state plan chooses to postpone receipt of benefits from age 62 to 65 by working three additional years, the absolute amount of the annuity expected will generally rise because the average salary increases if higher earnings are expected during these additional years and because the average is multiplied by three additional years of service. A person covered by a TIAA plan can usually expect additional accumulations both because of the contributions made on the additional year's salary and the dividends that will be earned on the undistributed accumulated amounts. In addition, benefits are actuarially adjusted to account for the shorter lifetime over which delayed benefits will be received.[11] Combined employer and employee contributions in TIAA covered institutions range from 5 to 20 percent in our sample of institutions.

For the person with this hypothesized earnings history, annual benefits would rise by 30 percent in the 174 public institutions covered by 43 state plans if retirement were postponed from 62 to 65 and by 37 percent in the 172 TIAA participating institutions. Annual social security benefits would rise by 44 percent. At age 64, this person would be eligible for a mean benefit of over $8,000 from social security, of about $12,000 from TIAA, and $18,000 from state plans. It appears that by postponing benefits faculty members gain. They do in terms of annual benefit amounts; it is less clear whether they do over their lifetime. In some plans, benefits lost during the three years of work between age 62 and 65 may never be matched by higher benefits beyond age 65. By looking at the present value of higher benefits postponed to an age to which survival is not certain and inflation may erode the worth of postponed dollars, we obtain a different picture of the value of postponing retirement benefits receipt. Under both the mean state and TIAA plans, the beneficiary will lose somewhat. Total lifetime retirement benefit income falls by 14 percent under state plans and 16 percent under TIAA.

Table 11.2 also demonstrates the relative advantage of being covered by TIAA and state plans. If salary schedules are identical under all plans, the person covered by the mean state pension plan can expect to receive a benefit higher by about 50 percent than will the faculty member covered by a TIAA plan. Even this difference is probably underestimated. State teachers are usually subject to the formulas in existence at retirement. Thus, our calculation of benefits using 1980 formulas reflects the benefits payable in that year to persons retiring at ages 62 and 65. Many TIAA plans, on the other hand, have increased employer and employee contribution rates since 1935. In estimating past contributions using current rates, we overestimate prior contributions for faculty members in institutions that have increased these rate schedules since the date for which contributions were estimated. The biggest contributor to annuity increases between ages 62 and 65 is earnings on prior contributions with additional contributions being of marginal importance, so we have in some cases overestimated the absolute gain from delayed retirement under TIAA plans.

Under both types of plans, inflation between age 62 and 65 will reduce the value of postponed benefits. The additional years of service and higher average earnings will increase benefits paid by public plans, but the most common inflation adjustment of 2 to 5 percent is clearly inadequate in light of recent inflation rates and our assumed 10 percent inflation. Retirees with TIAA contracts can expect some increase in benefits from additional earnings on these accumulated amounts, but TIAA dividends have been well below inflation in recent years. Inadequate Consumer Price Index adjustments are a major problem in all types of employer retirement plans. Current high rates increase the return to accepting retirement dollars as early as possible.

Social security benefits do not differ across institutions because we assume a single salary profile, except if coverage is not offered at all. For those covered by social security, annual income rises if benefits are postponed, and because benefits are fully adjusted to price changes, postponement translates into an increase in lifetime social security income.

RETIREMENT DETERMINANTS
AND THE DESIRE TO CONTINUE WORKING

It appears that in general pension plans provide an inducement to retire prior to age 65. If workers were primarily interested in maximizing lifetime income from retirement benefit programs, we would notice a far larger percentage of faculty members retiring at age 62 under these plans. This would be especially true for those not covered by social security; covered employees would find the lifetime loss in employer pension income partially offset by gains in social security income from retiring at age 65 rather than 62.

Clearly, faculty members are not maximizing retirement income alone. Despite relatively high pension incomes compared to the general work force and declines in lifetime pension income for many with delayed retirement, a high percentage of faculty members expect to retire well beyond age 65. Several reasons for their rejecting the early retirement incentives in pension plans are obvious. The two most important are (1) the gains in salary income from continued work and (2) the strong attachment of faculty members to professional work that extends beyond retirement and tends to delay their departure from academic duties.

Mean losses in lifetime income upon early retirement under state and TIAA plans are not large. Compared to the assumed salary of $33,000 during the final year of work, they fade in importance. However, there is considerable variation around these means: neither state nor TIAA plans are all alike. Under TIAA plans, the absolute loss in lifetime income ranges from $1,531 to $12,759. For state plans, the effect of postponing retirement from 62 to 65 ranges from a gain of $6,203 to a loss of $24,916 over their remaining lifetime. For some faculty members, these losses are significant and will be weighed against the salary to be earned during the additional three years of work. To others, the loss in lifetime benefits if retirement were delayed is insignificant.

Table 11.3 gives the total change in lifetime income that would result if a faculty member chose to retire at age 65 rather than 62. Salary income during the three years of work far outweighs the loss in lifetime pension income. In addition, faculty members in OASI-covered institutions will find pension losses partially offset by gains in lifetime social security income. The important point of these numbers is that salary loss upon early retirement is the major factor determining the comparative financial advantage of late versus early retirement. At the same time, our investigation of the role of financial variables on retirement timing casts considerable doubt on the ability of financial incentives alone to stimulate earlier retirements. Our sample of faculty members displays a strong attachment to professional work, and their desire to continue working appears to modify their willingness to trade income for institutional affiliation.

TABLE 11.3. Components of Change in Lifetime Income
             Because of a Change in Retirement from Age 62 to 65

Change[a]	State Plan OASI Covered	State Plan Not OSAI Covered	TIAA
State Plan	-$12,303	-$17,772	–
TIAA	–	–	-$8,414
Social Security	+6,823	–	+6,823
Salary	+80,316	+80,316	+80,316
Total change	+74,836	+62,544	+78,725

a. Changes in the present value of lifetime income at age 62 if
retirement occurs at age 65 rather than age 62.

In investigating the causal relationship between faculty members' retirement ages and various pension variables, controlling for other financial
variables, productivity measures, health, and key demographic characteristics, we find the relationship is weak but also works in a seemingly
curious way (detailed results given in Hansen & Holden, 1981). For faculty
members aged 56–61 in 1980, pension values (both the expected level and
change if postponed) have an effect on expected retirement age, but for
faculty members 62–64 years of age we find no significant effect of pensions
on their expected retirement age. For the younger age group, a higher pension causes a lower expected retirement age, but as the slope of this curve
flattens out, the benefit amount increases. One explanation for this difference by age is the selectivity bias probably present in our sample. The
younger faculty group includes some who will retire at age 62, the older
group does not, although all are below the customary normal age of retirement for institutions in the sample. If early and normal/late retirees are
different in that the former are those faculty members most sensitive in
planning retirement to pension incentives, while the latter group—those
planning retirement at 64 or later—are those who have ignored pension incentives for early retirement, we would expect to find these differences between the two age groups in the effects of pension variables on retirement
age.

A similar difference in the sensitivity of workers to financial incentives
is also found by Burkhauser and Quinn (1980). While pension variables
work well in explaining the two-year retirement transition rates for workers
59–64 in their sample, these variables do not work for a sample of workers
aged 65–67 in 1973. They also conclude that the explanation is that these
older workers have rejected the early retirement incentives built into social
security and private pensions, thereby showing through later retirement
their insensitivity to financial incentives of this type. In a sample of all

workers, this is clearly an unusual group of workers because they are a minority. In higher education, this potentially insensitive group is large— only 21 percent of the faculty members aged 56–61 expect to retire before age 65. While pension variables are not significant, variables explaining differences in the expected retirement age of faculty members 61–64 years of age are, for example, receipt of outside professional income (delays retirement), social security coverage (accelerates retirement), and mandatory retirement provisions (accelerates retirement). We conclude that institutional affiliation allows faculty members to continue not only their teaching and research activities but their outside earnings opportunities as well. The obvious kicker to retirement income provided by social security enables faculty to retire earlier, and a mandatory retirement at age 65 (legal at the time of the survey) forces earlier retirement at approximately 1.5 years earlier than otherwise.

The commitment of faculty members to professional activities is also shown in the responses to questions on postretirement work. Only 14 percent said they would not continue some professional activity after retirement; another 18 percent expected to maintain professional activities in some way but without pay. The remaining 67 percent expect to continue working full or part time for pay either by teaching at their current institution, working with another employer in an academic or nonacademic job, or working as a paid consultant. When we look only at those who expect to work on a part-time basis—thereby assuming that those who will work full time after retirement are not really retired and are somewhat different from their peers (and they are only 4.5 percent of the respondents)—we find that 63 percent expect to continue working for pay after retirement. It is interesting that for all ages of expected retirement, all fields, all ranks and regardless of whether they are primarily teachers or researchers, a majority expect to earn something after retirement from professional activities. There are some interesting variations. It is not surprising to find that only 51 percent of those in the humanities, versus 73 percent in professional fields (excluding education), expect to work for pay after retirement. Sixty-four percent of full professors expect to do so, but only 57 percent of assistant professors. Among those retiring at age 62, 57 percent expect to work compared to 61 and 62 percent of those expecting to retire at age 65 and 70, respectively. Sixty-four percent of those who primarily teach (or at least did during 1980) expect to work after retirement versus 57 percent of those then engaged solely in research. We find three significant determinants of postretirement work plans: professional income from noninstitutional sources is positively associated with postretirement work probabilities as is current involvement in publishable research. Those in the humanities are significantly less likely to expect to work for pay; there is no significant difference among the other major fields.

These findings are consistent with those about the determinants of expected retirement age for this same group of faculty members. In that analysis we found that the higher the professional income earned from noninstitutional sources, the later the expected age of retirement. This finding suggests that current consulting activities, part-time teaching commitments elsewhere, labor mediation, and so on, do not necessarily encourage faculty members to ease sooner and more easily into retirement. Rather, it appears that persons with these outside earning possibilities are both more likely to want to continue working in retirement (and will probably be able to do so) but also want to retain their institutional affiliation far longer than do those dependent entirely on institutional income sources.

EARLY RETIREMENT INCENTIVES

Financial incentives for early retirement are designed to encourage workers to phase down or separate entirely from teaching or research at an age some years earlier than they would otherwise have done. Besides providing a higher retirement income at the targeted early retirement age, an important characteristic of such programs is that they increase the relative advantage of retiring early compared to continuing their full-time work activities. The results of our investigation of faculty pensions and retirement age expectations suggest that economic incentives must be large enough to counteract the rather significant loss in lifetime income (due primarily to forgone income) from early retirement that is characteristic of most pension plans and these incentives should be combined with opportunities for continued institutional affiliation. At the time of our 1980 survey, few institutions offered early retirement incentive (ERI) programs that met these two objectives. Twenty percent of the institutions sampled reported an ERI that was integrated with the pension plan covering faculty members. Another 3 percent of institutions in our sample offered ERIs that are not part of the regular retirement program. In examining the particular provisions of both these types of plans, however, it was clear that almost half of the programs are, in fact, optional tax deferred annuities that are available to faculty members through salary reductions. Payments are made entirely by faculty members to these annuities and they are not available to early retirees alone. These programs are a method of increasing benefits available to faculty members at any age of retirement — they do not alter the relative gain to faculty members of retiring earlier. While they could enable those with otherwise low pensions to retire somewhat earlier, they do not increase the relative advantage of early retirement.

Despite the low percentage of institutions having early retirement programs at that time, a high percentage of faculty members in our sample expressed interest in early retirement incentives and at least claim that such offers would result in their retiring earlier than they now expect to. We asked about three early retirement options: (1) if pension benefits were identical at an earlier age to those they will receive at their probable age of retirement, (2) if an unchanged pension amount at retirement was fully adjusted for Consumer Price Index increases throughout retirement, and (3) if faculty members could reduce their academic responsibilities with a proportionate reduction in salary. The first option would increase lifetime pension income; lifetime benefits at an earlier age of retirement would be raised and as long as no further increases in pension could be gained from continuing to work, this option would come close to offsetting the mean change in lifetime pension income that would otherwise result from early retirement. It would not, however, offset earnings loss.

The second option would reduce the loss in lifetime retirement income because of price inflation. It would mean that faculty members could better maintain income during retirement. Finally, the third option would grant that faculty members continued institutional affiliation through part-time work and, depending on the particular salary-pension package, could result in only a small reduction in annual income.

The responses to the posed incentive programs suggest that a large fraction of faculty members who now have some idea of when they will retire would consider earlier retirement if offered an ERI. If all those interested did, in fact, retire earlier and at the ages given, institutions would find mean ages of retirement dipping by about two years under each of the three options (Table 11.4). For those who took the option, retirement would occur on average between four and five years earlier than now planned. There are few differences in the responses given to the hypothesized ERIs. While a somewhat higher percentage claim interest in the financial incentives, phased retirement would induce a somewhat greater shift in retirement age among those choosing that option and would encourage a slightly higher percentage of those now planning to retire at 70 or later to retire earlier than would the other two options.

What conclusions can we draw about the effectiveness of early retirement incentives in higher education? Incentives in current benefit programs appear to encourage only a small percentage of faculty members to retire prior to reaching age 65. Seventeen percent of the 56–61 year olds expect to retire prior to that age, and we know that the closer one is to actual retirement, the more likely it is that expected retirement age shifts upward (Reimers, 1977). Although economic incentives may encourage the early retirement of this small fraction, far larger incentives would be required to offset the loss in salary income over the remaining years of work planned by those delaying retirement.

The interest of faculty members in significant incentives for early re-

TABLE 11.4.   Distribution of Faculty Aged 56 to 64 by
              Current Expected Age of Retirement and Expected Age,
              with Three Alternative Early Retirement Plans

Age	Current Expected Age of Retirement	If Earlier Pension Higher	If COLA[a]	Phased Retirement
55–59	1.0%	6.2%	5.3%	5.8%
60–61	6.3	16.9	15.6	12.2
62	11.6	17.2	17.2	13.2
63–64	3.6	5.8	4.9	5.1
65	35.0	24.8	26.1	32.9
66–69	12.1	7.8	9.1	9.9
70	24.4	15.4	15.7	16.3
71+	7.0	5.8	6.0	4.6
Mean age of retirement	65.7	63.7	63.9	64.1
Mean change in retirement age with ERI		2.1	1.8	1.7
For those who would choose ERI		4.4	4.3	5.1
Percent of respondents who would retire early with ERI		45.7%	42.2%	32.6%

a.   Cost-of-living adjustment.

tirement is encouraging but must be viewed with some caution. The large percentage interested in higher retirement benefits at an earlier age is not consistent with our findings that current pension incentives have only a small and sometimes insignificant influence on retirement timing. We also found no evidence that current postretirement inflation adjustments in pension plans—and in some such adjustments are large—have any effect on retirement timing. On the other hand, the interest of faculty members in phased retirement options is consistent with our findings about the importance of continuing institutional affiliation as a means both of obtaining outside income and of continuing postretirement work activities.

It appears that the ERI most consistent with the way in which faculty members have already planned for retirement is one that would allow faculty members to reduce to part-time work, and several institutions are now developing such programs. In some, net income is reduced only slightly from full-time income, although the incomes from pension and salary allowed with part-time work vary. Most costly to the individual and least costly to the institution are arrangements by which faculty members receive a proportionate fraction of their salary, have additional contributions to pension plans or earnings, and have service increases based on their part-time hours and salary. In 1980, only 36 percent of institutions allowed faculty members to reduce to part-time work, although we suspect that such arrangements could be negotiated at other colleges and universities. However, these straightforward reductions in teaching programs are costly to the individual in terms of forgone earnings and future pensions, and they do not alter the relative advantage of late versus early retirement. It is not surprising that so few faculty members have been attracted by such phased retirement options.

More promising are ERIs that alter the salary and pension payments that are normally payable to part-time workers under the regular provision of the institution's pension plan. Programs that allow faculty members to phase into retirement with reductions in salary and work responsibilities — while maintaining retirement benefit contributions based on their full-time salary level — have been developed by some institutions including the University of Minnesota, Yale University, and the University of California. The University of California example shows that it is possible to structure such a program in defined benefit plans, although approval by the relevant political groups and state agencies may be difficult in some states.[12] Where faculty members are covered by TIAA, maintenance of contributions at the full-time salary rate is merely an implicit increase in the contribution rate on actual salary to a particular group of workers.

Other institutions have taken different approaches to early retirement. Under a temporary early retirement option, University of Wisconsin faculty members will be permitted to retire between age 62 and 65 without the reduction in benefits normally applied to benefits taken prior to 65. Minnesota will also allow early retirees to retire fully with a lump sum early retirement payment. Neither of these arrangements permits continued institutional affiliation.

The challenge of any designer of an ERI is to establish requirements for participation such that payments to those who would have retired earlier in any case will be minimized. Phased retirement options need not face this particular problem unless they are tied to significant changes in the partial pension paid. The planners of phased retirement options face a different problem. How can they ensure that a phased retirement option does not allow persons who would have otherwise retired completely to extend their work life? About 13 percent of our sample saw phased retirement as an opportunity not to retire earlier but to work part-time beyond their current expected age. The decision on how to do this may become more critical as mandatory retirement age legislation is changed and as enrollment declines result in sharp reductions in new hires at many institutions. It is necessary to carefully evaluate the net savings that will result from ERIs, and for this we need to have a better understanding of retirement behavior. ERIs will be more expensive than predicted if few new retirees are attracted by such offers and most payments are made to those who would have retired anyway, or if the most productive faculty members are induced to leave. The flexibility of phased retirement may be one way to reduce salary costs while opening up new positions and retaining the services of the most valued faculty members.

CONCLUSIONS

As in the early years of pension plan development, institutions of higher education are turning to financial incentives to help solve budget and age distribution problems. While the general assumption is made now, as it was then, that pension plan changes can make significant changes in retirement patterns, the results of current studies cast some doubt on the ability to manipulate retirement timing — and thereby budgets and age distributions — through financial incentives. The options are far more limited than administrators in higher education would like to assume, although there is some promise that particular types of financial incentives could prove successful in accelerating reductions in work by some faculty members.

Faculty members do not appear to be anxious to retire. They retire much later than does the average worker in the country's work force, early retirement is not increasing among them, and they wish to remain active professionally even after retirement. At the same time, virtually all faculty members are covered by pensions that on average will replace about 50 percent of earnings for long-term workers (COFHE, 1981), yet they are worried about the effects of inflation on postretirement incomes. These findings are both encouraging and discouraging. The desire to continue professional work is a welcome finding because it indicates that tenure contracts and the institutional environment continue to encourage research and teaching throughout a person's professional career. The majority of faculty members see their professional career as a lifetime commitment, not one that can be brought to an end at the convenience of the institution. This strong attachment to work implies that buy-out agreements must be generous and must be tied to alternative work opportunities in order to persuade faculty members to retire earlier than planned.

Despite the demand for continued professional work, only a small number of institutions in our sample extend office and clerical services to retired faculty members. While virtually all institutions grant library privileges and use of physical education facilities to retired faculty members, approximately 45 percent never provide secretarial, office, or laboratory facilities to them. Approximately 25 percent will grant these additional services upon special request, about 15 percent will grant them only to emeritus professors, and 5 percent will do so for all retirees. Yet the majority of the older faculty employed at these institutions want to and expect to continue professional involvement after retirement. The attractiveness, indeed the necessity, of continued institutional affiliation is apparent.

The options that institutions face in adapting retirement programs to changing demographics and budgets are limited. Faculty members are subject to past pension plan provisions and to state regulations in determining current pension benefits. While benefits are ample in comparison with other workers, inflation is a major concern. Inflation adjustments are expensive. A new TIAA program of inflation-adjusted pensions exacts a considerable cost in terms of the initial pension amount. A time of budget crunch is a difficult time in which to divert scarce funds to highly paid faculty members, some of whom may have retired early in any case. We studied three plans, the responses to which imply that some means exist for encouraging faculty to alter retirement plans. At the same time, our empirical results indicate that important groups of faculty members in the past have not responded to financial incentives. Highly paid and late retirees may be these whose behavior is most difficult to change through financial incentives. For these faculty members, phased retirement programs may be most successful in altering plans. However, phased retirement programs must be carefully designed, as indeed must all ERIs. Even though phased retirement may be somewhat more flexible than pure financial incentives, the programs release fewer positions per retiree and could have the unintended consequence of allowing faculty members to extend their work life well beyond the age at which they would otherwise have retired.

NOTES

1. See Carnegie Commission, 1973; Carnegie Council, 1980; Cartter, 1976; Dresch, 1975 for enrollment and faculty projections. See AAUP, 1978 for a summary of the concerns about the effects on institutions of changes in faculty age structure. The References cite articles that suggest the emphasis put on retirement programs for a solution.

2. The history of the development and expanding coverage of pension plans in higher education is described in greater detail in Graebner (1980), King and Cook (1980), Greenough and King (1969), and Pratt (forthcoming).

3. All joint statements have looked at replacement rates at retirement, recommending in 1950 a one-half replacement rate. In 1980 a two-thirds replacement was recommended. The only flexibility recognized in the replacement standard was that earlier retirees may require a higher replacement rate because of their longer retired life. In none of the joint statements is there any suggestion that the adequacy of a given replacement rate paid at retirement depends on the type of plan, guaranteed inflation adjustments, postretirement dividend payments, survivor benefits, and earn-

ings restrictions that affect the lifetime value of an initial benefit level. Not until 1980 was a footnote added suggesting that a study be done to examine the effect of inflation on pensions.

4. For all but tenured faculty, the age of mandatory retirement rose to age 70 on January 1, 1979. Prior to that date, nontenured faculty and staff could be retired in compliance with procedures not tied strictly to age. For tenured staff, a shift upward in the mandatory retirement age meant an extension in tenure by that number of additional years. In effect employment was guaranteed. An age 65 MRA implied a termination of tenure, with year-to-year appointments possible at the majority of institutions (Hansen & Holden, 1981b). As of July 1, 1982, the termination of tenure cannot occur until age 70.

5. Thus, the direction of causation built into these answers makes it difficult to study the effect of pensions on retirement timing. This feature may be one source of the large pension effect obtained in studies that use self-reported pension or social security information as an independent variable.

6. The same cannot be said for employer pension benefits. Since the passage of the Employee Retirement Income Security Act of 1974, all pension plans must make annual reports to participants about benefit formulas or contribution amounts. Thus, workers are now in a better position to estimate probable benefits given particular assumptions about future service and earnings. Workers are not given similar information on social security. They only know current tax rates and see employee contributions deducted from salary. Few workers appear to understand how benefits are calculated and contributions are not directly related to benefit amounts.

7. Burkhauser is not clear on exactly what factors a pension plan must take into account to assure "neutrality." As we will see below, fully accurate actuarial adjustments may still result in nonneutral pensions if higher earnings and longer years of service mean that the basic pension amount before the actuarial adjustment applied will rise with delayed retirement. Burkhauser implies that neutrality must consider wage and service increases, as they are included in his own calculations (Burkhauser and Quinn, 1980). The concept remains important—that actuarial adjustments, salary, and service increases may result in a net gain or loss in lifetime income. However, the particular policy that should then be followed by a pension plan is not as clear, because a neutral pension for one group of workers may not be so for others.

8. Over 90 percent of all full-time faculty (of all ages) are employed in institutions with TIAA or a state public employee plan, so the discussion is limited to these two types of plans and, for faculty in covered employment, to the federal social security system. A small percentage (4.6 percent) are covered only by other plans. These are primarily church plans that may be either defined benefit or contribution plans. An even smaller percentage (3.1 percent) work in institutions that either have no plan or gave us no information on their plan. Schools with no plan are usually church-related or specialty colleges.

9. This value may be on the high side, but was selected in order to compare our findings with those of two other mandatory retirement studies commissioned by the Department of Labor. Uniform assumptions make it possible to compare both pension plans and retirement behavior in higher education with the relevant findings of these two studies for the general work force (DOL, 1982).

10. Minnesota is an atypical state plan, inasmuch as a portion of employer and employee contributions for the Teachers' Retirement System is paid into the Supplemental Retirement Fund, a money purchase annuity whose value at retirement is determined by prior contribution and earnings. Minnesota is excluded from the following discussion.

11. Actuarial adjustments in state plans are not customary after age 62 and if made are usually at a flat rate that varies among plans.

12. More typical for state institutions may be the University of Utah's program that permits persons electing a phased retirement option to both draw an annuity and accumulate additional contributions (to TIAA) or service credits under the state plan based on their part-time salary.

Part IV

EPILOGUE

The concluding chapter in this volume reviews and summarizes demographic and external pressures that currently influence faculty vitality in higher education. The use of faculty vitality as a practical concept is also reviewed and posited as in need of institutional response. Suggestions are given for the use of policies and strategies that follow from the preceding chapters of the book. Focus is given to three basic sets of strategies that institutions must address in order to cope with the projected conditions of academe; namely, altering the rate and composition of new faculty entering higher education, altering the rate and composition of faculty leaving academe, and/or enhancing the vitality of existing faculty.

Chapter 12

Implications
for Institutional
Response

Shirley M. Clark and *Darrell R. Lewis*

CONDITIONS OF ACADEME

Changing demographic and economic conditions have brought hard times to academe. Well-documented declines and shifts in student enrollment have reduced the numbers of faculty positions available to recent and future cohorts of new doctorates (Carnegie Council on Policy Studies in Higher Education, 1980; Commission on Human Resources, 1979; Hansen, Chapter 2 of this book; National Science Foundation Advisory Council, 1978; and others). With the annual turnover rate in tenure track positions at less than 2 percent at present, the faculty market is fast becoming immobilized (Hansen, Chapter 2; Hellweg & Churchman, 1981), and the consequences of a "lost generation of scholars" are considered to border on a national tragedy (Radner & Kuh, 1978). Faculty members who do have security of employment find their institutions caught in straitened financial circumstances (Hansen, Chapter 2) and their hegemony threatened by student consumer demands (Riesman, 1980) and, increasingly, by centralized governance processes (Becker, Chapter 10; Baldridge et al., 1978). Many faculty also perceive increasing constraints and accountability on both their work (Clark & Corcoran, Chapter 6) and their outside professional activities (Boyer & Lewis, Chapter 9). Similarly, they perceive little encouragement with few incentives to either change careers (Patton & Palmer, Chapter 8) or select alternative work patterns or early retirement options (Holden, Chapter 11). Furthermore, the faculty work force is aging slowly but relentlessly (Hansen, Chapter 2), raising concern among those who argue that efforts must be made to improve institutional productivity in both the instructional (Leslie, Swiren, & Flexner, 1977) and research realms (Reskin, Chapter 4).

These new and problematic circumstances, which are affecting both faculty members and their institutions, albeit differentially, are increasingly drawing attention to the character of work life as experienced by faculty and to the institution as employer and workplace. If we agree with Smith (1978) and Bailey (1974) that the most important resource of a college or university is the quality of its faculty, we must be concerned with the vitality of both individuals and institutions. Vitality issues are among the most frequently noted problems in the popular and scholarly higher education literature today.

FACULTY VITALITY AS A PRACTICAL CONCEPT

From the review of the literature and the descriptions, assessments, and effective uses of the concept of faculty and institutional vitality in this volume, we can conclude that although the concept tends to be rather imprecise and primitive, it is, nevertheless, highly useful. At the least, it sensitizes us to a complex, multivariable, interactive phenomenon that does not easily lend itself to precise methodological inquiry or standardized programs of resolution (Clark, Boyer, & Corcoran, Chapter 1). As commentators, scholars and faculty developers work toward a more shared agreement about the concept, several vitality guidelines from this volume can serve usefully to inform policy making and personnel management for enhanced institutional effectiveness and productivity.

First and foremost, clear recognition must be given to the fact that individual and organizational vitality are interrelated. The individual pursues a career that is structured by the organization. Individual career vitality is affected by organizational and professional socialization as well as by personal variables such as intelligence and personality. Organizational strategies, opportunity, and reward structures all provide career paths, tracks, and escalators. As the professoriate becomes immobilized, greater attention needs to be paid to the quality and efficacy of the socialization experience, to the provision of structured opportunities for career development, to appropriate recognition and rewards for performance in the full range of domains, and to growth and renewal—including possible resocialization or respecialization options.

Second, it is essential to note that vital institutions are not synonymous with so-called elite institutions relative to institutional type, resource status, student body, or mission. Prestigious institutions may indeed be vital institutions, but many will also face slow or no growth, shifting interests of students and constricted futures for their faculty. The ideas of vitality and of prestige refer to different phenomena.

Relatedly, ideal types of faculty and performance emphases will differ according to institutional type and mission. Institutions that emphasize teaching and/or service will need to focus more on faculty development policies, which revitalize routine teaching and retrain faculty for shifting curricular emphases. Those that emphasize the research and scholarly orientation will need to consider more attentively the adequacy of sponsorship and resources to sustain scholarly productivity. The point here is that situational and contextual aspects must be given special attention in the customization of faculty vitality policies and programs.

Fourth, productivity and efficiency are inherent in the idea of vitality, but they are not the whole of it. Measures of effectiveness as well as efficiency must be developed. Moving beyond quantitative estimates of faculty output in publications or student credit hours, we raise the question of quality and effectiveness. How well are the faculty performing? How well is the institution functioning in its mission? What obstacles or conditions either facilitate or block the productive efforts of the faculty?

Finally, systematic consideration must be given to the dimension of vitality variously termed enthusiasm, energy, or esprit. The reference is to the embodiment of a set of values in the spirit of the organization that energizes people to work productively and creatively. Kanter (1979) asserts that people who conceive of themselves as among the "moving" rather than the "stuck" in the career structure of the organization will keep their aspirations high, will have positive self-esteem, will work hard, will take appropriate risks, will remain engaged in their interests, will remain involved with their students and their colleagues, and will advocate constructive organizational change. How to keep faculty among the moving will require the development and maintenance of an opportunity and power structure that opens career paths, that provides developmental activities, that facilitates lateral movement across fields if vertical movement is impossible, that involves people in goal-setting, planning and governance, that deliberately builds sponsorship (old hand–newcomer) relationships within the institution, and that recognizes good performance in a variety of ways.

Thus, we argue for shared agreement on a concept of vitality that is true to the specific context of higher education institutions; one that includes but goes beyond concerns with efficiency to those of productivity, effectiveness, and quality; one that recognizes the broad-scale concerns with quality of work life in postindustrial societies. Measures of vitality such as this argument would support should include value-added, quality-associated concerns with careers over the long term in organizations, skill development at different career stages, internal opportunities for both vertical and lateral mobility, relationships that promote both the psychological sense of community or collegium and sponsor-mentor generative activity, and participation in shaping the direction of one's unit or the institution at large. Policies that acknowledge this value-added approach are necessary to prevent the demoralization of today's and tomorrow's faculty members and to enhance long-term institutional productivity.

ALTERNATIVES FOR INSTITUTIONAL RESPONSE

In order to respond to the various problematic conditions identified in this volume and elsewhere concerning faculty vitality, the range of both new and old ideas being put forth about what might be done is enormous. According to W. Todd Furniss (1981), recent solutions have included

> special and expensive programs to provide jobs for 250 hand-picked scientists and engineers each year until the generation gap is closed in the 1990s; career counseling programs—institutional, regional, consortial, and national, non-profit and commercial, from a day-long workshop to six-week residential programs; new policies on leaves of absence, part-time employment, consulting, moonlighting, patent and royalty rights, nonacademic internships, and other off-campus activities to create more options for the faculty member stuck on his home campus; faculty development programs covering everything from better teaching to planning one's life; information networks and mutual support groups and emeriti centers, and programs, programs, programs. (p. 130)

In spite of all these varied prescriptions, very little of a systematic nature has been developed to assist policy development and personnel management in these matters. Most responses have tended to be more idiosyncratic to the short-term interests of selected faculty or administrators than to the focused long-term interests of the institution and its vitality. In reviewing the collective works in this volume, it is clear that focus must be given to institutional strategies which go beyond single shot solutions and quick cures.

The condition of academe in terms of projected faculty vitality is generally bleak in outlook and long-term solutions are generally few in number. Drawing from the contributed chapters to this volume, it is evident that institutions have available basically three sets of strategies that they might adopt to assure or improve the vitality of their faculty under present and near-future conditions. They can (1) alter the rate and composition of any new faculty entering their institutions, (2) alter the rate and composition of faculty leaving academe, and/or (3) enhance the vitality of existing faculty.

Strategies for Increasing New Faculty

Strategies for increasing new faculty members at present are obviously linked with strategies for increasing faculty exits, thereby creating replacement opportunities. We will comment upon these strategies in turn.

Given the complexities of faculty demography described in this volume, the near-universal, American tradition of tenure provisions in academic personnel systems, declining enrollments, the less than favorable economic situation for faculty, and the commitment of academics (and other professionals) to the one life–one career imperative (Sarason, 1977), it should surprise no one that nearly closed communities of faculty are aging with little prospect of alteration. The traditional faculty career, as an almost perfect example of Sarason's imperative, has assumed that upon receipt of tenure a faculty member moved into a mature period of consolidation and deepening of expertise, participation in the collegial life-style, performance in teaching, research and service activities, and participated generally in a busy and productive manner until retirement. Some variation from this pre-scription has been permitted in the form of leaves of absence for relevant public or private service and consultation or moonlighting. Strategies to alter traditional careers are one matter; strategies to add new faculty without changing the personnel traditions that now hold sway are another.

Concerns about both the personal and national consequences of the loss of a generation of scientist scholars have prompted proposals to federal agencies and to private philanthropic foundations for support of young doctorates in regular institutional positions at least to the point of the ten-ure decision when the institutions themselves might accept the fiscal respon-sibilities for their salaries (Radner & Kuh, 1978). The total number of young faculty members supported by such externally funded programs at this time is unknown; without a doubt, however, it is relatively low.

Other proposals for increasing the numbers of young academics in-clude reserving some positions as they become vacant for nontenure track positions and for a few years offering them to highly qualified "nomads" (Furniss, 1981). The situation of the nomads who would "churn" as sociological marginals in the lower faculty ranks in one institution and then another raises questions of equity over the long term and, of course, the subsequent management of the inevitable hostility of those who are af-fected.

Creation of new research positions, either for young doctorates or for senior faculty, has been another proposal intended to make room for the young, recently trained PhDs (Hansen, Chapter 2). In fact, many univer-sities have moved in the past decade to develop nonfaculty personnel sys-tems for professional, research, and administrative positions, some of which have received federal funding. These proposals do seem to enlarge the institution's and the nation's research capacities, while leaving relatively untouched the traditional faculty personnel prerogatives and systems of accountability.

Stimulation of demand for higher education is, of course, another ap-proach and the more traditional one to adding younger faculty, although the two are not necessarily coupled in most cases made by advocates for de-mand stimulation (Hansen, Chapter 2; H. Bowen, 1981). Cultivating adult learners (over age 25), working hard to reduce attrition rates of undergraduate students, increasing interest in continuing, graduate, and professional education, expanding access to lower percentiles of high school graduating classes — all of these approaches are being tried or talked about.

Strategies for Increasing Faculty Exits

Strategies for altering the rate and composition of faculty leaving academe, as indicated in the previous section, are intended to address the financial solvency problems of institutions and result in open positions that less costly, younger, more recently trained doctorates might fill. At the outset, it is important to note that many conventional assumptions about the high vitality of younger faculty as compared with the diminishing vitality and flagging productivity of older faculty are weak at best. The evidence and recent findings by Reskin (Chapter 4) and Havighurst (Chapter 5) indicate that (1) increasing age does not necessarily lower scholarly productivity, (2) relationships between productivity and age differ by fields and disciplines, (3) scholarly productivity does not decline monotonically, but for most groups appears to have two peaks, and (4) any simple effects of aging appear to be small for most faculty under retirement age. Nonetheless, it is clear that many institutions already have begun to attempt the difficult process of altering faculty demography by freezing the number of tenured positions permitted and thus imposing de facto tenure quotas (Hansen, Chapter 2). This action is unpopular but sometimes fiscally prudent and may have to be taken by institutions — for reasons quite apart from those that fall within our concerns for faculty vitality. It must be recognized, however, that putting the brakes on the tenuring-in process may create inequities and career dislocations for probationary individuals, and it provides no guarantees of vitality to the institution beyond stabilization of the present situation.

More attractive options than simply securing the status quo, as essential as that may be, are those which address ways to release the faculty member from the normative grasp of the one life–one career imperative through midcareer change opportunities, through early retirement options, and through more flexible retirement programs generally.

A substantial minority of today's academics may not be happy with their careers; they may feel blocked, stuck, demoralized, or dissatisfied. Of these, some may be reluctant to consider voluntary career change, whereas others may be willing and even interested in considering change to nonacademic positions outside of the college or university under favorable circumstances. Whether sufficient jobs at comparable status and income levels will be available for the age-mature academics who may be interested in seeking them is an important and unknown factor that institutional planners should keep in mind as they, with affected faculty members, move in the direction of facilitating out-placement.

Several principles or tasks have been identified for institutional consideration by Patton and Palmer (Chapter 8) in order for midcareer options to work. Perhaps most importantly, more information from many sources must be obtained and made available to faculty members and graduate students regarding employment patterns and prospects outside academe. Faculty members should be provided with a range of opportunities for self-assessment of their personal and career goals in order to assist them in their decision making. Since each institution's problem will differ in terms of where staff reductions might best occur, or whether some minor shifting of staff into other curricular areas would be best, the focus of any career change program must be responsive to programmatic needs. Faculty support of career change may come slowly in individual cases and may require the social support of colleagues and the financial support of the institution to cushion the financial risk in the transition process. Departments and colleges must not receive negative sanctions (e.g., loss of positions, loss of more valuable rather than less valuable personnel), if their participation is to be encouraged. Finally, the financial viability of midcareer change programs should be assessed. On this principle, as with others preceding it, the cautionary reminder must be given that each individual institution must first assess its own unique circumstances; perhaps analysis of the age composition of a specific institution would indicate that a program to encourage faculty exits via career change options is *not* needed.

Early retirement incentives and more flexible retirement policies also promise to result in changes in the faculty age composition. However, we are cautioned by contributing authors Hansen, Havighurst, and Holden (Chapters 2, 5, and 11, respectively) that early retirement incentives may be very costly to make retirement attractive and to induce many faculty to forgo their regular salaries, that faculty members generally do not appear to be eager to retire, that phased retirement programs might have the unintended consequences of later retirements than might have been the case without the "easing-out" provisions; moreover, even with a successfully implemented early retirement program, the institution will gain only a one-time effect on its faculty demography. Institutional flexibility in adapting retirement programs to changing demographics and fixed or reduced budgets is limited in turn by pension plan rules, by law, and by availability of funds (Holden, Chapter 11). However, if institutions were resolved to accommodate to the needs and wishes of many older faculty members for part-time or phased retirement options congruent with their professional commitments and life-style preferences, perhaps the vitality in continued but limited role activities of these individuals might be sustained. When institutional options are greatly limited, on the other hand, and the case for employing qualified young men and women is pressing, perhaps early retirement options with professional perquisites such as availability of office space, library and laboratory facilities, and other forms of professional assistance will be as much of a balance as can be struck.

Strategies for Enhancing the Vitality of Existing Faculty

Although the various strategies that are directed toward changes in faculty demography may result in at least a modest degree of success in the near future, it is a certainty that the majority of faculty members now in regular positions in academic institutions will remain there pursuing relatively traditional career paths. Thus, the question remains: what might be done to enhance the vitality of existing faculty in whom resources have been invested and to whom institutional commitments have been made?

In spite of the intensity and extensity of interest in arguing the need for faculty development programs in the current literature, Centra (Chapter 7) has concluded that institutional programs and funds for faculty development have been greatly reduced in recent years from the previous levels established in the mid-1970s. Development program staff numbers have been reduced, fewer sabbaticals are being awarded, and less money is being made available to support participation in conferences of the various professional associations. These data are assumed to be associated with a faculty malaise, sometimes called "burnout," which is described in terms that parallel Kanter's (1979) concept of "stuckness," lack of opportunity, or immobilization. In discussing several vitality guidelines in an earlier section, we noted that keeping faculty "moving" would require the development or protection of opportunity and power structures that, among other things, involve people in goal setting, planning, and governance, and that recognize good performance in a variety of ways. Both Kanter (1979) and Becker (Chapter 10) speculate on the vulnerability of persons who feel immobilized to unionization efforts. If people feel that there is little prospect for personal progress in positions that are not apt to change and that the leaders of their institutions are not responsive to faculty concerns, unionization and perhaps devitalization are likely to occur.

One area that often has been treated as a problem in the literature and the popular press as allegedly affecting the vitality of faculty and institutions in negative ways has been examined in this volume in a new and far more positive light. This area is faculty consulting (Boyer and Lewis, Chapter 9). Consulting has been and is an integral part of traditional faculty roles and responsibilities; the case has been made for its contributions to faculty and institutional vitality. Unfortunately, faculty consulting in the past has been overestimated in its extent and underappreciated in its benefits to those who do the consulting, to the institutions that receive the bridging effects, and, of course, to those who receive the consulting services per se. With appropriate policy and procedures, faculty consulting can and ought to be permissive rather than tightly restrictive.

In summary, policy and action areas for enhancing the vitality of existing faculty from an institutional perspective may be grouped around three general themes: providing environmental support for the scholarly development of the faculty, providing institutional support for faculty research and instructional development activities, and providing differentiated support for individual faculty needs. The first of these policy areas, derived in this book from an institutional case study of highly active faculty in a research-oriented multiversity (Clark and Corcoran, Chapter 6), concerns the importance of administrative attitudes and behavior as reflective of scholarly concerns, of recognizing the full range of faculty accomplishments, and of encouraging development of an intellectually stimulating community of colleagues. The second thematic policy area focuses on support of faculty in their high valuation on freedom of inquiry and their research activities, their need for adequate concentrated time for research, provision of "seed" money to initiate research and new instructional activities, and adequate facilities for both research and teaching. Since research and graduate training are bound together, concerns about quality of and support for graduate students also enters this policy domain. The third of the thematic policy areas focuses on provision of support for individual faculty needs such as those of faculty whose research interests have run dry, those whose research is not currently attractive to the programmatic emphases of external funding agencies, those whose instructional areas are weak in student and programmatic demand, those who experience role and performance/reward system discontinuities, and those probationary faculty members who confront rigorous expectations in a time of uncertain rewards. More concrete policy actions are suggested throughout the book relative to each of these thematic areas.

CONCLUSION

In constructing this epilogue, we have attempted to be realistic in our assessment of faculty and institutional vitality and in strategies to affect it. As we think about options and opportunities, the agenda is not to advocate simply for more faculty development programs, although many worthy programs deserve full support. We must learn more about adult development, the professional socialization of faculty members, how their careers are structured, and how the academic organization affects their vitality. Above all, we must probe into the nature of individual and organizational circumstances. The contextual, situational variables may not be as generalizable from one institution to another as the rather prescriptive literature on faculty development programs has conventionally assumed. And we must acknowledge that the faculty person—himself or herself—is the most important actor and decision maker in preserving and enhancing both faculty and institutional vitality.

About the Editors
Contributors
References
Index

About the Editors

SHIRLEY M. CLARK is professor of education and sociology at the University of Minnesota, having previously served as assistant vice-president for academic affairs at Minnesota. Her research interests are in sociology of education, including higher education, youth studies, and women's studies. She is author or coauthor of numerous articles, and is coauthor of *Youth in Modern Societies.*

DARRELL R. LEWIS is an economist and associate dean of education at the University of Minnesota. His research interests are in economic education and the economics of education with a current focus on higher education. He is author or coauthor of numerous articles, monographs, and books. His recent books include *Educational Games and Simulations in Economics, Current Issues of Economic Policy, The Professor as Teacher: University Staff Development,* and *Academic Rewards in Higher Education.*

Contributors

William E. Becker, Jr., associate professor of economics, Indiana University

Robert T. Blackburn, professor of higher education, University of Michigan

Carol M. Boyer, senior policy analyst, Education Commission of the States

John A. Centra, senior research psychologist, Educational Testing Service

Shirley M. Clark, professor of education and sociology, University of Minnesota

Mary Corcoran, professor of educational psychology and higher education, University of Minnesota

W. Lee Hansen, professor of economics, University of Wisconsin — Madison

Robert J. Havighurst, professor emeritus of education and human development, University of Chicago

Karen C. Holden, project associate of economics, University of Wisconsin — Madison

Darrell R. Lewis, professor of economic and higher education, University of Minnesota

David D. Palmer, assistant professor of management and organization, University of Connecticut

Carl V. Patton, dean of the School of Architecture and Urban Planning, University of Wisconsin-Milwaukee

Barbara Reskin, professor of sociology, University of Illinois — Champaign-Urbana

References

Aggarwal, R. "Faculty Members as Consultants: A Policy Perspective," *Journal of the College and University Personnel Association*, Summer 1981, *32*(2), 17-20.

Alderfer, C. P. "Change Processes in Organizations." In Marvin Dunnette (ed.), *Handbook of Industrial and Organizational Psychology*. Chicago: Rand McNally, 1976, 1591-1638.

Aldrich, H. E. *Organizations and Environments*. Englewood Cliffs, NJ: Prentice-Hall, 1979.

Alexander, L. T. and Yelon, S. L. (eds.). "Instructional Development Agencies in Higher Education." (Occasional paper from the Conference on Instructional Development Agencies in Higher Education, Michigan State University, 1971.) East Lansing, MI: Learning Service, Educational Development Program, Michigan State University, 1972.

Allison, P. D. and Stewart, J. A. "Productivity Differences Among Scientists: Evidence for Accumulative Advantage," *American Sociological Review*, August 1974, *39*(4), 596-606.

Altbach, P. G. "The Crisis of the Professoriate," *Annals of the American Academy of Political Social Sciences*, March 1980, *448*, 1-14.

American Association for Higher Education. *Academic Careers, Unlimited*. Washington, DC: American Association for Higher Education, n.d.

American Association for Higher Education. *Expanding Faculty Options*. Washington, DC: American Association for Higher Education, 1981.

American Association of University Professors. "Academic Retirement and Related Subjects," *AAUP Bulletin*, Spring 1950, 97-117.

American Association of University Professors. "Academic Retirement and Insurance Programs," *AAUP Bulletin*, Summer 1958, 508-515.

American Association of University Professors. "Impact of Federal Retirement-Age Legislation on Higher Education." Report of special committee on age discrimination and retirement. In *AAUP Bulletin*, Spring 1978, *64*, 181-192. (Also in *Journal of College and University Personnel Association*, Winter 1978, *29*, 14-20.)

American Association of University Professors. "Statement of
    Principles on Academic Retirement and Insurance Plans," Academe:
    Bulletin of the AAUP, August-September 1980.
American Association of University Professors (Committee Z on the
    Economic Status of the Profession). "The Rocky Road Through the
    1980s: Annual Report on the Economic Status of the Profession,
    1980-81," Academe: Bulletin of the AAUP, August 1981, 67(4),
    210-230.
American Association of University Professors (Committee Z on the
    Economic Status of the Profession). "Surprises and Uncertainties:
    Annual Report on the Economic Status of the Profession, 1981-82,"
    Academe: Bulletin of the AAUP, July-August 1982a, 68(4), 3-23.
American Association of University Professors (Committee A on
    Academic Freedom and Tenure). "Uncapping the Mandatory
    Retirement Age," Academe: Bulletin of the AAUP, September-
    October 1982b, 68(5), 14a-18a.
Arbeiter, S. "Mid-Life Career Change: A Concept in Search of
    Reality," AAHE Bulletin, October 1979, 1, 11-13, 16.
Argyris, C. Understanding Organizational Behavior. Homewood, IL:
    Dorsey Press, 1960.
Astin, A. W. Predicting Academic Performance in College:
    Selective Data on 2300 Colleges. New York: Free Press, 1971.
Astin, H. S. The Woman Doctorate in America. New York: Russell
    Sage Foundation, 1969.
Astin, H. S. "Factors in Women's Scholarly Productivity." In
    H. S. Astin and W. Z. Hirsch (eds.), The Higher Education of
    Women. New York: Praeger, 1978.
Atkinson, J. W. "Motivation for Achievement." In T. Blass (ed.),
    Personality Variables in Social Behavior. Hillsdale, NJ:
    Erlbaum Associates, 1977.
Atselek, F. J. and Gomberg, I. L. Young Doctorate Faculty in
    Selected Science and Engineering Departments, 1975 to 1980.
    Higher Education Panel Reports, No. 30. Washington, DC:
    American Council on Education, August 1976.
Atselek, F. J. and Gomberg, I. L. Young Doctoral Faculty in
    Science and Engineering: Trends in Composition and Research
    Activity. Higher Education Panel Reports, No. 43. Washington,
    DC: American Council on Education, February 1979.
Bacharach, S. B. and Lawler, E. J. Power and Politics in
    Organizations. San Francisco: Jossey-Bass, 1980.
Back, K. W. (ed.). Life Course: Integrative Theories and
    Exemplary Populations. AAAS Selected Symposium 41. Boulder,
    CO: Westview Press, 1980.
Bailey, S. K. "The Effective Use of Human Resources." In The
    Effective Use of Resources: Financial and Human. Washington,
    DC: Association of Governing Boards, 1974.
Bailey, S. K. "People Planning in Postsecondary Education: Human
    Resources Development." In J. N. Nesmith (ed.), More for Less:
    Academic Planning with Faculty Without New Dollars. New York:
    Society for College and University Planning, 1975.
Bailey, T. "Industrial Outplacement at Goodyear, Part I: The
    Company's Position," Personnel Administrator, March 1980, 42-45.
Baldridge, J. V. "Reflections on 'Dual Track' Governance," Academe:
    Bulletin of the AAUP, January-February 1982a, 68, 8A-9A.
Baldridge, J. V. "Shared Governance: A Fable About the Lost Magic
    Kingdom," Academe: Bulletin of the AAUP, January-February 1982b,
    68, 12-15.

Baldridge, J. V., Curtis, D. V., Ecker, G., and Riley, G. L.
    Policy Making and Effective Leadership. San Francisco:
    Jossey-Bass, 1978.
Baldwin, R. G. "Adult and Career Development: What are the
    Implications for Faculty?," Current Issues in Higher Education,
    1979a, (2), 13-20.
Baldwin, R. G. "The Faculty Career Process--Continuity and Change:
    A Study of College Professors at Five Stages of the Academic
    Career." Unpublished PhD dissertation, University of Michigan,
    1979b.
Baldwin, R. G. "Fostering Faculty Vitality: Options for
    Institutions and Administrators," Administrator's Update, Fall
    1982, 4(1), 1-5.
Baldwin, R. G. and Blackburn, R. T. "The Academic Career as a
    Developmental Process: Implications for Higher Education,"
    Journal of Higher Education, November/December 1981, 52(6),
    598-614.
Baldwin, R., Brakeman, L., Edgerton, R., Hagberg, J., and Maher, T.
    Expanding Faculty Options: Career Development Projects
    at Colleges and Universities. Washington, DC: American
    Association for Higher Education, 1981.
Barry, R. M. and Naftzger, B. "Career Development Program."
    Chicago: Loyola University, n.d.
Baugh, W. and Stone, J. "Teachers, Unions, and Wages in the 1970s:
    Unionism Now Pays," Industrial and Labor Relations Review, April
    1982, 3, 368-376.
Bayer, A. E. Teaching Faculty in Academe: 1972-73. Washington,
    DC: American Council on Education, 1973.
Bayer, A. E. and Dutton, J. E. "Career Age and Research-
    Professional Activities of Academic Scientists: Tests of
    Alternative Nonlinear Models and Some Implications for Higher
    Education Faculty Policies," Journal of Higher Education,
    May/June 1977, 48(3), 259-282.
Becker, W. E., Jr. "The University Professor as a Utility
    Maximizer and Producer of Learning, Research and Income,"
    Journal of Human Resources, 1975, 10, 109-115.
Becker, W. E., Jr. "Professorial Behavior Given a Stochastic
    Reward Structure," American Economic Review, December 1979,
    69, 1010.
Begin, J. P. "Faculty Bargaining and Faculty Reward Systems."
    In Darrell R. Lewis and William E. Becker, Jr. (eds.), Academic
    Rewards in Higher Education. Cambridge, MA: Ballinger, 1979.
Bennis, W. "Toward a 'Truly' Scientific Management: The Concept
    of Organizational Health," General Systems Yearbook, 1962, 7,
    269-282.
Bergquist, W. H. and Phillips, S. R. "Components of An Effective
    Faculty Development Program," Journal of Higher Education, 1975,
    46, 177-211.
Bergquist, W. H., Phillips, S. R., and Quehl, G. A Handbook for
    Faculty Development 1. Washington, DC: Council for the
    Advancement of Small Colleges, 1975.
Bergquist, W. H., Phillips, S. R., and Quehl, G. A Handbook for
    Faculty Development 2. Berkeley, CA: Pacific Soundings Press,
    1977.
Bess, J. L. "Patterns of Satisfaction of Organizational
    Prerequisites and Personal Needs in University Academic
    Departments," Sociology of Education, 1973a, 46, 99ff.

Bess, J. L. "Integrating Faculty and Student Life Cycles," Review of Educational Research, Fall 1973b, 43, 377-403.

Bess, J. and Lodahl, T. M. "Career Patterns and Satisfactions in University Middle-Management," Educational Record, Spring 1969, 50, 200-229.

Birnbaum, R. "Unionization and Faculty Compensation: Part I," Educational Record, 1974, 55, 29-33.

Birnbaum, R. "Unionization and Faculty Compensation: Part II," Educational Record, 1976, 57, 116-118.

Blackburn, R. T. Tenure: Aspects of Job Security on the Changing Campus. Atlanta, GA: Southern Regional Education Board, Research Monograph No. 19, July 1972.

Blackburn, R. T. "Expert Rating on Academic Leadership as a Measure of Institutional Quality," Sociology of Education, Fall 1974, 47, 535-540.

Blackburn, R. T. "Academic Careers: Patterns and Possibilities," Current Issues in Higher Education, 1979, (2), 25-27.

Blackburn, R. T. "Career Phases and Their Influence on Faculty Motivation." In James Bess (ed.), Faculty Motivation to Teach Effectively. San Francisco: Jossey-Bass, 1982.

Blackburn, R. T., Behymer, C. E., and Hall, D. E. "Research Note: Correlates of Faculty Publications," Sociology of Education, April 1978, 51, 132-141.

Blackburn, R. T., Chapman, D., and Cameron, S. "Cloning in Academe: Mentorship and Academic Careers," Research in Higher Education, 1981, 15(4), 315-327.

Blackburn, R. T. and Clark, M. J. "An Assessment of Faculty Performance: Some Correlates Between Administrator, Colleague, Student and Self-Ratings," Sociology of Education, Spring 1975, 48, 242-256.

Blackburn, R. T. and Fox, T. G. "Physicians' Values and Their Career Stage," Journal of Vocational Behavior, April 1983, 22(2), 159-173.

Blackburn, R. T. and Havighurst, R. J. "Career Patterns of U.S. Male Academic Social Scientists," Higher Education, Spring 1979, 8, 553-572.

Blackburn, R. T., Pellino, G., Boberg, A., and O'Connell, C. "Faculty Development Programs, the Improvement of Instruction, and Faculty Goals: An Evaluation." Paper presented at the Annual Meeting of the American Educational Research Association, Boston, Massachusetts, 1980.

Blackburn, R. T. and Schluckebier, D. "Faculty Quality in Black and White Public Colleges and Universities in Selected Southern States: 1954-1980." Paper presented at Finley Carpenter Research Conference, University of Michigan, May 1982.

Blau, P. M. The Organization of Academic Work. New York: John Wiley & Sons, 1973.

Blau, P. M. "Recruiting Faculty and Students," Sociology of Education, Winter 1974, 47, 93-113.

Bobbitt, H. R., Jr. and Behling, O. C. "Organizational Behavior: A Review of the Literature," Journal of Higher Education, January/February 1981, 52(1), 29-44.

Boberg, A. L. "Faculty Under Stress: Person-Environment Fit Theory." Unpublished PhD dissertation, University of Michigan, 1982.

Bognanno, M. R., Estenson, D. L., and Suntrup, E. L. Faculty Collective Bargaining Agreements in Four-Year Colleges and Universities (Working Paper 77-01). Minneapolis: University of Minnesota, Industrial Relations Center, 1977.

Bowen, H. R. Academic Compensation: Are Faculty and Staff in
    American Higher Education Adequately Paid? New York: Teachers
    Insurance and Annuity Association, College Retirement Equities
    Fund, 1978.
Bowen, H. R. The State of the Nation and An Agenda For Higher
    Education. San Francisco: Jossey-Bass, 1981.
Bowen, W. G. Graduate Education in the Arts and Sciences:
    Prospects for the Future. Report of the President, Princeton
    University, April 1981.
Bragg, A. K. The Socialization Process in Higher Education.
    AAHE-ERIC/Higher Education Report No. 7, 1976.
Braskamp, L. A., Fowler, D., and Ory, J. C. "Faculty Development
    and Achievement: A Faculty's [sic] View." Paper presented at
    the Annual Meeting of the American Educational Research
    Association, New York, March 1982.
Brenneman, D. An Economic Theory of Ph.D. Production: The Case at
    Berkeley. Berkeley: University of California, Office of the
    Vice President-Planning and Analysis, June 1970.
Brim, O. G., Jr. "Theories of the Male Mid-Life Crisis," Counseling
    Psychologist, 1976, 6, 2-9.
Brim, O. G., Jr. and Wheeler, S. (eds.). Socialization After
    Childhood. New York: John Wiley & Sons, 1966.
Broudy, H. S. "Faculty Study in a Second Discipline." Urbana, IL:
    University of Illinois, Advisory Committee on Interdisciplinary
    Programs, 18 September 1978.
Brown, D. G. The Mobile Professor. Washington, DC: American
    Council on Education, 1967.
Brown, D. G. and Hanger, S. "Pragmatics of Faculty Self-
    Development," Educational Record, Summer 1975, 56, 201-206.
Brown, J. C. (trans.). "Justus von Liebig: An Autobiographical
    Sketch." In Annual Report of the Board of Regents of the
    Smithsonian Institution, July 1891. Washington, DC: Government
    Printing Office, 1893, 257-268.
Brown, W. W. and Stone, C. C. "Faculty Compensation Under
    Unionization: An Analysis of Current Research Methods and
    Findings." Working Paper No. 77501, School of Business
    Administration and Economics, California State University,
    Northridge, March 1977.
Bruss, E. A. and Kutina, K. L. "Faculty Vitality Given
    Retrenchment: A Policy Analysis," Research in Higher Education,
    1981, 14, 19-30.
Buhl, L. C. and Greenfield, A. "Contracting for Professional
    Development in Academe," Educational Record, Summer 1975, 56,
    111-121.
Burkhauser, R. V. "The Pension Acceptance Decision of Older
    Workers," Journal of Human Resources, Winter 1979, 14(1).
Burkhauser, R. V. "The Early Acceptance of Social Security--An
    Asset Maximization Approach," Industrial Labor Relations Review,
    July 1980, 33(5).
Burkhauser, R. V. and Quinn, J. "Mandatory Retirement Study
    (Part I): Task Completion Report on the Relationship Between
    Mandatory Retirement Age Limits and Pension Rules in the
    Retirement Decision." Washington, DC: Urban Institute, June
    1980.
Cameron, K. "Measuring Organizational Effectiveness in Institutions
    of Higher Education," Administrative Science Quarterly, December
    1978, 23(4), 604-626.

Cameron, S. W. and Blackburn, R. T. "Sponsorship and Academic Career Success," Journal of Higher Education, July/August 1981, 52(4), 369-377.

Carlson, G. and Karlsson, K. "Age, Cohorts and Generation of Generations," American Sociological Review, 1970, 35, 710-718.

Carnegie Commission on Higher Education. A Classification of Institutions of Higher Education (Technical Report). New York: McGraw-Hill, 1973a.

Carnegie Commission on Higher Education. New Students and New Places: Policies for the Future Growth and Development of American Higher Education. New York: McGraw-Hill, 1973b.

Carnegie Council on Policy Studies in Higher Education. A Classification of Institutions of Higher Education. Berkeley, CA: Carnegie Council on Policy Studies in Higher Education, 1976.

Carnegie Council on Policy Studies in Higher Education. Three Thousand Futures. The Next Twenty Years for Higher Education. San Francisco: Jossey-Bass, 1980.

Carnegie Foundation for the Advancement of Teaching. Missions of the Curriculum: A Contemporary Review with Suggestions. San Francisco: Jossey-Bass, 1977.

Cartter, A. M. "Science Manpower for 1970-1985," Science, 1971, 172, 132-140.

Cartter, A. M. "The Academic Labor Market." In M. S. Gordon (ed.), Higher Education and the Labor Market. New York: McGraw-Hill, 1974.

Cartter, A. M. Ph.D.'s and the Academic Labor Market. New York: McGraw-Hill, 1976.

Cartter, A. M. and Solmon, L. C. "Implications for Faculty," Change, 1976, 8, 37-38.

Cattell, R. B., Eber, H. W., and Tatsuoka, M. M. Handbook for the Sixteen Personality Factor Questionnaire (16PF). Champaign, IL: Institute for Personality and Ability Testing, 1970.

Centra, J. A. Women, Men and the Doctorate. Princeton, NJ: Educational Testing Service, 1974.

Centra, J. A. Faculty Development Practices in U.S. Colleges and Universities. Princeton, NJ: Educational Testing Service, November 1976.

Centra, J. A. "Types of Faculty Development Programs," Journal of Higher Education, 1978, 49(2), 151-162.

Centra, J. "Maintaining Faculty Vitality Through Development." Paper presented at Higher Education Symposium on Faculty Vitality, University of Minnesota, Minneapolis, May 1982.

Centra, J. A. (ed.). Renewing and Evaluating Teaching. New Directions for Higher Education, No. 17. San Francisco: Jossey-Bass, 1977.

Centra, J. A. and Creech, F. R. The Relationship Between Student, Teacher, and Course Characteristics and Student Ratings of Teacher Effectiveness. Princeton, NJ: Educational Testing Service (Research Bulletin 76-1), March 1976.

Chambers, J. A. "Relating Personality and Biographical Factors to Scientific Creativity," Psychological Monographs, 1964, 78, 1-20.

Chickering, A. W. and Havighurst, R. J. "The Life Cycle." In Arthur W. Chickering and Associates, The Modern American College, 16-50. San Francisco: Jossey-Bass, 1981.

Child, J. "Organization Structure, Environment and Performance-- The Role of Strategic Choice," Sociology, January 1972, 6, 1-22.

Chronicle of Higher Education. "In Brief: Faculty-Union Membership
   at an All-Time High," 28 April 1982, p. 2.
Chronicle of Higher Education. "Estimated Earnings of Faculty
   Members Beyond Their Basic Salaries for 1980-81," 9 December
   1981, 23(15), p. 14.
Chronicle of Higher Education. "Facts About Universities' Career
   Programs," 16 February 1983, p. 24.
Clark, R., Kreps, J., and Spengler, J. "Economics of Aging:
   A Survey," Journal of Economic Literature, September 1978.
Clark, S. and Corcoran, M. (Interviews with University of
   Minnesota faculty, research in progress, 1982.)
Clemente, F. "Early Career Determinants of Research Productivity,"
   American Journal of Sociology, September 1973, 79(2), 409-419.
Clemente, F. and Sturgis, R. B. "Quality of Department of Doctoral
   Training and Research Productivity," Sociology of Education,
   Spring 1974, 47, 287-299.
COFHE (Consortium on Financing Higher Education). Potential
   Financial and Employment Impact of Age 70 Mandatory Retirement
   Legislation on COFHE Institutions. Cambridge, MA: Tillinghas,
   Nelson and Warren, Inc. for COFHE, 1979.
COFHE (Consortium on Financing Higher Education). Faculty
   Retirement at the COFHE Institutions: An Analysis of the Impact
   of Age 70 Mandatory Retirement and Options for Institutional
   Response. Cambridge, MA: John O. Blackburn and Susan Schiffman
   for COFHE, 1980a.
COFHE (Consortium on Financing Higher Education). The Report of
   the COFHE Study on Faculty Retirement: An Overview. Cambridge,
   MA: COFHE, June 1980b.
COFHE (Consortium on Financing Higher Education). Uncapping and
   Faculty Retirement: A Closer Look at the Issues. Cambridge,
   MA: COFHE, 1981.
Cohen, M. D. and March, J. G. Leadership and Ambiguity: The
   American College President. New York: McGraw-Hill for the
   Carnegie Commission on the Future of Higher Education, 1974.
Cole, J. R. "Patterns of Intellectual Influence in Scientific
   Research," Sociology of Education, 1973, 46, 377-403.
Cole, J. R. Fair Science: Women in the Scientific Community.
   New York: Free Press, 1979.
Cole, J. R. and Cole, S. "Measuring the Quality of Scientific
   Research." In J. R. Cole and S. Cole (eds.), Social
   Stratification in Science. Chicago: University of Chicago
   Press, 1973a.
Cole, J. R. and Cole, S. (eds.). Social Stratification in Science.
   Chicago: University of Chicago Press, 1973b.
Cole, S. "Age and Scientific Behavior: A Comparative Analysis."
   Paper presented at the Annual Meeting of the American
   Sociological Association, New Orleans, Louisiana, 1972.
Cole, S. "Age and Scientific Performance," American Journal of
   Sociology, January 1979, 84(4), 958-977.
Cole, S. and Cole, J. R. "Scientific Output and Recognition: A
   Study in the Operation of the Reward System in Science,"
   American Sociological Review, 1967, 39, 377-390.
Conrad, C. F. "A Grounded Theory of Academic Change," Sociology
   of Education, April 1978, 51, 101-112.
Corwin, T. W. and Knepper, P. R. Finance and Employment
   Implications of Raising the Mandatory Retirement Age for
   Faculty. Washington, DC: American Council on Education, 1978.

Crane, D. "Scientists at Major and Minor Universities: A Study of
    Productivity and Recognition," American Sociological Review,
    1965, 30(5), 699-714.
Danziger, S., Haveman, R., and Plotnick, R. "How Income Transfer
    Programs Affect Work, Savings, and the Income Distribution: A
    Critical Review," Journal of Economic Literature, September
    1981, 19, 975-1028.
Davis, R. A. "Note on Age and Productive Scholarship of a
    University Faculty," Journal of Applied Psychology, 1954, 38,
    318-319.
Debrief. "The Southwest Field Training Project" (Prescott, AZ:
    Learninghouse, Inc.), December 1979.
Dennis, W. "Age and Achievement: A Critique," Journal of
    Gerontology, 1956a, 11, 331-337.
Dennis, W. "Age and Productivity among Scientists," Science,
    1956b, 123, 724.
Dennis, W. "The Age Decrement in Outstanding Scientific
    Contributions: Fact or Artifact?," American Psychologist, 1958,
    13, 457-460.
Dennis, W. "Creative Productivity Between the Ages of 20 and 80,"
    Journal of Gerontology, 1966, 21, 1-8.
Dennis, W. and Girden, E. "Current Scientific Activities of
    Psychologists as a Function of Age," Journal of Gerontology,
    1974, 9, 175-178.
Department of Labor. Interim Report to Congress on Age
    Discrimination in Employment Act Studies. Submitted to Congress
    by Employment Standards Administration, Department of Labor,
    1982.
DeVries, D. L. "The Relationship of Role Expectations to Faculty
    Behavior," Research in Higher Education, 1975, 3(2), 111-127.
Dillon, K. E. "Outside Professional Activities," National Forum:
    Phi Kappa Phi Journal, 1979, 69(4), 38-42.
Dillon, K. E. and Bane, K. L. "Consulting and Conflict of Interest:
    A Compendium of the Policies of Almost One Hundred Major
    Colleges and Universities," Educational Record, Spring 1980,
    61(2), 52-72.
Dorfman, L. T. "Emeritus Professors: Correlates of Professional
    Activity in Retirement," Research in Higher Education, 1980,
    12(4), 301-316.
Dresch, S. P. "Demography, Technology, and Higher Education:
    Toward a Formal Model of Educational Adaptation," Journal of
    Political Economy, June 1975, 83(3), 535-569.
Dunham, R. E., Wright, P. S., and Chandler, M. O. Teaching
    Faculty in Universities and Four-Year Colleges. Washington, DC:
    US Office of Education, 1966.
Dunlop, J. T. Testimony to the Subcommittee on Labor, Committee on
    Labor and Human Resources, US Senate, 18 August 1982.
Dunnette, M. D. (ed.). Handbook of Industrial and Organizational
    Psychology. Chicago: Rand McNally, 1976.
Ebben, J. and Maher, T. H. "Capturing Institutional Vitality."
    Paper presented at the Association for Institutional Research
    Annual Forum, San Diego, California, May 1979.
Eble, K. E. Career Development of the Effective College Teacher.
    Washington, DC: American Association of University Professors,
    November 1971.
Eble, K. E. Professors as Teachers. San Francisco: Jossey-Bass,
    1972.

Eble, K. E. The Craft of Teaching. San Francisco: Jossey-Bass, 1976.

Eckert, R. E. and Stecklein, J. E. Job Motivations and Satisfactions of College Teachers: A Study of Faculty Members in Minnesota Colleges. Washington, DC: US Government Printing Office, 1961.

Eddy, M. S. "Faculty Response to Retrenchment," AAHE-ERIC/Higher Education Research Currents, June 1982, 33(10), 7-10.

Edgerton, R. "Perspectives on Faculty." Keynote Address to the Kansas Conference on Postsecondary Education, Topeka, Kansas, 18 November 1980.

Elmore, C. J. and Blackburn, R. T. "Black and White Faculty in White Research Universities," Journal of Higher Education, January/February 1983, 54(1), 1-15.

Epstein, C. F. Woman's Place: Options and Limits in Professional Careers. Berkeley: University of California Press, 1970.

Epstein, J. (ed.). Masters: Portraits of Great Teachers. New York: Basic Books, 1981.

Erikson, E. H. Identity and the Life Cycle. New York: International Universities Press, 1959.

Erikson, E. H. (ed.). Adulthood. New York: Norton, 1978.

Farber, S. "The Earnings and Promotion of Women Faculty: Comment," American Economic Review, 1977, 67, 199-217.

Feinberg, L. "The Retrofitting of the Ph.D.," Washington Post, 19 July 1982.

Felder, N. and Blackburn, R. T. "Student Reactions to the Faculty Pedagogical Role." Paper presented at the Annual Meeting of the American Educational Research Association, Los Angeles, California, April 1981.

Ferber, M. A. "Professors, Performance and Rewards," Industrial Relations, 1974, 13, 69-77.

Filstead, W. J. "Qualitative Methods: A Needed Perspective in Evaluation Research." In C. S. Reichardt and T. S. Cook (eds.), Qualitative and Quantitative Methods in Evaluation Research. Beverly Hills, CA: Sage Publications, 1979.

Freeman, R. B. "Demand for Labor in a Nonprofit Market: University Faculty." In D. S. Hamermesh (ed.), Labor in the Public and Nonprofit Sectors. Princeton, NJ: Princeton University Press, 1975.

Freeman, R. B. "Employment Opportunities and Doctorate Manpower." Report (Mimeograph) to National Academy of Science, Washington, DC, 1977.

Freeman, R. B. "Should We Organize? Effects of Faculty Unionism on Academic Compensation." NBER Working Paper No. 301 and Discussion Paper No. 671, Harvard Institute of Economic Research, November 1978.

French, J. R. P., Jr., Tupper, C. J., and Mueller, E. F. "Work Load of University Professors." Unpublished paper, University of Michigan, Ann Arbor, 1965.

Friedkin, N. E. "University Social Structure and Social Networks Among Scientists," American Journal of Sociology, May 1978, 83, 1444-1465.

Friedson, E. (ed.). The Professions and Their Prospects. Beverly Hills, CA: Sage Publications, 1973.

Froomkin, J. "Full-Time Faculty in Higher Education—Numbers and Ages," Proceedings of the Social Statistics Section, American Statistical Association, 1978, 657-662.

Fulton, O. and Trow, M.   "Research Activity in American Higher
   Education," Sociology of Education, Winter 1974, 47(1), 29-73.
Furniss, W. T.   "New Opportunities for Faculty Members,"
   Educational Record, Winter 1981a, 62(1), 8-15.
Furniss, W. T.   Reshaping Faculty Careers.   Washington, DC:
   American Council on Education, 1981b.
Gaff, J. G.   Toward Faculty Renewal.   San Francisco: Jossey-Bass,
   1975.
Gaff, J. G.   Institutional Renewal through the Improvement of
   Teaching.   New Directions for Higher Education, No. 24.   San
   Francisco: Jossey-Bass, 1978.
Gaff, S. S., Festa, C., and Gaff, J. G.   Professional Development:
   A Guide to Resources.   New Rochelle, NY: Change Magazine Press,
   1978.
Garbarino, J. W.   "Creeping Unionism and the Faculty Labor Market."
   In M. S. Gordon (ed.), Higher Education and the Labor Market.
   New York: McGraw-Hill, 1974.
Garbarino, J. W.   Faculty Bargaining: Change and Conflict.   A
   report prepared for the Carnegie Commission on Higher Education
   and the Ford Foundation.   New York: McGraw-Hill, 1975a.
Garbarino, J. W.   "Faculty Union Activity in Higher Education--
   1974," Industrial Relations, 1975b, 14, 110-111.
Garbarino, J. W.   "Faculty Unionism: The First Ten Years,"
   Annals of the American Academy of Political and Social Sciences,
   March 1980a, 448, 74-85.
Garbarino, J. W.   "Faculty Unionization: The Pre-Yeshiva Years,
   1966-1979," Industrial Relations, Spring 1980b, 19, 221-230.
Garbarino, J. W. and Aussieker, B.   Faculty Bargaining: Change and
   Conflict.   New York: McGraw-Hill, 1975.
Garbarino, J., Feller, D. E. and Finkin, M. W.   Faculty Bargaining
   in Public Higher Education: A Report and Two Essays.   San
   Francisco: Jossey-Bass, 1977.
Gardner, J. W.   Self-Renewal.   New York: Harper & Row, 1963.
Gardner, J. W.   Morale.   New York: Norton, 1978.
Gavin, J. F.   "Organizational Climate as a Function of Personal
   and Organizational Variables," Journal of Applied Psychology,
   February 1974, 60, 135-139.
"Generations," Daedalus, Fall 1978, 107, 205 pp. (See especially
   the papers by L. Nash, A. Kriegel, M. W. Riley, and T. K.
   Hareven.)
Glaser, B. G.   "Variations in the Importance of Recognition in
   Scientists' Careers," Social Problems, 1963, 268-276.
Glaser, B. G.   Organizational Scientists: Men with Professional
   Careers.   Indianapolis, IN: Bobbs-Merrill, 1964.
Glaser, B. G. and Strauss, A. L.   The Discovery of Grounded Theory:
   Strategies for Qualitative Research.   Chicago: Aldine, 1967.
Glass, G. V.   "Teacher Effectiveness."   In H. Walberg (ed.),
   Evaluating Educational Performance.   Berkeley, CA: McCutchan,
   1974.
Goldner, F. H. and Ritti, R. R.   "Professionalization as Career
   Immobility," American Journal of Sociology, March 1967, 72(5),
   489-502.
Golomb, S. W.   "Faculty Consulting: Should It Be Curtailed?,"
   National Forum: Phi Kappa Phi Journal, 1979, 69(4), 34-37.
Gooding, J.   "Out-placement . . .," Across the Board, April 1979,
   14-22.

Goodman, P. S., Pennings, J. M., et al. New Perspectives on
    Organizational Effectiveness. San Francisco: Jossey-Bass, 1977.
Gottschalk, E. C. "Some Frustrated Humanities Ph.D.s Find Success
    after Being Retrained for Business," Wall Street Journal, 16
    December 1982, p. 27.
Graebner, W. A History of Retirement: The Meaning and Function
    of an American Institution, 1885-1978. New Haven, CT: Yale
    University Press, 1980.
Grant, G. and Riesman, D. The Perpetual Dream: Reform and
    Experiment in the American College. Chicago: University of
    Chicago Press, 1978.
Greenough, W. C. College Retirement and Insurance Plans. New
    York: Columbia University Press, 1948.
Greenough, W. C. and King, F. P. Benefit Plans in American
    Colleges. New York: Columbia University Press, 1969.
Gronau, R. "Leisure, Home Production, and Work--The Theory of the
    Allocation of Time Revisited," Journal of Political Economy,
    1977, 85, 1099-1123.
Gross, A. "Twilight in Academe: The Problem of the Aging
    Professoriate," Phi Delta Kappan, 1977, 58, 752-755.
Group for Human Development in Higher Education. Faculty
    Development in a Time of Retrenchment. New Rochelle, NY:
    Change Magazine Press, 1974.
Gustad, J. W. The Career Decisions of College Teachers. Atlanta,
    GA: Southern Regional Education Board, Research Monograph No. 2,
    November 1960.
Guthrie-Morse, B., Leslie, L. L., and Hu, T. W. "Assessing the
    Impact of Faculty Unions: The Financial Implications of
    Collective Bargaining," Journal of Higher Education, May/June
    1981, 52, 237-255.
Hagberg, J. and Leider, R. The Inventurers. Reading, MA:
    Addison-Wesley, 1978.
Hage, J. Techniques and Problems of Theory Construction in
    Sociology. New York: John Wiley & Sons, 1972.
Hall, D. J. Careers in Organizations. Santa Monica, CA:
    Goodyear, 1976.
Hall, R. H. Organizations: Structure and Process (2nd Ed.).
    Englewood Cliffs, NJ: Prentice-Hall, 1977.
Hammer, T. H. and Bacharach, S. B. Reward Systems and Power
    Distribution. Ithaca, NY: New York State School of Industrial
    and Labor Relations, Cornell University, 1977.
Hansen, W. L. "The Implications of Declining Enrollments and the
    Higher Mandatory Retirement Age." Unpublished paper for the
    Midwest Economics Association, Chicago, Illinois, 1979.
Hansen, W. L. and Holden, K. C. "Faculty Responses to Mandatory
    Retirement." Paper presented at the American Economic
    Association Meeting, Washington, DC, 29 December 1981a.
Hansen, W. L. and Holden, K. C. Mandatory Retirement in Higher
    Education. Final report (unpublished), submitted to US
    Department of Labor, 1981b.
Hargens, L. L. "The Social Contexts of Scientific Research."
    Unpublished PhD Dissertation, University of Wisconsin, Madison,
    1971.
Hargens, L. L. Patterns of Scientific Research: A Comparative
    Analysis of Research in Three Scientific Fields. American
    Sociological Association Rose Monograph Series, 1975.

Hargens, L. L. and Hagstrom, W. O. "Sponsored and Contest Mobility of American Academic Scientists," _Sociology of Education_, Winter 1967, 40(1) 24-38.

Hargens, L. L., McCann, J. C., and Reskin, B. F. "Productivity and Reproductivity: Fertility and Professional Achievement Among Research Scientists," _Social Forces_, September 1978, 57(1), 154-163.

Harmon, L. R. _Profiles of Ph.D.'s in the Sciences (1935-1960)_. Washington, DC: National Academy of Sciences, National Research Council, 1965.

Havighurst, R. J., McDonald, W. J., Perun, P. J., and Snow, R. B. _Social Scientists and Educators: Lives After Sixty_. Chicago: University of Chicago Press, 1976.

Havighurst, R. J., McDonald, W. J., Maeulen, L., and Mazel, J. "Male Social Scientists: Lives After Sixty," _Gerontologist_, February 1979, 19(1), 55-60.

Heist, P. and Yonge, G. _The Omnibus Personality Inventory, Form E (Manual)_. New York: Psychological Corporation, 1968.

Hellweg, S. A. and Churchman, D. A. "The Academic Tenure System: Unplanned Obsolescence in an Era of Retrenchment," _Planning for Higher Education_, 1981, 10(1), 16-18.

Hipps, G. M. and Winstead, P. C. _Faculty Development in Academic Planning: An Approach to Institutional Self-Renewal_. Greenville, SC: Furman University, 1978.

Hitch, E. J. "Similarity of Student Ratings for Instructors and Courses Across Time." Unpublished PhD dissertation, University of Michigan, 1980.

Hodgkinson, H. L. "Adult Development: Implications for Faculty and Administrators," _Educational Record_, Fall 1974, 55(4), 263-274.

Hodgkinson, H. L. "Beyond Productivity to Quality." Paper presented at the Annual Meeting of the American Association for Higher Education, Washington, DC, March 1981.

Hofstadter, R. and Hardy, C. D. _The Development and Scope of Higher Education in the United States_. New York: Columbia University Press, 1952.

Holley, J. W. "Tenure and Research Productivity," _Research in Higher Education_, April 1977, 6(2), 181-192.

Horn, J. L. and Cattell, R. B. "Refinement and Test of the Theory of Fluid and Crystallized Intelligence," _Journal of Educational Psychology_, 1966, 57, 253-270.

Horn, J. L. and Cattell, R. B. "Age Differences in Fluid and Crystallized Intelligence," _Acta Psychologica_, 1967, 26, 107-129.

Hoyt, D. and Howard, G. "The Evaluation of Faculty Development Programs," _Research in Higher Education_, 1978, 8, 25-38.

Hull, D. L., Tessner, P. D., and Diamond, A. M. "Planck's Principle: Do Younger Scientists Accept New Scientific Ideas with Greater Alacrity than Older Scientists?," _Science_, 1978, 202, 717-723.

Improving College and University Teaching. "Professor and Profession," symposium, Autumn 1976, 24, 197-254.

Jackson, T. "Industrial Outplacement at Goodyear, Part 2: The Consultant's Viewpoint," _Personnel Administrator_, March 1980, 43-47.

Jacobson, R. L. "Looking Beyond Academe: What Scholars Can Do When Their Careers Don't Work," _Chronicle of Higher Education_, 16 February 1983, pp. 21-23.

Jenny, H. H., Heim, P., and Hughes, G. C. Another Challenge, Age
    70 Retirement in Higher Education. New York: Teachers
    Insurance and Annuity Association, 1979.
Kanter, R. M. Men and Women of the Corporation. New York: Basic
    Books, 1977.
Kanter, R. M. "Changing the Shape of Work: Reform in Academe,"
    Current Issues in Higher Education, 1979, (1), 3-10.
Katz, D. A. "Faculty Salaries, Promotion, and Productivity at a
    Large University," American Economic Review, 1973, 63, 469-477.
Katz, D. A. and Kahn, R. L. The Social Psychology of Organizations.
    New York: John Wiley & Sons, 1968.
Katz, D. A. and Kahn, R. L. The Social Psychology of Organizations
    (2nd Ed.). New York: John Wiley & Sons, 1978.
Kell, D. and Patton, C. V. "Reaction to Induced Early Retirement."
    Gerontologist, April 1978, 18, 173-179.
Kemerer, F. R. and Baldridge, J. V. Unions on Campus. San
    Francisco: Jossey-Bass, 1975.
Kemerer, F. R. and Baldridge, J. V. "Senates and Unions:
    Unexpected Peaceful Coexistence," Journal of Higher Education,
    May/June 1981, 52(3), 256-264.
Kenen, P. B. and Kenen, R. H. "Who Thinks Who's in Charge Here:
    Faculty Perceptions on Influence and Power in the University,"
    Sociology of Education, April 1978, 51, 113-123.
King, F. P. and Cook, T. J. Benefit Plans in Higher Education.
    New York: Columbia University Press, 1980.
Kirschling, W. R. "Conceptual Problems and Issues in Academic
    Labor Productivity." In Darrell R. Lewis and William E. Becker,
    Jr. (eds.), Academic Rewards in Higher Education. Cambridge, MA:
    Ballinger, 1979.
Kirschling, W. R. (ed.). Evaluating Faculty Performance and
    Vitality. New Directions for Institutional Research, 5(4).
    San Francisco: Jossey-Bass, 1978.
Koerin, B. B. "Teaching Effectiveness and Faculty Development
    Programs: A Review," Journal of General Education, Spring 1980,
    32, 40-51.
Krantz, D. L. Radical Career Changers: Life Beyond Work. New
    York: Free Press, 1978.
Kreinin, M. E. "Preserving Tenure Commitments in Hard Times:
    The Michigan State Experience," Academe: Bulletin of the AAUP,
    March-April 1982, 68, 37-45.
Kuhn, T. S. The Structure of Scientific Revolutions. Chicago:
    University of Chicago Press, 1970.
Ladd, E. C., Jr. "The Economic Position of the American
    Professoriate: A Survey Portrait." Paper presented at the
    Third Annual Academic Planning Conference, University of
    Southern California, Office of Institutional Studies, January
    1978.
Ladd, E. C., Jr. "The Work Experience of American College
    Professors: Some Data and an Argument," Current Issues in
    Higher Education, 1979, (2), 3-12.
Ladd, E. C., Jr. and Lipset, S. M. Technical Report: 1975 Survey
    of the American Professoriate. Storrs, CT: University of
    Connecticut, Social Science Data Center, November 1975a.
Ladd, E. C., Jr. and Lipset, S. M. The Divided Academy:
    Professors and Politics. New York: McGraw-Hill, 1975b.
Ladd, E. C., Jr. and Lipset, S. M. The 1977 Survey of the American
    Professoriate. For information regarding the entire survey,

see Technical Report: 1977 Survey of the American Professoriate by R. K. MacDonald. Storrs, CT: Institute for Social Inquiry, University of Connecticut, February 1978.

Lanning, A. W. "Some Correlates of Paid Faculty Consultants at Major Universities: An Analysis of their Cosmopolitan-Local Orientation." Unpublished PhD dissertation, University of Michigan, 1977.

Larson, M. S. The Rise of Professionalism: A Sociological Analysis. Berkeley: University of California Press, 1977.

Lawler, E. E., III. "Control Systems in Organizations." In Marvin Dunnette (ed.), Handbook of Industrial and Organizational Psychology, 1247-1291. Chicago: Rand McNally, 1976.

Lawrence, P. R. and Lorsch, J. W. Organization and Environment. Cambridge, MA: Harvard Business School, 1967.

Lehman, H. C. "The Creative Years in Science and Literature," Scientific Monthly, 1936, 43, 162.

Lehman, H. C. "Man's Most Creative Years: Quality vs. Quantity of Output," Scientific Monthly, 1944, 59, 384-398.

Lehman, H. C. Age and Achievement. Princeton, NJ: Princeton University Press, 1953.

Lehman, H. C. "The Influence of Longevity upon Curves Showing Man's Creative Production Rate at Successive Age Levels," Journal of Gerontology, 1958, 13, 187-191.

Leslie, L. L. and Hu, T. W. "Collective Bargaining and Faculty Compensation Revisited: A Response and a Reaffirmation," Sociology of Education, October 1977a, 31, 315-317.

Leslie, L. L. and Hu, T. W. "The Financial Implications of Collective Bargaining," Journal of Educational Finance, 1977b, 3, 32-53.

Leslie, L. L., Swiren, J. M., and Flexner, H. "Faculty Socialization and Instructional Productivity," Research in Higher Education, October 1977, 7(2), 127-143.

Levinson, D. J., Darrow, C. M., Klein, E. B., Levinson, M. H., and McKee, B. "Periods in the Adult Development of Men: Ages 18 to 45," Counseling Psychologist, 1976, 6(1), 21-25.

Levinson, D. J., Darrow, C. M., Klein, E. B., Levinson, M. H., and McKee, B. The Seasons of a Man's Life. New York: Knopf, 1978.

Lewis, D. R. and Becker, W. E., Jr. (eds.). Academic Rewards in Higher Education. Cambridge, MA: Ballinger, 1979.

Lewis, D. R. and Kellogg, T. E. "Planning and Evaluation Criteria for Allocating Departmental and Collegiate Resources in a University Setting." In Darrell R. Lewis and William E. Becker, Jr. (eds.), Academic Rewards in Higher Education. Cambridge, MA: Ballinger, 1979.

Lewis, L. S. "Academic Tenure: Its Recipients and Its Effects," Annals of the American Academy of Political Social Sciences, March 1980, 448, 86-101.

Lewis, L. S. and Ryan, M. N. "Professionalization and the Professoriate," Social Problems, December 1976, 24, 282-297.

Liebert, R. J. "Productivity, Favor and Grants Among Scholars," American Journal of Sociology, November 1976, 82, 664-673.

Lienemann, W. H. and Bullis, B. Collective Bargaining in Higher Education Systems: A Study of Four States. Washington, DC: American Association of State Colleges and Universities, 1980.

Light, D., Jr. "Introduction: The Structure of the Academic Professions," Sociology of Education, Winter 1974, 47(1), 2-28.

Light, D. W., Jr., Marsden, L. R., and Corl, T. C. The Impact of Academic Revolution on Faculty Careers. Washington, DC: American Association for Higher Education, 1973.

Linnell, R. H. "Age, Sex and Ethnic Trade-offs in Faculty Employment: You Can't Have Your Cake and Eat it Too," Current Issues in Higher Education, 1979, (4), 3-10.

Linsky, A. S. and Straus, M. A. "Student Evaluation, Research Productivity and Eminence of College Faculty," Journal of Higher Education, January 1975, 46(1), 89-102.

Lipset, S. M. "The Myth of the Conservative Professor: A Reply to Michael Faia," Sociology of Education, Spring 1974, 47(2), 203-213.

Locke, Edwin. "The Nature and Causes of Job Satisfaction." In Marvin Dunnette (ed.), Handbook of Industrial and Organizational Psychology. Chicago: Rand McNally, 1976, 1297-1349.

Long, J. S. "Productivity and Academic Position in the Scientific Career," American Sociological Review, December 1978, 43, 889-908.

Long, J. S., Allison, P. D., and McGinnis, R. "Entrance into the Academic Career," American Sociological Review, October 1979, 44(4), 816-830.

Lortie, D. C. Schoolteacher: A Sociological Study. Chicago: University of Chicago Press, 1975.

Lovett, C. M. Difficult Journey: Senior Academics and Career Change. The City University of New York, Baruch College and Graduate School, 1980. (Mimeograph.)

Lowenthal, M. F., Fiske, M., Thurnher, M., Chiriboga, D., et al. Four Stages of Life. San Francisco: Jossey-Bass, 1975.

Lowenthal, M. F. and Weiss, L. "Intimacy and Crisis in Adulthood," Counseling Psychologist, 1976, 6, 10-15.

Lublin, J. S. and King, M. L. "Invited Out," Wall Street Journal, 12 November 1980.

Mackie, M. "Professional Women's Collegial Relationships and Productivity: Female Sociologists' Journal Publications, 1976 and 1973," Sociology and Social Research, April 1977, 61, 277-293.

Maher, T. H. "Institutional Vitality in Higher Education." AAHE-ERIC/Higher Education Research Currents, AAHE Bulletin, June 1982, 34(10).

Mandelbaum, S. J. "The Intelligence of Universities," Journal of Higher Education, November/December 1979, 50(6), 697-725.

Many, W. A., Ellis, J. R., and Abrams, P. In-Service Education in American Senior Colleges and Universities: A Status Report. DeKalb, IL: College of Education, Northern Illinois University, 1969.

March, J. G. and Olsen, J. P. Ambiguity and Choice in Organizations. Oslo, Norway: Universitetsforlaget, 1976.

Margolis, J. "Productivity, Performance and Professionalism," Training and Development Journal, October 1979, 33(10), 22-25.

Marsh, H. W. and Dillon, K. E. "Academic Productivity and Faculty Supplemental Income," Journal of Higher Education, September/October 1980, 51(5), 546-555.

Marshall, J. L. "The Effects of Collective Bargaining on Faculty Salaries in Higher Education," Journal of Higher Education, May/June 1979, 50(3), 310-322.

Marver, J. D. and Patton, C. V. "The Correlates of Consultation: American Academics in 'The Real World,'" Higher Education, 1976, 5, 319-335.

Mathis, B. C. "Academic Careers and Adult Development: A Nexus for Research," Current Issues in Higher Education, 1979, (2), 21-24.

McAllister, R. J. "Service, Teaching and Research: Old Elements in a New Academic Melting Pot," Journal of Higher Education, July 1976, 47, 471-480.

McCormmach, R. Night Thoughts of a Classical Physicist. Cambridge, MA: Harvard University Press, 1982.

McGrath, E. J. "Fifty Years in Higher Education: Personal Influences on my Professional Development," Journal of Higher Education, January/February 1980, 51(1), 76-93.

McGrath, J. "Stress and Behavior in Organizations." In Marvin Dunnette (ed.), Handbook of Industrial and Organizational Psychology, 1351-1396. Chicago: Rand McNally, 1976.

McHenry, D. E., et al. Academic Departments. San Francisco: Jossey-Bass, 1977.

McKeachie, W. J. "Financial Incentives are Ineffective for Faculty." In Darrell R. Lewis and William E. Becker, Jr. (eds.), Academic Rewards in Higher Education, 3-20. Cambridge, MA: Ballinger, 1979.

McKeachie, W. J. "Enhancing Productivity in Postsecondary Education," Journal of Higher Education, July/August 1982, 53(4), 460-464.

McLaughlin, G. W., Montgomery, J. R., and Mahan, B. T. "Pay, Rank, and Growing Old With More of Each," Research in Higher Education, 1979, 11(1), 23-35.

Menges, R. J. and Levinson-Rose, J. "Improving College Teaching: A Critical Review of Research," Review of Educational Research, 1981, 51(3), 403-434.

Meyer, M. W., et al. Environments and Organizations: Theoretical and Empirical Perspectives. San Francisco: Jossey-Bass, 1978.

Miller, J. G. "Living Systems: Basic Concepts, Structure and Process, Cross-Level Hypotheses," Behavioral Science, 1965, 10, 193-237, 337-379, and 380-411.

Miller, R. I. (ed.). "Institutional Assessment for Self-Improvement," New Directions for Institutional Research, No. 29. San Francisco: Jossey-Bass, 1981.

Miller, W. S. and Wilson, K. W. Faculty Development Procedures in Small Colleges. Atlanta, GA: Southern Regional Education Board, 1963.

Minter, W. J. and Bowen, H. "Despite Economic Ills, Colleges Weathered the 70s with Larger Enrollments and Stronger Programs," Chronicle of Higher Education, 12 May 1982a.

Minter, W. J. and Bowen, H. "Colleges' Achievements in Recent Years Came Out of the Hides of Professors," Chronicle of Higher Education, 19 May 1982b, pp. 7-8.

Mitchell, J. R. "Expectancy Models of Job Satisfaction, Occupational Preference and Effort: A Theoretical, Methodological and Empirical Approach," Psychological Bulletin, 1974, 81, 1053-1077.

Montgomery, S. "Faculty Plans, Institutional Costs, and Later Mandatory Retirement: Some Findings of the COFHE Studies." Paper presented at the American Economic Association Meeting, Washington, DC, 29 December 1981.

Morgan, D. R. and Kearney, R. C. "Collective Bargaining and Faculty Compensation: A Comparative Analysis," Sociology of Education, January 1977, 50, 28-39.

Mortimer, J. and Simmons, R. "Adult Socialization," Annual Review
 of Sociology, 1978, 4, 421-454.
Mortimer, K. P. "Academic Government at Berkeley: The Academic
 Senate." Unpublished PhD dissertation, University of
 California, Berkeley, 1969.
Mulanaphy, J. M. Plans and Expectations for Retirement of TIAA-CREF
 Participants. New York: Teachers Insurance and Annuity
 Association, Educational Research Division, 1981.
Murray, J. R., Powers, E. A., and Havighurst, R. J. "Personal and
 Situational Factors Producing Flexible Careers," Gerontologist,
 1971, 11, Pt. 2, 4-12.
National Center for the Study of Collective Bargaining in Higher
 Education. "Merit Clauses in College Contracts," Newsletter,
 1975, 3, 1-7.
National Research Council. Mobility of Ph.D.'s Before and After
 the Doctorate. Career Patterns Report No. 3, prepared in the
 Research Division of the Office of Scientific Personnel.
 Washington, DC: National Academy of Sciences, 1971.
National Research Council. Field Mobility of Doctoral Scientists
 and Engineers. Washington, DC: National Academy of Sciences,
 Commission on Human Resources, 1975.
National Research Council (Commission on Human Resources).
 Research Excellence Through the Year 2000: The Importance of
 Maintaining a Flow of New Faculty into Academic Research.
 Washington, DC: National Academy of Sciences, 1979.
National Research Council. Science, Engineering, and Humanities
 Doctorates in the United States: 1981 Profile. Washington, DC:
 National Academy Press, 1982.
National Science Board. Report to the Subcommittee in Science,
 Research and Technology, U.S. House of Representatives
 Regarding Peer Review Procedures at the National Science
 Foundation. Washington, DC: National Science Board (NSB
 77-468), 1977.
National Science Foundation Advisory Council. Report of Task
 Group #1: Continued Viability of Universities as Centers for
 Basic Research. Washington, DC: National Science Foundation,
 October 1978.
Neff, C. B. "Faculty Retraining: A Four State Perspective."
 Paper presented at the American Association for Higher
 Education National Conference, Chicago, Illinois, March 1978a.
Neff, C. B. "Faculty Retraining in Four States," American
 Association of Higher Education, October 1978b, 31(2).
Nelsen, W. C. "Faculty Development: Prospects and Potential for
 the 1980s," Liberal Education, Summer 1979, 65, 141-149.
Nelsen, W. C. "AAC Prospect on Faculty Development: Content,
 Process, and Motivation in Faculty Renewal," Liberal Education,
 Summer 1980, 66, 208-209.
Nelsen, W. C. and Siegel, M. E. (eds.). Effective Approaches to
 Faculty Development. Washington, DC: Assocation of American
 Colleges, 1980.
Nelson, J. L. "Collective Bargaining's Myth and Realities,"
 Academe: Bulletin of the AAUP, January-February 1982, 68,
 9-12.
Neumann, Y. Structural Constraints, Power Perception, Research
 Performance and Rewards: An Organizational Perspective of
 University Graduate Departments. Ithaca, NY: Cornell
 University, 1976.

New York Times. "Coast Teachers Warned on Ties to Corporations,"
    8 February 1983, p. 8.
Newman, F. "Can There be Anything Affirmative about Affirmative
    Action in the 1980s?," Current Issues in Higher Education, 1979,
    (4), 15-18.
Niland, J. Where Have All the Ph.D.'s Been Going? Ithaca, NY:
    Cornell University, 1973.
Oi, Walter Y. "Academic Tenure and Mandatory Retirement Under the
    New Law," Science, December 1979, 206(21), 1373-1378.
Orzack, L. H. "Work as a 'Central Life Interest' of Professionals,"
    Social Problems, 1959, 7.
Ouchi, W. Theory Z: How American Business can Meet the Japanese
    Challenge. Reading, MA: Addison-Wesley, 1981.
Palmer, D. D. "Basic Age Distributions by Field by Type of
    Institution." University of Connecticut, School of Business
    Administration, 20 October 1976. (Mimeograph.)
Palmer, D. D. "Faculty Responses to the Higher Mandatory Retirement
    Age: Which Faculty Members Will Stay?" Paper presented at the
    Midwest Economics Association Meeting, Chicago, Illinois,
    6 April 1979.
Palmer, D. D., and Patton, C. V. "Attitudes toward Incentive Early
    Retirement Schemes." In Current Issues in Higher Education:
    Changing Retirement Policies. Washington, DC: American
    Association for Higher Education, 1978.
Palmer, D. D. and Patton, C. V. "Mid-Career Change Options in
    Academe: Experience and Possibilities," Journal of Higher
    Education, July/August 1981, 52(4), 378-398.
Parker, C. A. and Lawson, J. "From Theory to Practice to Theory:
    Consulting with College Faculty," Personnel and Guidance Journal,
    March 1978, 424-427.
Parsons, T. and Platt, G. M. The American Academic Profession:
    A Pilot Study. Washington, DC: National Science Foundation
    Grant GS-B, March 1968.
Parsons, T. and Platt, G. M. The American University. Cambridge,
    MA: Harvard University Press, 1973.
Pascal, A. H., Bell, D., Dougharty, L. A., Dunn, W. L., and Montoya,
    V., with contributions by Olson, L. S. and Prusoff, L. L.
    An Evaluation of Policy-Related Research Programs for Career
    Redirection. Santa Monica, CA: Rand, 1975.
Patton, A. "Industry's Misguided Shift to Staff Jobs," Business
    Week, 5 April 1982, 12-15.
Patton, C. V. "Early Retirement in Academia: Making the Decision,"
    Gerontologist, August 1977, 17, 347-354.
Patton, C. V. Academia in Transition: Mid-Career Change or Early
    Retirement. Cambridge, MA: Abt Books, 1979.
Patton, C. V. "Consulting by Faculty Members," Academe: Bulletin
    of the AAUP, 1980, 66(4), 181-185.
Patton, C. V., and Foertsch, R. "Some Impacts of Raising the
    Mandatory Retirement Age." Paper (unpublished) presented at the
    American Council on Education Conference on Retirement Policy
    and Higher Education, Washington, DC, February 1978.
Patton, C. V. and Marver, J. D. "Paid Consulting by American
    Academics," Educational Record, 1979, 60, 175-184.
Payne, R. and Pugh, D. S. "Organizational Structure and Climate."
    In Marvin Dunnette (ed.), Handbook of Industrial and
    Organizational Psychology, 1125-1173. Chicago: Rand McNally,
    1976.

Pellino, G. R., Boberg, A., and Blackburn, R. T. Planning and
    Evaluating Professional Growth Programs for Faculty. Ann Arbor:
    Center for the Study of Higher Education (Monograph), University
    of Michigan, 1981.
Pelz, D. C. and Andrews, F. M. Scientists in Organizations:
    Productive for Research and Development. Ann Arbor: Institute
    for Social Research, University of Michigan, 1966.
Pelz, D. C. and Andrews, F. M. Scientists in Organizations
    (Revised Ed.). New York: John Wiley & Sons, 1976.
Peterson, M. "Faculty and Academic Responsiveness in a Period of
    Decline: An Organizational Perspective, Journal of the College
    and University Personnel Association, Spring 1980, 31, 95-104.
Peterson, R. E., Centra, J. A., Hartnett, R. T., and Linn, R. L.
    Institutional Functioning Inventory. Princeton, NJ:
    Educational Testing Service, 1970.
Peterson, R. E. and Loye, D. E. Conversations Toward a Definition
    of Institutional Vitality. Princeton, NJ: Educational Testing
    Service, 1967.
Pfeffer, J. "Organizational Demography." In L. L. Cummings (ed.),
    Research in Organizational Behavior, Vol. 5. Greenwich, CT:
    JAI Press, 1983.
Pfeffer, J., Leong, A., and Strehl, K. "Publication and Prestige
    Mobility of University Departments in Three Scientific
    Disciplines," Sociology of Education, July 1976, 49, 212-218.
Planning Council. "A Proposal for a Study on 'The Future Vitality
    of the Faculties of the University.'" Memorandum to President
    C. Peter Magrath, University of Minnesota, February 1980.
Polishook, I. H. "Unions and Governance--The CUNY Experience,"
    Academe: Bulletin of the AAUP, January-February 1982, 68, 15-17.
Pratt, H. "History of Pensions, Tenure and Mandatory Retirement
    Provisions." In W. Lee Hansen and Karen C. Holden (eds.),
    The Future of Pensions and Retirement Provisions in Higher
    Education. Madison, WI: Wisconsin University Press
    (forthcoming).
Presthus, R. The Organizational Society (Revised Ed.).
    New York: St. Martin's Press, 1978.
PROD. "Career Renewal." Harrisburg, PA: Pennsylvania State
    College, Educational Services Trust Fund, Winter 1980.
Radner, R. and Kuh, C. V. "Preserving a Lost Generation: Policies
    to Assume A Steady Flow of Young Scholars Until the Year 2000."
    A report and recommendations to the Carnegie Council on Policy
    Studies in Higher Education, October 1978.
Raymond, J. C. "Publications, Production of Knowledge, and Career
    Patterns of American Economists." Unpublished PhD dissertation,
    University of Virginia, 1967.
Reichardt, C. S. and Cook, T. D. (eds.). Qualitative and
    Quantitative Methods in Evaluation Research. Beverly Hills, CA:
    Sage Publications, 1979.
Reimers, C. "The Timing of Retirement of American Men."
    Unpublished Ph.D. dissertation, Columbia University, 1977.
Reskin, B. F. "Scientific Productivity and the Reward Structure of
    Science," American Sociological Review, 1977, 42, 491-504.
Reskin, B. F. "Scientific Productivity, Sex, and Location in the
    Institution of Science," American Journal of Sociology, 1978,
    83, 1235-1243.
Reskin, B. F. "Academic Sponsorship and Scientists' Careers,"
    Sociology of Education, July 1979a, 52, 129-146.

Reskin, B. F. "Review of the Literature on the Relationship Between Age and Scientific Productivity." Appendix C in National Research Council, Research Excellence Through the Year 2000: The Importance of Maintaining a Flow of New Faculty into Academic Research. Washington, DC: National Academy of Sciences, 1979b, 187-207.

Reynolds, P. D. A Primer in Theory Construction. Indianapolis, IN: Bobbs-Merrill, 1971.

Rice, R. E. "Dreams and Actualities: Danforth Fellows in Mid-Career," AAHE Bulletin, April 1980a, 32, 3-5 and 14-16.

Rice, R. E. "Recent Research on Adults and Careers: Implications for Equity, Planning, and Renewal." Paper presented at The American Association for Higher Education Conference, Spring Hill, Minnesota, November 1980b.

Rice, R. E. "Maintaining Faculty Vitality in the 1980s." An Interim Report to the Northwest Area Foundation, St. Paul, Minnesota, September 1981.

Rich, H. E. and Jolicoeur, P. M. "Faculty Role Perceptions and Preferences in 70's," Sociology of Work and Occupations, 1978, 5(4), 423-445.

Richardson, R. C., Jr. "Staff Development: A Conceptual Framework," Journal of Higher Education, May/June 1975, 46, 303-312.

Ricklefs, R. "How Bosses on the Brink are Rescued," Wall Street Journal, 28 January 1981.

Riesman, D. On Higher Education: The Academic Enterprise in an Era of Rising Student Consumerism. San Francisco: Jossey-Bass, 1980.

Riley, M. W. "Aging and Cohort Succession: Interpretations and Misinterpretations," Public Opinion Quarterly, Spring 1973, 35-49.

Riley, M. W. (ed.). Aging From Birth to Death: Introductory Perspectives. Boulder, CO: Westview Press, 1979.

Robbins, P. I. Successful Midlife Career Change: Self-Understanding and Strategies for Action. New York: AMACOM, 1978.

Roe, A. "Changes in Scientific Activities with Age," Science, 1965, 150, 313-318.

Roizen, J., Fulton, O., and Trow, M. Technical Report: 1975 Carnegie Council National Surveys of Higher Education. Berkeley, CA: University of California, Center for Studies in Higher Education, 1978.

Rossi, A. and Calderwood, A. Academic Women on the Move. New York: Russell Sage Foundation, 1973.

Rowe, A. R. "Retired Academics and Research Activity," Journal of Gerontology, July 1976, 31, 456-461.

Rudolph, F. The American College and University, A History. New York: Alfred A. Knopf, 1962.

Rynder, N. B. and Westhoff, C. F. Reproduction in the United States, 1965. Princeton: Princeton University Press, 1971.

Sandler, B. R. "You've Come a Long Way, Maybe -- Or Why it Still Hurts to be a Woman in Labor," Current Issues in Higher Education, 1979, 11-18.

Sarason, S. B. Work, Aging and Social Change: Professionals and the One Life-One Career Imperative. New York: Free Press, 1977.

Schein, E. H. Organizational Psychology. Englewood Cliffs, NJ: Prentice-Hall, 1965.

Schein, E. H. "The Individual, the Organization and the Career:
    A Conceptual Scheme," Journal of Applied Behavioral Science,
    1971, 7, 401-426.
Scherba, J. "Outplacement: An Established Personnel Function,"
    Personnel Administrator, July 1978, 47-49.
Schmid, M. "The Tenure System," Landmarks in Collective Bargaining
    in Higher Education, Proceedings, April 1979, 108.
Schuman, H. and Laumann, E. O. "Do Most Professors Support the
    War?," Trans-action, November 1967, 5, 32-35.
Scott, R. A. "Indicators of Institutional Vitality." A Report to
    the Indiana Commission for Higher Education, March 1980.
Sheehy, G. Passages. New York: Dutton, 1976.
Sherlock, B. J. "Socialization Cycles in Professional Schools."
    Paper presented at meeting of the American Sociological
    Association, San Francisco, California, September 1967.
Sherlock, B. J. and Morris, R. T. Becoming a Dentist. Springfield,
    IL: Charles C. Thomas, 1972.
Shively, P. and Swan, C. "Faculty Salaries and Unionization."
    Minneapolis, MN: Faculty Governance Caucus, University of
    Minnesota, May 1981.
Simpson, W. A. "Steady State Effects of a Later Mandatory
    Retirement Law for Tenured Faculty," Research in Higher
    Education, 1979, 11(1), 37-44.
Smart, J. C. "Diversity of Academic Organizations: Faculty
    Incentives," Journal of Higher Education, September/October
    1978, 49(5), 404-419.
Smith, A. B. Faculty Development and Evaluation in Higher
    Education. AAHE-ERIC/Higher Education Research Report No. 8,
    1972.
Smith, D. K. "Faculty Vitality and the Management of University
    Personnel Policies." In Wayne R. Kirschling (ed.), Evaluating
    Faculty Performance and Vitality. New Directions for
    Institutional Research, 5(4), 1-16. San Francisco: Jossey-Bass,
    1978.
Smith, R. and Fiedler, F. E. "The Measurement of Scholarly Work:
    A Critical Review of Literature," Educational Record, Summer
    1971, 52(3), 225-232.
Snyder, R. A., Howard, A., and Hammer, L. H. "Mid-Career Change
    in Academia: The Decision to Become an Administrator," Journal
    of Vocational Behavior, October 1978, 13(2), 229-241.
Solmon, L. C. "Ph.D.'s in Nonacademic Careers: Are There Good
    Jobs?" Los Angeles: Higher Education Research Institute,
    17 April 1979.
Solmon, L. C., Kent, L., Ochsner, N. L., and Hurwicz, M. L.
    Underemployed Ph.D.'s. Lexington, MA: Lexington Books, 1981.
Souerwine, A. H. Career Strategies: Planning for Personal
    Achievement. New York: AMACOM, 1979.
Spilerman, S. "Careers, Labor Market Structure, and Socioeconomic
    Achievement," American Journal of Sociology, 1977, 83(3),
    551-593.
Starup, R. and Gruneberg, M. "The Rewards of Research,"
    Universities Quarterly, 1976, 30, 227-238.
Stern, N. "Age and Achievement in Mathematics: A Case Study in
    the Sociology of Science," Social Studies of Science, 1978, 8,
    127-140.
Teague, G. V. "Faculty Consulting: Do Universities Have
    'Control'?," Research in Higher Education, 1982, 17(2), 179-186.

Texas Bureau for Economic Understanding and Career Design
    Associates. "Campus to Corporate Careers Program." Garland,
    TX: Texas Bureau for Economic Understanding and Career Design
    Associates, 1980.
Thompson, M. S. Benefit-Cost Analysis for Program Evaluation,
    Beverly Hills, CA: Sage Publications, 1980.
Thompson, V. M. "A Government Policy to Induce Efficient
    Retraining during Unemployment." Santa Monica, CA: Rand,
    1977a.
Thompson, V. M. "Unemployed Aerospace Professionals: Lessons for
    Programs for Mid-Life Career Redirection," Policy Analysis,
    Summer 1977b, 3, 375-385.
Time. "Are Whizzes Washed Up at 35?," 18 October 1982.
Time. "Open Windows: Incentives to Resign or Retire," 21 February
    1983, p. 56.
Toevs, A. L., and Hanhardt, A. M., Jr. "The Effect of Early
    Retirement Incentives on Faculty Quality," Collegiate Forum,
    Fall 1982, 6.
Toombs, W. E. Productivity: Burden of Success. AAHE-ERIC/Higher
    Education Research Report No. 2, 1973.
Toombs, W. E. "Faculty Career Change: A Pilot Study of Individual
    Decisions." Paper presented at the American Association for
    Higher Education National Conference, Washington, DC, April
    1979.
Trent, J. W. and Cohen, A. M. "Research on Teaching in Higher
    Education." In R. N. W. Travers (ed.), Second Handbook of
    Research on Teaching. Chicago: Rand McNally, 1973.
Trow, M. Technical Report: National Survey of Higher Education.
    Berkeley, CA: Carnegie Commission on Higher Education, 1972.
Trow, M. (ed.). Teachers and Students: Aspects of American Higher
    Education. (A volume of essays sponsored by Carnegie Commission
    on Higher Education.) New York: McGraw-Hill, 1975.
Trumble, R. R. "Young Instructors: Concerns, Options, and
    Opportunities," Research in Higher Education, 1980, 12(4),
    335-345.
Van Maanen, J. "People Processing: Strategies of Organizational
    Socialization," Organizational Dynamics, Summer 1978, 7(1),
    19-36.
Van West, P. E. "The Greying Professoriate: Theories, Perceptions
    and Policies." Paper presented at the annual meeting of the
    American Educational Research Association, New York, March 1982.
Vollmer, H. M. and Mills, D. L. Professionalization. Englewood
    Cliffs, NJ: Prentice-Hall, 1966.
Von Moltke, K. and Schneevoigt, N. Educational Leaves for
    Employees: European Experience for American Consideration.
    San Francisco: Jossey-Bass, 1977.
Walden, T. "Tenure and Academic Productivity," Improving College
    and University Teaching, Fall 1979, 27, 154-171.
Walden, T. "Tenure: A Review of the Issues," Educational Forum,
    March 1980, 44, 363-372.
Wall Street Journal. "Pan Am Falls Short of Goal to Reduce Work
    Force by 15%," 3 November 1982.
Wallhaus, R. A. (issue ed.). Measuring and Increasing Academic
    Productivity. San Francisco: Jossey-Bass, 1975.
Watkins, B. T. "A New Academic Disease: Faculty Burnout,"
    Chronicle of Higher Education, 24 March 1982a, 24(4), pp. 1, 8.

Watkins, B. T. "NLRB Rules Professors at 3 Private Institutions Are Managers, Those at 2 Others May Bargain," Chronicle of Higher Education, 12 May 1982b, pp. 1, 12.

Weathersby, R. and Tarule, J. M. Adult Development: Implications for Higher Education. Washington, DC: ERIC Clearinghouse on Higher Education, 1980.

Webster's New International Dictionary (2nd Ed.), unabridged version. Springfield, MA: Merriam, 1959.

Weick, K. E. "Educational Organizations as Loosely Coupled Systems," Administration Science Quarterly, 1976, 21, 1-19.

Wertheimer, R. F. "Differences in Retirement Behavior Between Academics and Nonacademics: Is There a Case for Mandatory Retirement?" Paper (unpublished) presented at the Conference on Mandatory Retirement Policy in Higher Education, Brookings Institution, March 1982.

Weston, M. C. "'Outside' Activities of Faculty Members," Journal of College and University Law, 1980-81, 7(1-2), 68-77.

Wheeler, S. "The Structure of Formally Organized Socialization Systems." In Orville G. Brim, Jr. and Stanton Wheeler (eds.), Socialization after Childhood, 53-116. New York: John Wiley & Sons, 1966.

White, S. W. "Work and Productivity," National Forum, Spring 1982, 62(2), 2 and 47.

Wildavsky, A. "Viewpoint 2: The Debate Over Faculty Consulting," Change, June-July 1978, 10(6), 13-14.

Williams, G., Blackstone, T., and Metcalf, D. The Academic Labor Market. New York: Elsevier, 1974.

Wilson, L. The Academic Man. New York: Oxford University Press, 1942.

Wilson, R. C., Gaff, J. G., Dienst, E., Wood, L., and Bavry, J. College Professors and Their Impact on Students. New York: John Wiley & Sons, 1975.

Wortley, D. B. and Amatea, E. S. "Mapping Adult Life Changes: A Conceptual Framework for Organizing Adult Development Theory," Personnel and Guidance Journal, April 1982, 476-482.

Wright, J. D. and Hamilton, R. F. "Work Satisfaction and Age: Some Evidence for the Job-Change Hypothesis," Social Forces, June 1978, 56, 1140-1158.

Yankelovich, Daniel. New Rules: Searching for Self-Fulfillment in a World Turned Upside Down. New York: Random House, 1981.

Yuker, H. E. Faculty Workload: Facts, Myths, and Commentary. Washington, DC: American Association for Higher Education, 1974.

Zambrano, A. L., and Entine, A. D. A Guide to Career Alternatives for Academics. New Rochelle, NY: Change Magazine Press, 1976.

Zuckerman, H. Scientific Elite: Nobel Laureates in the United States. New York: Free Press, 1977.

Zuckerman, H. and Merton, R. "Age, Aging and Age Structure in Science." In R. Merton (ed.), The Sociology of Science: Theoretical and Empirical Investigation. Chicago: University of Chicago Press, 1973.

Index

NOTE: Italicized page numbers refer to material in tables. Page numbers followed by *n* refer to notes.

Faculty (*continued*)
consequences of changing conditions on, 12–13, 113–117
consulting by. *See* Consulting
demographic issues concerning. *See* Demographic issues, faculty
development of. *See* Faculty development
differentiated support for needs of, 137–138
intellectual performance of, 99–100, 134–135
life-style, 103–107
measuring effectiveness of, 21–22
motivation, 128–129
productivity. *See* Productivity
retirement. *See* Retirement
salary. *See* Salary
strategies for increasing exits of, 252–254
strategies for increasing new, 250–252
student ratings of, 61, 73
tenure. *See* Tenure
unionization. *See* Collective bargaining
vitality of existing, 254–255
Faculty development, 156
career development in. *See* Career development
evaluation of programs for, 153–155
history of, 143–145
present status of, 155
study of, 146–153
Faculty Development in a Time of Retrenchment, 145
Faculty flow model, 32–34
Faculty-student ratio, 37
Feinberg, L., 172
Felder, N., 73
Fiedler, F. E., 22
"Fifty Years in Higher Education" (McGrath), 12
Filstead, W. J., 121
Flexner, H., 247
Foertsch, R., 159, 227
Fowler, D., 77
Fox, T. G., 57
Freedom, vitality and, 130–132, 135–137
Freeman, R. B., 212
Freudenberger, H. J., 155
Froomkin, J., 34, *35*
Fulton, O., 10, 85*n*, 117, 118, 138*n*, 168
Fund for the Improvement of Postsecondary Education, 162
Furniss, W. T., 14, 164, 173, 250, 251

Gaff, J. G., 144–145, 150
Garbarino, J. W., 198–200, *201*, 203, 206, 209, 219, 222*n*
Gardner, J. W., 6–8, 116, 141, 142, 158, 179, 196*n*
Geology, 95
Glaser, B. G., 57, 121
Goals, organizational, 9–10
Golomb, S. W., 181–183
Gooding, J., 161, 174
Gottschalk, E. C., 170, 172
Graebner, W., 224, 242*n*
Grant, G., 4, 11
Greenough, W. C., 225, 242*n*
Gustad, J. W., 81
Guthrie-Morse, B., 211–215, 218, 222*n*

Hage, J., 6
Hall, D. E., 65, 69, *70*, *71*, 73, *74*, *75*, 85*n*, 88
Hall, R. J., 24*n*
Hanger, S., 145
Hanhardt, A. M., Jr., 159, 170
Hansen, S. A., 251–253
Hansen, W. L., 28, 30, 36–38, 168, 227, 230, 231, 235, 243*n*, 247
Hardy, C. D., 143
Haveman, R., 231
Havighurst, R. J., 57, 69, 77, 79, 252, 253
Heim, P., 227
Heist, P., 101
Hellweg, S. A., 4, 5, 247
Higher education, stimulation of demand for, 52–53, 251–252
Hitch, E. J., 73
Hodgkinson, H. L., 23, 57
Hofstadter, R., 143
Holden, K. C., 28, 30, 36–38, 168, 227, 230, 231, 235, 243*n*, 247, 253
Horn, J. L., 99–100
Hu, T. W., 211–215, 218, 222*n*
Hughes, G. C., 227
Humanities
career change and, 166
case study of faculty productivity in, 122–138

Incompetence, 30
Inflation, 5, 29–30, 50, 141, 219, 231–233, 238, 241–242
Institutions
benefits of faculty consulting for, 182